Hands-On Data Structures and Algorithms with Rust

Learn programming techniques to build effective, maintainable, and readable code in Rust 2018

Claus Matzinger

BIRMINGHAM - MUMBAI

Hands-On Data Structures and Algorithms with Rust

Commissioning Editor: Richa Tripathi
Acquisition Editor: Shahnish Khan
Content Development Editor: Zeeyan Pinheiro
Technical Editor: Romy Dias
Copy Editor: Safis Editing
Project Coordinator: Vaidehi Sawant
Proofreader: Safis Editing
Indexer: Priyanka Dhadke
Graphics: Alishon Mendonsa
Production Coordinator: Tom Scaria

First published: January 2019

Production reference: 1230119

Published by Packt Publishing Ltd.
Livery Place
35 Livery Street
Birmingham
B3 2PB, UK.

ISBN 978-1-78899-552-8

www.packtpub.com

`mapt.io`

Mapt is an online digital library that gives you full access to over 5,000 books and videos, as well as industry leading tools to help you plan your personal development and advance your career. For more information, please visit our website.

Why subscribe?

- Spend less time learning and more time coding with practical eBooks and Videos from over 4,000 industry professionals

- Improve your learning with Skill Plans built especially for you

- Get a free eBook or video every month

- Mapt is fully searchable

- Copy and paste, print, and bookmark content

Packt.com

Did you know that Packt offers eBook versions of every book published, with PDF and ePub files available? You can upgrade to the eBook version at `www.packt.com` and as a print book customer, you are entitled to a discount on the eBook copy. Get in touch with us at `customercare@packtpub.com` for more details.

At `www.packt.com`, you can also read a collection of free technical articles, sign up for a range of free newsletters, and receive exclusive discounts and offers on Packt books and eBooks.

Foreword

Rust is not an easy language to learn. Ask why, and you'll hear that Rust was designed to solve almost any complex problem in system programming, a complicated domain to begin with. It was designed to do it safely, to be incredibly fast, and be very strict; "ease of use" is a necessary sacrifice. Rust reads like any other imperative language, but it incorporates a number of special concepts that ask you to think through your problems in greater depth and with a different spin than you're used to. It's brutally honest about the complicated parts a system language has to address.

Those are the typical reasons cited for why Rust is hard. The more honest answer is that those people may not have the right teacher.

I met Claus at my first event as an open source developer for Microsoft. He had joined just a few months before, and could show me the ropes. It didn't occur to me until a few weeks later that, as his manager, I was supposed to be teaching him! I've discovered that this is a common situation for Claus: he falls naturally into a teaching role. Not a lecturing bore, either—the kind of teaching where the student doesn't realize that's what's happening until they find themselves using newly acquired knowledge. We've long since moved into other roles, but I've seen the pattern repeated over and over again.

Early in his career as an open source developer, Claus found himself diving deep into documentation. And fair enough: it's often the most important part of a project! "Just three lines," he said to me once. "I just lost a whole day of my life because someone didn't bother to write three lines of good documentation. I can fix that."

Claus's background was in academic software development, but in his professional life, he has rejected the dry, abstract computer science theory often taught in that environment. He is one of those rare developers who cares deeply about making this easy for people to understand. It's important that it makes sense, it's important that it looks nice, it's important that it's easy to follow—and how to make it that way is intuitive to him. I think it honestly doesn't occur to him that other people struggle to explain things the way he does naturally.

One of the aspects of this book that I appreciated the most when reading it is the balance Claus strikes. It stays focused on the teaching goal without getting sidetracked by more technical detail than is required. We all know the feeling of reading that kind of documentation—the kind that demands to be skimmed. Most readers, including myself, are simply confused by too much theory or detail at the outset. As Claus puts it, "most teachers make it sound like something really fancy is going on, but, in reality, it's quite simple."

This practical approach has made Claus an in-demand speaker, community member, and contributor in the Rust world. This book is his next step into teaching for a broader audience, and I'm excited to see its impact.

You've chosen a great teacher! Rust is difficult to learn, but it doesn't have to be. Just ask Claus.

Campbell Vertesi

Principal Software Engineer Manager

twitter: @ohthehugemanatee
ohthehugemanatee.org

Contributors

About the author

Claus Matzinger is a software engineer with a very diverse background. After working in a small company maintaining code for embedded devices, he joined a large corporation to work on legacy Smalltalk applications. This led to a great interest in programming languages early on, and Claus became the CTO for a health games start-up based on Scala technology.

Since then, Claus' roles have shifted toward customer-facing roles in the IoT database-technology start-up crate.io and, most recently, Microsoft. There, he hosts a podcast, writes code together with customers, and blogs about the solutions arising from these engagements. For more than 5 years, Claus has implemented software to help customers innovate, achieve, and maintain success.

> *Any large project is a joint effort, and many people have helped me create this book. There is the Rust community, who eagerly helped with my questions; the Packt team, who provided comments on my writing; my colleagues, with whom I kept discussing language details; and—above all—my future wife, who gave me the space and support to write every day.*
>
> *Thank you, all!*

About the reviewer

Ivo Balbaert is a former lecturer in (web) programming and databases at CVO Antwerpen, a community college in Belgium. He received a Ph.D. in applied physics from the University of Antwerp in 1986. He worked in the software industry for 20 years, as a developer and consultant in several companies, and for 10 years as a project manager at Antwerp University Hospital. From 2000 onward, he switched to part-time teaching, developing software, and writing technical books.

In 2012, he authored *The Way To Go*, a book on the Go programming language. He also wrote a number of introductory books on new programming languages, including Dart, Crystal, Julia, Rust, and Red, most of them published by Packt.

Packt is searching for authors like you

If you're interested in becoming an author for Packt, please visit authors.packtpub.com and apply today. We have worked with thousands of developers and tech professionals, just like you, to help them share their insight with the global tech community. You can make a general application, apply for a specific hot topic that we are recruiting an author for, or submit your own idea.

Table of Contents

Preface

When I first made the effort of learning one programming language a year, I started with Ruby, then learned a bit of Scala, until, in 2015, I started with a very new language: Rust. My first attempts at creating a Slack (a team chat program) bot were somewhat successful but very frustrating. Being used to Python's flexibility with JSON data and permissive compiler, Rust's steep learning curve quickly took its toll.

The next projects were more successful. A database driver, as well as my very own **Internet of Things (IoT)**-type client and server application for the Raspberry Pi, allowed me to collect temperature data in a rock-solid manner. Unlike Python, if the program compiled, it would almost certainly work as expected—and I loved it.

Since then, a lot has changed. Big companies such as Microsoft and Amazon are picking up Rust as a way to create safe and fast code on embedded devices as well as in the cloud. With **WebAssembly (Wasm)**, Rust is gaining traction in the web frontend space, and gaming companies are starting to build game engines in Rust. 2018 has been a great year for the technology and the Rust community, both of which will continue to grow in 2019 (and beyond).

For this reason, I hope to provide a learning resource for creating more sophisticated Rust code from a practical angle. Wherever your journey leads you, learning about Rust and its various programming models will change your view of code for the better.

Who this book is for

Rust has great tutorials for learning the fundamentals of the language. There are workshops at every conference, regular meetups in many cities, and a very helpful online community. However, many developers find themselves beyond these resources but still don't feel ready for more complex solutions. Especially coming from different backgrounds with years of experience, the transition can be daunting: examples on the one side feature some type of a "Hello World!" program; on the other side, there are huge Rust open source projects with thousands of lines of code – impossible to learn from quickly. If you feel like this, then this book is for you.

What this book covers

Chapter 1, *Hello Rust!*, gives a short recap of the Rust programming language and what changed in the 2018 edition.

Chapter 2, *Cargo and Crates*, discusses Rust's `cargo` build tool. We will explore the configuration as well as the build process and modularization options.

Chapter 3, *Storing Efficiently*, looks at how in Rust, knowing where values are stored is not only important for performance, but also important for understanding error messages and the language in general. In this chapter, we think about stack and heap memory.

Chapter 4, *Lists, Lists, and More Lists*, covers the first data structures: lists. Using several examples, this chapter goes into variations of sequential data structures and their implementations.

Chapter 5, *Robust Trees*, continues our journey through popular data structures: trees are next on the list. In several detailed examples, we explore the inner workings of these efficient designs and how they improve application performance considerably.

Chapter 6, *Exploring Maps and Sets*, explores the most popular key-value stores: maps. In this chapter, techniques surrounding hash maps; hashing; and their close relative, the set; are described in detail.

Chapter 7, *Collections in Rust*, attempts to connect to the Rust programmer's daily life, going into the details of the Rust `std::collections` library, which contains the various data structures provided by the Rust standard library.

Chapter 8, *Algorithm Evaluation*, teaches you how to evaluate and compare algorithms.

Chapter 9, *Ordering Things*, will look at sorting values, an important task in programming—this chapter uncovers how that can be done quickly and safely.

Chapter 10, *Finding Stuff*, moves onto searching, which is especially important if there is no fundamental data structure to support it. In these cases, we use algorithms to be able to quickly find what we are looking for.

Chapter 11, *Random and Combinatorial*, is where we will see that, outside of sorting and searching, there are many problems that can be tackled algorithmically. This chapter is all about those: random number generation, backtracking, and improving computational complexities.

Chapter 12, *Algorithms of the Standard Library*, explores how the Rust standard library does things when it comes to everyday algorithmic tasks such as sorting and searching.

To get the most out of this book

This book comes with a lot of code examples and implementations. For you to learn the most that you can, it is recommended to install Rust (any version later than 1.33 should do) and run all of the examples. Here are a few recommendations for text editors and other tools:

- Microsoft's Visual Studio Code (https://code.visualstudio.com/), arguably one of the best Rust code editors
- Rust support for Visual Studio Code via a plugin (https://github.com/rust-lang/rls-vscode)
- **Rust Language Server** (**RLS**), found at https://github.com/rust-lang/rls-vscode, installed via rustup (https://rustup.rs/)
- Debugging support using the LLDB frontend plugin (https://github.com/vadimcn/vscode-lldb) for Visual Studio Code

Having this environment set up and being familiar with it is great for your daily Rust programming, and will let you debug and inspect the workings of the code provided in this book. For you to get the most out of this book, we recommend that you do the following:

- Check out the source code in the repository to get the whole picture. The snippets are only isolated examples to show specifics.
- Don't blindly trust our results; run the tests and benchmarks of each sub-project (chapters) to reproduce the findings yourself.

Download the color images

We also provide a PDF file that has color images of the screenshots/diagrams used in this book. You can download it here https://www.packtpub.com/sites/default/files/downloads/9781788995528_ColorImages.pdf.

Download the example code files

You can download the example code files for this book from your account at www.packt.com. If you purchased this book elsewhere, you can visit www.packt.com/support and register to have the files emailed directly to you.

You can download the code files by following these steps:

1. Log in or register at www.packt.com.
2. Select the **SUPPORT** tab.

3. Click on **Code Downloads & Errata**.
4. Enter the name of the book in the **Search** box and follow the onscreen instructions.

Once the file is downloaded, please make sure that you unzip or extract the folder using the latest version of:

- WinRAR/7-Zip for Windows
- Zipeg/iZip/UnRarX for Mac
- 7-Zip/PeaZip for Linux

The code bundle for the book is also hosted on GitHub at https://github.com/ PacktPublishing/Hands-On-Data-Structures-and-Algorithms-with-Rust. In case there's an update to the code, it will be updated on the existing GitHub repository.

We also have other code bundles from our rich catalog of books and videos available at https://github.com/PacktPublishing/. Check them out!

Conventions used

There are a number of text conventions used throughout this book.

CodeInText: Indicates code words in text, database table names, folder names, filenames, file extensions, pathnames, dummy URLs, user input, and Twitter handles. Here is an example: "The reason is that the passing_through variable outlives x."

A block of code is set as follows:

```
fn my_function() {
    let x = 10;
    do_something(x); // ownership is moved here
    let y = x; // x is now invalid!
}
```

When we wish to draw your attention to a particular part of a code block, the relevant lines or items are set in bold:

```
fn main() {
    let mut a = 42;
    let b = &a; // borrow a
    let c = &mut a; // borrow a again, mutably
    // ... but don't ever use b
}
```

Any command-line input or output is written as follows:

```
$ cargo test
```

Bold: Indicates a new term, an important word, or words that you see onscreen. For example, words in menus or dialog boxes appear in the text like this. Here is an example: "Select **System info** from the **Administration** panel."

Warnings or important notes appear like this.

Tips and tricks appear like this.

Get in touch

Feedback from our readers is always welcome.

General feedback: If you have questions about any aspect of this book, mention the book title in the subject of your message and email us at customercare@packtpub.com.

Errata: Although we have taken every care to ensure the accuracy of our content, mistakes do happen. If you have found a mistake in this book, we would be grateful if you would report this to us. Please visit www.packt.com/submit-errata, selecting your book, clicking on the Errata Submission Form link, and entering the details.

Piracy: If you come across any illegal copies of our works in any form on the Internet, we would be grateful if you would provide us with the location address or website name. Please contact us at copyright@packt.com with a link to the material.

If you are interested in becoming an author: If there is a topic that you have expertise in and you are interested in either writing or contributing to a book, please visit authors.packtpub.com.

Reviews

Please leave a review. Once you have read and used this book, why not leave a review on the site that you purchased it from? Potential readers can then see and use your unbiased opinion to make purchase decisions, we at Packt can understand what you think about our products, and our authors can see your feedback on their book. Thank you!

For more information about Packt, please visit packt.com.

1
Hello Rust!

First, thank you for picking up a copy of this book! Many of you will only have talked about the topic of algorithms and data structures back in university. In fact, regardless of whether this is your first endeavor in programming or not, we worked hard to make this book a great learning experience. Our primary focus will be the unique influence of Rust on algorithm and data structure design, so we would like to start with a recap of important fundamentals.

Starting off with the Rust 2018 edition changes, we will cover how borrowing and ownership, mutability, and concurrency influence how and where data can be held, and what algorithms can be executed. In this chapter, you can look forward to learning about the following:

- A quick refresh on Rust and what awaits in the 2018 edition (Rust 1.31)
- The latest and greatest about borrowing and ownership
- How we can leverage concurrency and mutability properly
- References (not pointers!) to where Rust lives

Rust in 2018

How old is Rust? It started off in 2006 as a side project of Graydon Hoare, an engineer at Mozilla, and was later (in 2009) adopted by the company. Fast forward to less than a decade later to May 15, 2015, and the Rust team announced a stable version 1.0!

During its journey, there have been many features that have been added and removed again (for example, a garbage collector, classes, and interfaces) to help it become the fast and safe language that it is today.

Before getting deeper into borrowing and ownership, mutability, concurrency, safety, and so on in Rust, we would like to recap some major concepts in Rust and why they change architectural patterns significantly.

The 2018 edition

Rust in the 2015 edition is essentially the 1.0 version with a few non-breaking additions. Between 2015 and 2018, however, features and **Requests for Comments (RFCs)**, Rust's way of changing core features with the community, accumulated, and worries about backward compatibility arose.

With the goal of keeping this compatibility, editions were introduced and, with the first additional edition, many major changes made it into the language:

- Changes to the module path system
- `dyn Trait` and `impl Trait` syntax
- `async`/`await` syntax
- Simplifications to the lifetime syntax

With these additions, Rust will introduce asynchronous programming into its syntax (`async`/`await` keywords) and improve the language's usability. This book uses the Rust 2018, released on December 6, 2018 (`https://blog.rust-lang.org/2018/12/06/Rust-1.31-and-rust-2018.html`) edition by default, so all the following snippets will already include these new language features!

The Rust language

Many of the established programming languages today are multi-paradigm languages, but still remain focused on the principles of object orientation. This means that they have classes, methods, interfaces, inheritance, and so on, none of which can be found in Rust, giving it a steep learning curve for many established developers.

 More experienced readers will miss many aspects of what makes Rust an excellent language, such as static versus dynamic method invocation, memory layouts, and so on. I recognize the importance of those things, yet for brevity and focus chose to leave it to you to explore these things further. Check the *Further reading* section for resources.

As a multi-paradigm language, Rust has many functional concepts and paradigms that guide it, but they make traditional object-oriented patterns more difficult to apply. Other than organizing code without classes and interfaces, there are various methods to handle errors, change the code itself, or even work with raw pointers.

In the following sections, we want to explore a few concepts that make Rust unique and have a major influence on the way we develop algorithms and data structures.

Objects and behavior

Organizing code in Rust is a bit different from regular object-oriented languages such as C#. There, an object is supposed to change its own state, interfaces are simple contract definitions, and specialization is often modeled using class inheritance:

```
class Door {
    private bool is_open = false;

    public void Open() {
        this.is_open = true;
    }
}
```

With Rust, this pattern would require constant mutability of any `Door` instance (thereby requiring explicit locking for thread safety), and without inheritance `GlassDoor` would have to duplicate code, making it harder to maintain.

Instead, it's recommended to create traits to implement (shared) behavior. Traits have a lot in common with abstract classes in traditional languages (such as default implementations of methods/functions), yet any `struct` in Rust can (and should) implement several of those traits:

```
struct Door {
    is_open: bool
}

impl Door {
    fn new(is_open: bool) -> Door {
        Door { is_open: is_open }
    }
}

trait Openable {
    fn open(&mut self);
}

impl Openable for Door {
    fn open(&mut self) {
        self.is_open = true;
    }
}

#[cfg(test)]
mod tests {
    use super::*;
```

```
    #[test]
    fn open_door() {
        let mut door = Door::new(false);
        door.open();
        assert!(door.is_open);
    }
}
```

This pattern is very common in the standard library, and often third-party libraries will even add behavior to existing types by implementing traits in their code (also known as extension traits).

Other than a typical class, where data fields and methods are in a single construct, Rust emphasizes the separation between those by declaring a struct for data and an impl part for the methods/functions. Traits name and encapsulate behaviors so they can easily be imported, shared, and reused.

Going wrong

Other than classes, Rust comes without another well-known companion: null. In the absence of pointers and with a very different memory management model, there is no typical null pointer/reference.

Instead, the language works with Option and Result types that let developers model success or failure. In fact, there is no exception system either, so any failed execution of a function should be indicated in the return type. Only in rare cases when immediate termination is required does the language provide a macro for panicking: panic!().

Option<T> and Result<T, E> both encapsulate one (Option<T>) or two (Result<T, E>) values that can be returned to communicate an error or whether something was found or not. For example, a find() function could return Option<T>, whereas something like read_file() would typically have a Result<T, E> return type to communicate the content or errors:

```
    fn find(needle: u16, haystack: Vec<u16>) -> Option<usize> {
        // find the needle in the haystack
    }

    fn read_file(path: &str) -> Result<String, io::Error> {
        // open the path as a file and read it
    }
```

Handling those return values is often done with `match` or `if let` clauses in order to handle the cases of success or failure:

```
match find(2, vec![1,3,4,5]) {
    Some(_) => println!("Found!"),
    None => println!("Not found :(")
}

// another way
if let Some(result) = find(2, vec![1,2,3,4]) {
    println!("Found!")
}

// similarly for results!
match read_file("/tmp/not/a/file") {
    Ok(content) => println!(content),
    Err(error) => println!("Oh no!")
}
```

This is due to `Option<T>` and `Result<T, E>` both being enumerations that have generic type parameters; they can assume any type in their variants. Matching on their variants provides access to their inner values and types to allow a branch of the code to be executed and handle the case accordingly. Not only does this eliminate the need for constructs such as try/catch with multiple—sometimes cast—exception arms, it makes failure part of the normal workflow that needs to be taken care of.

Macros

Another aspect of Rust is the ability to do metaprogramming—basically programming programming—using macros! Macros are expanded in Rust code before compilation, which gives them more power than a regular function. The generated code can, for instance, create functions on the fly or implement traits for a structure.

These pieces of code make everyday life a lot easier by reducing the need to create and then initialize vectors, deriving the ability to clone a structure, or simply printing stuff to the command line.

This is a simplified example for the declarative `vec![]` macro provided in the *Rust Book* (second edition, Appendix D):

```
#[macro_export]
macro_rules! vec {
    ( $( $x:expr ),* ) => {
        {
```

```
                let mut temp_vec = Vec::new();
                 $( temp_vec.push($x); )*
                temp_vec
            }
        };
    }
```

Declarative macros work on patterns and run code if that pattern matches; the previous example matches *0 - n* expressions (for example, a number, or a function that returns a number) and inserts `temp_vec.push(...)` *n* times, iterating over the provided expressions as a parameter.

The second type, procedural macros, operate differently and are often used to provide a default trait implementation. In many code bases, the `#[derive(Clone, Debug)]` statement can be found on top of structures to implement the `Clone` and `Debug` traits automatically.

Later in this chapter, we are going to use a structure, `FileName`, to illustrate reference counting, but for printing it to the command line using the debug literal `"{:?}"`, we need to derive `Debug`, which recursively prints all members to the command line:

```
#[derive(Debug)]
struct FileName {
    name: Rc<String>,
    ext: Rc<String>
}
```

The Rust standard library provides several macros already, and by creating custom macros, you can minimize the boilerplate code you have to write.

Unsafe

Rust's code is "safe" because the compiler checks and enforces certain behavior when it comes to memory access and management. However, sometimes these rules have to be forgone, making the code unsafe. `unsafe` is a keyword in Rust and declares a section of code that can do most of the things the C programming language would let you do. For example, it lets the user do the following (from the *Rust Book*, chapter 19.1):

- Dereference a raw pointer
- Call an `unsafe` function or method
- Access or modify a mutable static variable
- Implement an `unsafe` trait

These four abilities can be used for things such as very low-level device access, language interoperability (the compiler can't know what native libraries do with their memory), and so on. In most cases, and certainly in this book, `unsafe` is not required. In fact, the Rustonomicon (`https://doc.rust-lang.org/nomicon/what-unsafe-does.html`) defines a list of issues the language is trying to prevent from happening by providing the safe part:

- Dereferencing null, dangling, or unaligned pointers.
- Reading uninitialized memory.
- Breaking the pointer aliasing rules.
- Producing invalid primitive values:
    - Dangling/null references
    - Null `fn` pointers
    - A bool that isn't 0 or 1
    - An undefined `enum` discriminant
    - A char outside the ranges [0x0, 0xD7FF] and [0xE000, 0x10FFFF]
    - A non-UTF8 string
- Unwinding into another language.
- Causing a data race.

The fact that these potential issues are prevented in safe Rust certainly makes the life of a developer easier, especially when designing algorithms or data structures. As a consequence, this book will always work with safe Rust.

Borrowing and ownership

Rust is famous for its memory management model, which replaces runtime garbage collection with compile-time checks for memory safety. The reason why Rust can work without a garbage collector and still free the programmer from error-prone memory management is simple (but not easy): borrowing and ownership.

While the particulars are quite complex, the high-level view is that the compiler inserts any "provide *x* amounts of memory" and "remove *x* amounts of memory" (somewhat like `malloc()` and `free()` for C programmers) statements for the developer. Yet how can it do that?

The rules of ownership are as follows:

- The owner of a value is a variable
- At any time, only a single owner is allowed
- The value is lost once the owner goes out of scope

This is where Rust's declarative syntax comes into play. By declaring a variable, the compiler knows—at compile time—that a certain amount of memory needs to be reserved. The lifetime is clearly defined too, from the beginning to end of a block or function, or as long as the `struct` instance lives. If the size of this variable is known at compile time, the compiler can provide exactly the necessary amount of memory to the function for the time required. To illustrate, let's consider this snippet, where two variables are allocated and removed in a deterministic order:

```
fn my_func() {
    // the compiler allocates memory for x
    let x = LargeObject::new();
    x.do_some_computation();
    // allocate memory for y
    let y = call_another_func();
    if y > 10 {
        do_more_things();
    }
} // deallocate (drop) x, y
```

Is this not what every other compiler does? The answer is yes—and no. At compile time, the "provide *x* amounts of memory" part is fairly simple; the tricky part is keeping track of how much is still in use when references can be passed around freely. If, during the course of a function, a particular local reference becomes invalid, a static code analysis will tell the compiler about the lifetime of the value behind the reference. However, what if a thread changes that value at an unknown time during the function's execution?

At compile time, this is impossible to know, which is why many languages do these checks at runtime using a garbage collector. Rust forgoes this, with two primary strategies:

- Every variable is owned by exactly one scope at any time
- Therefore, the developer is forced to pass ownership as required

Especially when working with scopes, the nature of stack variables comes in handy. There are two areas of memory, stack and heap, and, similar to other languages, the developer uses types to decide whether to allocate heap (`Box`, `Rc`, and so on) or stack memory.

Stack memory is usually short-lived and smaller, and operates in a first-in, last-out manner. Consequently, a variable's size has to be known before it is put on the stack:

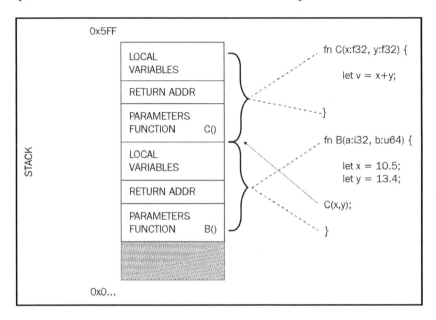

Heap memory is different; it's a large portion of the memory, which makes it easy to allocate more whenever needed. There is no ordering, and memory is accessed by using an addresses. Since the pointer to an address on the heap has a known size at compile time, it fits nicely on the stack:

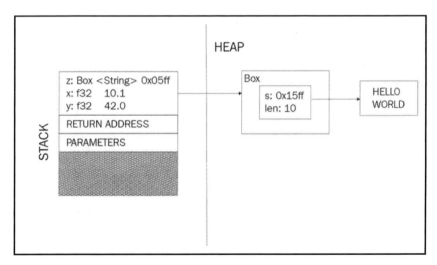

Stack variables are typically passed by value in other languages, which means that the entire value is copied and placed into the stack frame of the function. Rust does the same, but it also invalidates further use of that variable in the—now parent—scope. Ownership moves into the new scope and can only be transferred back as a return value. When trying to compile this snippet, the compiler will complain:

```
fn my_function() {
    let x = 10;
    do_something(x); // ownership is moved here
    let y = x;       // x is now invalid!
}
```

Borrowing is similar but, instead of copying the entire value, a reference to the original value is moved into the new scope. Just like in real life, the value continues to be owned by the original scope; scopes with a reference are just allowed to use it as it was provided. Of course, this comes with drawbacks for mutability, and some functions will require ownership for technical and semantic reasons, but it also has advantages such as a smaller memory footprint.

These are the rules of borrowing:

- Owners can have immutable or mutable references, but not both
- There can be multiple immutable references, but only one mutable reference
- References cannot be invalid

By changing the previous snippet to borrow the variable to `do_something()` (assuming this is allowed, of course), the compiler will be happy:

```
fn my_function() {
    let x = 10;
    do_something(&x); // pass a reference to x
    let y = x;        // x is still valid!
}
```

Borrowed variables rely heavily on lifetimes. The most basic lifetime is the scope it was created in. However, if a reference should go into a struct field, how can the compiler know that the underlying value has not been invalidated? The answer is explicit lifetimes!

Exceptional lifetimes

Some lifetimes are different and Rust denominates them with a '. While this could be the predefined 'static, it's equally possible to create your own, something that is often required when working with structures.

This makes sense when thinking about the underlying memory structure: if an input parameter is passed into the function and returned at the end, its lifetime surpasses the function's. While the function owns this part of the memory during its lifetime, it cannot borrow a variable for longer than it actually exists. So, this snippet cannot work:

```
fn another_function(mut passing_through: MyStruct) -> MyStruct {
    let x = vec![1, 2, 3];

    // passing_through cannot hold a reference
    // to a shorter lived x!
    // the compiler will complain.
    passing_through.x = &x;

    return passing_through;
} // x's life ends here
```

The reason is that the passing_through variable outlives x. There are several solutions to this problem:

- Change the type definition of MyStruct to require ownership. This way, the structure now owns the variable and it will live as long as the structure:

    ```
    fn another_function(mut passing_through: MyStruct) -> MyStruct {
        let x = vec![1, 2, 3];

        // passing_through owns x and it will be
        // dropped together with passing_through.
        passing_through.x = x;

        return passing_through;
    }
    ```

- Clone x to pass ownership into passing_through:

    ```
    fn another_function(mut passing_through: MyStruct) -> MyStruct {
        let x = vec![1, 2, 3];
        let y = &x;

        // passing_through owns a deep copy of x'value that is be
        // dropped together with passing_through.
        passing_through.x = y.clone();
    ```

```
            return passing_through;
    }
```

- In this case, `vec![]` is statically defined, so it could make sense to add it as a function parameter. This is not only more allocation-efficient, but also can enforce an appropriate lifetime:

```
fn another_function<'a>(mut passing_through: MyStruct<'a>, x: &'a
Vec<u32>) -> MyStruct<'a> {

    // The compiler knows and expects a lifetime that is
    // at least as long as the struct's
    // of any reference passed in as x.
    passing_through.x = x;

    return passing_through;
}
```

Lifetimes cause a lot of strange errors for many Rust users, and in the 2018 edition there is one less to worry about. With the introduction of non-lexical lifetimes, the borrow checker got a lot smarter and it is now able to check—up to a certain degree—semantically whether the variable was used. Recall from the rules of borrowing that, if a mutable reference is created, no immutable references can exist.

This code did not compile before Rust 1.31:

```
fn main() {
    let mut a = 42;
    let b = &a; // borrow a
    let c = &mut a; // borrow a again, mutably
    // ... but don't ever use b
}
```

Now it will compile since the compiler does not just check the beginning and ending of a scope, but also if the reference was used at all.

Multiple owners

As powerful as single ownership is, it does not work for every use case. Large objects or shared objects that other instances need to own are examples where immutable ownership makes life easier. Consider a function that requires an owned object to be passed in:

```
#[derive(Debug)]
struct FileName {
    name: String,
```

```
        ext: String
    }

    fn no_ref_counter() {
        let name = String::from("main");
        let ext = String::from("rs");

        for _ in 0..3 {
            println!("{;?}", FileName {
                        name: name,
                        ext: ext
            });
        }
    }
```

When trying to compile `no_ref_counter()`, the compiler creates a scope for each iteration of the loop and owns any value that is used within it. This works exactly once, since afterward, the variable has been moved and is inaccessible for subsequent iterations.

Consequently, these values (in this case, `name` and `ext`) are gone and compilation will yield two errors, one for each "second" move of a string:

```
error[E0382]: use of moved value: `name`
  --> src/main.rs:63:33
   |
63 | let _ = FileName { name: name, ext: ext };
   |                          ^^^^ value moved here in previous iteration
of loop
   |
   = note: move occurs because `name` has type `std::string::String`, which
does not implement the `Copy` trait

error[E0382]: use of moved value: `ext`
  --> src/main.rs:63:44
   |
63 | let _ = FileName { name: name, ext: ext };
   |                                     ^^^ value moved here in previous
iteration of loop
   |
   = note: move occurs because `ext` has type `std::string::String`, which
does not implement the `Copy` trait
```

One solution is to clone the object in every iteration, but that causes a lot of slow memory allocations. For this, the Rust standard library provides a solution: reference counting.

A reference counter (`std::rc::Rc<T>`) encapsulates a variable of type `T` allocated on the heap and returns an **immutable** reference when created. This reference can be cloned with low overhead (it's only a reference count that is incremented) but never transformed into a mutable reference. Regardless, it acts just like owned data, passing through function calls and property lookups.

While this requires a change to the variable types, a call to `clone()` is now far cheaper than cloning the data directly:

```
use std::rc::Rc;

#[derive(Debug)]
struct FileName {
    name: Rc<String>,
    ext: Rc<String>
}

fn ref_counter() {
    let name = Rc::new(String::from("main"));
    let ext = Rc::new(String::from("rs")));

    for _ in 0..3 {
        println!("{;?}", FileName {
                    name: name.clone(),
                    ext: ext.clone()
        });
    }
}
```

Running this snippet prints the debug version of the `FileName` object three times:

```
FileName { name: "main", ext: "rs" }
FileName { name: "main", ext: "rs" }
FileName { name: "main", ext: "rs" }
```

This approach works great for single-threaded and immutable scenarios, but will refuse to compile multithreaded code. The solution to this will be discussed in the next section.

Concurrency and mutability

Rust's approach to managing memory is a powerful concept. In fact, it is powerful enough to also facilitate concurrency and parallel execution. However, first things first: how do threads work in the Rust standard library?

Concurrency and parallelism are two different modes of execution. While concurrency means that parts of a program run independently of each other, parallelism refers to these parts executing at the same time. For simplicity, we will refer to both concepts as concurrency.

Due to its low-level nature, Rust provides an API to the operating system's threading capabilities (for example, POSIX on Linux/Unix systems). If no variables are passed into the scope, their usage is very straightforward:

```
use std::thread;

fn threading() {
    // The to pipes (||) is the space where parameters go,
    // akin to a function signature's parameters, without
    // the need to always declare types explicitly.
    // This way, variables can move from the outer into the inner scope
    let handle = thread::spawn(|| {
        println!("Hello from a thread");
    });
    handle.join().unwrap();
}
```

However, when passing data back and forth, more work has to be done to hold up Rust's safety guarantees, especially when mutability comes into play. Before getting into that, it is important to recap immutability.

Immutable variables

Rust—like many functional languages—embraces immutable variables. They are the default, and changing mutability requires explicit declaration with mut, which tells the compiler what the variable is going to be used for (reading or writing).

Functional programming languages are known for facilitating the ability to work concurrently, thanks to immutability guarantees; reading data does not produce side effects! Requiring explicit mutability gives the compiler a chance to check where and if mutability is required, and therefore whether a data race may occur.

This results in compile-time warnings and errors instead of crashes and strange race conditions at runtime, something that many production users appreciate. In short, it's easier to think through your code if mutability is a (rare) option instead of the norm.

Shadowing

Instead of changing variable properties, it's often more readable to overwrite a variable with a different value (for example, a changed copy of the original). This technique is called **shadowing**.

Typically, this is used to reuse a variable name, even though the actual value has changed, to work in the current situation. This snippet sanitizes String and, by using the same name throughout the function, it's always clear that it's the input parameter that is changed:

```
fn sanitize(s: String) -> String {
    let s = s.trim();
    let s = s.replace(" ", "_");
    s
}
```

While this is akin to changing the value of a variable, shadowing does not replace mutability, especially when it's less costly to actually change properties of that variable; Rust has a specific design pattern for that!

Interior mutability

Can a variable be immutable and mutable at the same time? Of course. Boxed variables (Box, Rc, and so on) are an immutable reference to the heap and they contain the actual value.

For these kinds of containers, there is no reason why the inner variable cannot be changed—a task that can be done safely in Rust using RefCell. RefCell maintains single ownership of a value but allows mutable borrowing **checked at runtime.** Instead of compiler errors, violating the rules of borrowing will lead to a runtime panic!, crashing the program.

This entire concept is called **interior mutability** and is often used in combination with Rc in order to provide a value to multiple owners with mutability at will. Clearly, to provide a great user experience, it is strongly recommended to make sure the borrowing rules can't be violated in other ways.

Wrapping a RefCell in an Rc acts as the gatekeeper for having multiple owners, including a way to change the contents. This is actually similar to more traditional programming languages such as Java or C#, where typically references are moved between method calls, pointing to the object's instance on the heap memory.

This pattern is very important for implementing complex programs and data structures, since ownership of a specific variable is not always clear. For example, later in the book we will examine doubly linked lists, which famously have a pointer to the preceding and succeeding node. Which node *should* have ownership of which pointer? Interior mutability allows us to say both. Consider the node declaration we will use later:

```
use std::cell::RefCell;
use std::rc::Rc;

#[derive(Clone)]
struct Node {
    value: String,
    next: Link,
    prev: Link,
}

type Link = Option<Rc<RefCell<Node>>>;
```

With this list declaration, we can see the pattern in this simpler version of the append function:

```
pub fn append(&mut self, value: String) {
    let new = Rc::new(RefCell::new(Node::new(value)));
    match self.tail.take() {
        Some(old) => {
            old.borrow_mut().next = Some(new.clone());
            new.borrow_mut().prev = Some(old);
        }
        None => self.head = Some(new.clone()),
    };
}
```

This code adds a new node at the front (head) of the list, which contains all data in the form of nodes stored on the heap. In order to add a node at the head of the list, the references have to be set properly, so the previous and next pointers actually refer to the same nodes instead of copies. A more detailed exploration is going to be covered in Chapter 3, *Lists, Lists, and More Lists*. For now, the important part is setting the variables using borrow_mut(). This mutable reference only lives as long as the assignment takes, thereby ruling out creating a too-large scope and violating the borrowing rules.

By using the RefCell function's borrow_mut(), it will check for and enforce borrowing rules and panic in the case of a violation. Later on, we will also talk about the Mutex type, which is essentially a multithreaded version of these cells.

Moving data

The introductory snippet showed code that spawns a thread but did not pass any data into the scope. Just like any other scope, it requires either ownership of a value or at least a borrowed reference in order to work with that data. In this case, passing ownership is what we want, something that is called **moving data** into the scope.

If we change the snippet from the introduction to include a simple variable to print from within the thread, compilation is going to fail:

```
use std::thread;

fn threading() {
    let x = 10;
    let handle = thread::spawn(|| {
        println!("Hello from a thread, the number is {}", x);
    });
    handle.join().unwrap();
}
```

The reason for this is simple: the compiler cannot determine the lifetimes of each of the scopes (will x still be there when the thread needs it?), so it refuses to compile the code:

```
Compiling ch1 v0.1.0 (file:///code/ch1)
error[E0373]: closure may outlive the current function, but it borrows `x`,
which is owned by the current function
  --> src/main.rs:5:32
   |
5  |     let handle = thread::spawn(|| {
   |                                ^^ may outlive borrowed value `x`
6  |         println!("Hello from a thread, the number is {}", x);
   |                                                           - `x` is
borrowed here
help: to force the closure to take ownership of `x` (and any other
referenced variables), use the `move` keyword
   |
5  |     let handle = thread::spawn(move || {
   |                                ^^^^^^^
```

As the compiler messages indicate, adding the move keyword will solve the issue! This keyword lets a thread pass ownership to a different thread; it "moves" the memory area:

```
fn threading() {
    let x = 10;
    let handle = thread::spawn(move || {
        println!("Hello from a thread, the number is {}", x);
    });
```

```
        handle.join().unwrap();
}
```

When running this snippet, the output is as follows:

Hello from a thread, the number is 10

However, for passing multiple messages into a thread or implementing *an actor model*, the Rust standard library offers channels. Channels are single-consumer, multi-producer queues that let the caller send messages from multiple threads.

This snippet will spawn 10 threads and have each send a number into the channel, where it will be collected into a vector after the senders have finished executing:

```
use std::sync::mpsc::{channel, Sender, Receiver};

fn channels() {
    const N: i32 = 10;
    let (tx, rx): (Sender<i32>, Receiver<i32>) = channel();
    let handles = (0..N).map(|i| {
        let _tx = tx.clone();
        thread::spawn(move || {
            // don't use the result
            let _ = _tx.send(i).unwrap();
        })
    });
    // close all threads
    for h in handles {
        h.join().unwrap();
    }
    // receive N times
    let numbers: Vec<i32> = (0..N).map(|_|
            rx.recv().unwrap()
        ).collect();
    println!("{:?}", numbers);
}
```

As expected, the output is as follows:

[0, 1, 2, 3, 4, 5, 6, 7, 8, 9]

With these tools, a multithreaded application can move data between threads without the need for manual locking or the dangers of inadvertently creating side effects.

Sharing data

Other than sending data into threads one way, many programs operate on a shared state where multiple execution streams have to access and change one or more shared variables. Typically, this warrants a **mutex** (short for **mutual exclusion**), so that any time something is accessed within this locked mutex, it is guaranteed to be a single thread.

This is an old concept and implemented in the Rust standard library. How does that facilitate accessing a variable? Wrapping a variable into a Mutex type will provide for the locking mechanism, thereby making it accessible from multiple concurrent writers. However, they don't have ownership of that memory area yet.

In order to provide that ownership across threads—similar to what Rc does within a single thread—Rust provides the concept of an Arc, an atomic reference counter. Using this Mutex on top, it's the thread-safe equivalent of an Rc wrapping a RefCell, a reference counter that wraps a mutable container. To provide an example, this works nicely:

```
use std::thread;
use std::sync::{Mutex, Arc};

fn shared_state() {
    let v = Arc::new(Mutex::new(vec![]));
    let handles = (0..10).map(|i| {
        let numbers = Arc::clone(&v);
        thread::spawn(move || {
            let mut vector = numbers
                .lock()
                .unwrap();
            (*vector).push(i);
        })
    });

    for handle in handles {
        handle.join().unwrap();
    }
    println!("{:?}", *v.lock().unwrap());
}
```

When running this example, the output is this:

```
[0, 1, 2, 3, 4, 5, 6, 7, 8, 9]
```

While the preferred way of doing concurrent programming is still to use immutable variables as often as possible, safe Rust provides the tools for working with shared data without side effects.

Send and Sync

These marker traits are fundamental to Rust's multithreading policies. They have distinct purposes:

- Send: A data type is safe to send (move) from one thread to the other
- Sync: The data type can be shared across threads without manual locks or mutex areas

These marker traits are implemented in all basic types of the standard library and can be inherited for custom types (if all properties of a type are Sync, then the type itself is Sync too).

Implementing Sync or Send is unsafe because there is no way for the compiler to know if you are right and the code can be shared/sent between threads, which is why it's very unusual to do this.

In case your program requires this depth of Rust programming, be sure to read up on this topic in the *Rust Book*, chapter 16 (`https://doc.rust-lang.org/1.31.0/book/ch16-04-extensible-concurrency-sync-and-send.html`).

Deeper into Rust

Another one of Rust's strong points is its thriving community. Many users actively participate in their local community (by going to or organizing meetups) or online via working groups, the IRC/Discord channel, or the official forum. The most important online resources are as follows:

- The main website with pointers to various resources: `https://www.rust-lang.org`
- The Rust user forum: `https://users.rust-lang.org`
- The official Twitter account: `https://twitter.com/rustlang`
- A collection of IRC channels at `https://wiki.mozilla.org/Rust`
- Rust's official blog: `https://blog.rust-lang.org`
- The Rust Book: `https://doc.rust-lang.org/book/`

Other than that, users have created additional content, such as podcasts, blogs, and various tools and libraries. The most impressive user contributions, however, can be found in the core language!

Rust's official GitHub repository at `https://github.com/rust-lang` holds the source code for many of the resources (for example, the website, blog, book, and documentation), and contributions are very welcome.

Mozilla has an impressive record of creating and fostering open source communities, and Rust is no different. As active members of these communities, we encourage everyone to take part and help make Rust the most enjoyable and useful language around!

Requests for Comments (RFCs)

Due to the open source nature of Rust, there are some governance rules in place to maintain stable and flexible interfaces, yet encourage change and discussion as the language evolves.

For something as sensitive as a programming language and its standard library, a more rigid process than the regular pull request approval is required to have deeper discussions. Imagine the impact of changing a single keyword and how many projects would stop working immediately!

This is where RFCs come in. They provide a way for all stakeholders to contribute to the discussion with an equal chance to comment. A typical workflow for integrating change in open source projects uses the fork and pull method where the contributor creates a **pull request (PR)** to propose changes (`https://help.github.com/articles/about-pull-requests/`). Unlike in the RFC process, this gets hard to manage in larger code bases and only starts the discussion *after* a solution has been proposed, narrowing the focus considerably.

A repository of active and past RFCs can be found here: `https://github.com/rust-lang/rfcs`.

Summary

Rust is a multi-paradigm language with exceptional concepts: the language emphasizes data and behavior separation with structures and traits, uses macros for metaprogramming, and leverages explicit ownership of memory to determine variable lifetimes. Knowing these lifetimes removes the need for runtime garbage collection and, at the same time, greatly facilitates concurrency by allowing mutable borrowing only in certain circumstances.

Consequently, threads and other asynchronous processes can change variables only when they have mutable ownership of them, something that is mostly enforced at compile time, but can also be done at runtime! Therefore, safe Rust is effectively free of data races.

Another strong point of the Rust ecosystem is its diverse and welcoming community. Sponsored by Mozilla, development is guided by RFCs, events are organized and centrally advertised, and learning resources are available online. Another way to be a part of the ecosystem is to contribute packages to `crates.io` (https://crates.io/), Rust's public package repository. Read the next chapter to find out more about `cargo`, Rust's universal tool to build and package.

Questions

- What are traits and how are they different from interfaces?
- Why doesn't Rust have a garbage collector?
- Name three examples of how lifetimes are created in Rust (explicitly and implicitly)!
- Why is immutability for variables important?
- What does the Sync marker trait do?
- Where can you go to participate in the Rust community?
- Why are RFCs preferred over PRs?

Further reading

Refer to the following books for more information:

- *Hands-On Concurrency with Rust* by Brian L. Troutwine (Packt)
- *Functional Programming in Rust* by Andrew Johnson (Packt)

2
Cargo and Crates

Rust is a rather young language that has been designed from scratch to be a practical and useful tool for programmers. This is a great situation to be in: there are no legacy applications to care about, and many lessons learned from other languages have been incorporated in Rust—especially around tooling.

Integrating and managing third-party packages has been an issue in the past for a lot of languages, and there are a few different approaches out there:

- **NPM**: The package manager for Node, which has been very popular with the JavaScript community
- **Maven**: Enterprise-grade Java package management, based on the XML format
- **NuGet**: .NET's package management
- **PyPI**: The Python package index

Each of these has different styles of configuration, naming guidelines, publishing infrastructure, features, plugins, and so on. The Rust team learned from all of these approaches and built their own version: `cargo`. This chapter will be all about the power of `cargo` of how and where to integrate with the wealth of packages (called crates) out there. Whether you are working on your own small library or you are building a large enterprise-grade system, `cargo` will be a central piece of the project. By reading this chapter, you can look forward to the following:

- Learning more about `cargo`, its configuration, and plugins
- Knowing more about the different types of crates
- Benchmarking and test integration done in `cargo`

Cargo

The basic Rust tooling is composed of three programs:

- `cargo`: The Rust package manager
- `rustc`: The Rust compiler
- `rustup`: The Rust toolchain manager

Most users will never touch (or even see) `rustc` directly, but will usually use `rustup` to install it and then let `cargo` orchestrate the compilation.

Running `cargo` without any arguments reveals the subcommands it provides:

```
$ cargo
Rust's package manager

USAGE:
 cargo [OPTIONS] [SUBCOMMAND]

OPTIONS:
    -V, --version           Print version info and exit
        --list              List installed commands
        --explain <CODE>    Run `rustc --explain CODE`
    -v, --verbose           Use verbose output (-vv very verbose/build.rs
output)
    -q, --quiet             No output printed to stdout
        --color <WHEN>      Coloring: auto, always, never
        --frozen            Require Cargo.lock and cache are up to date
        --locked            Require Cargo.lock is up to date
    -Z <FLAG>...            Unstable (nightly-only) flags to Cargo, see
'cargo -Z help' for details
    -h, --help              Prints help information

Some common cargo commands are (see all commands with --list):
    build       Compile the current project
    check       Analyze the current project and report errors, but don't
build object files
    clean       Remove the target directory
    doc         Build this project's and its dependencies' documentation
    new         Create a new cargo project
    init        Create a new cargo project in an existing directory
    run         Build and execute src/main.rs
    test        Run the tests
    bench       Run the benchmarks
    update      Update dependencies listed in Cargo.lock
    search      Search registry for crates
```

```
publish      Package and upload this project to the registry
install      Install a Rust binary
uninstall    Uninstall a Rust binary
```

There are a few clues here as to what the package manager can do. Other than resolving different types of dependencies for projects, it acts as a test runner for benchmarks and unit/integration tests, and provides access to registries such as crates.io (https://crates.io/). Many of these properties can be configured in a .cargo/config file in the TOML (https://github.com/toml-lang/toml) syntax, either in your home directory, the project directory, or the hierarchy in between.

The individual properties that can be configured can easily evolve over time, so we'll focus on some core parts.

Local repositories can be customized with a paths property (an array of paths) in the root section of the file, whereas any command-line arguments for the cargo new command can be found in the [cargo-new] section of the file. If these custom repositories are remote, this can be configured in [registry] and [http] for the proxy address and port, custom certificate authority (cainfo), or high latencies (timeout).

These are handy configurations for enterprise systems with private repositories, or CI builds with shared drives acting as caches. However, there are options to **customize the toolchain,** by letting the user provide some configuration in a [target.$triple] section (for example, [target.wasm32-unknown-unknown] to customize a Wasm target). Each of those sections contains the following properties:

- A linker specific to the selected triple
- Another archiver by customizing ar
- A runner for running the program and associated tests
- Flags for the compiler in rustflags

Lastly, the **build configuration** is set within the [build] section, where the number of jobs, binaries, such as rustc or rustdoc, the target triple, rustflags, or incremental compilation can be set. To learn more about configuring cargo and to obtain a sample of this configuration, go to https://doc.rust-lang.org/cargo/reference/config.html.

In the next sections, we are going to explore the core of cargo: the project.

Project configuration

In order to recognize a Rust project, `cargo` requires its manifest to be present, where most of the other aspects (metadata, source code location, and so on) can be configured. Once this has been done, building the project will create another file: `Cargo.lock`. This file contains the dependency tree of a project with library versions and locations in order to speed up future builds. Both of these files are essential to a Rust project.

The manifest – Cargo.toml

The `Cargo.toml` file follows—as the name suggests—the TOML structure. It's handwritten and contains metadata about the project as well as dependencies, links to other resources, build profiles, examples, and much more. Most of them are optional and have reasonable defaults. In fact, the `cargo new` command generates the minimal version of a manifest:

```
[package]
name = "ch2"
version = "0.1.0"
authors = ["Claus Matzinger"]
edition = "2018"

[dependencies]
```

There are many more sections and properties, and we will present a few important ones here.

Package

This manifest section is all about metadata for the package, such as name, version, and authors, but also a link to the documentation that defaults to the corresponding page (`https://docs.rs/`). While many of these fields are there to support `crates.io` and display various indicators (categories, badges, repository, homepage, and so on), some fields should be filled regardless of whether they are published there, such as license (especially with open source projects).

Another interesting section is the metadata table in `package.metadata`, because it's ignored by `cargo`. This means that projects can store their own data in the manifest for project- or publishing-related properties—for example, for publishing on Android's Google Play Store, or information to generate Linux packages.

Profiles

When you run `cargo build`, `cargo build --release`, or `cargo test`, `cargo` uses profiles to determine individual settings for each stage. While these have reasonable defaults, you might want to customize some settings. The manifest provides these switches with the `[profile.dev]`, `[profile.release]`, `[profile.test]`, and `[profile.bench]` sections:

```
[profile.release]
opt-level = 3
debug = false
rpath = false
lto = false
debug-assertions = false
codegen-units = 16
panic = 'unwind'
incremental = false
overflow-checks = false
```

These values are the defaults (as of writing this book) and are already useful for most users.

Dependencies

This is probably the most important section for most developers. The dependencies section contains a list of values that represent crate names on `crates.io` (or your configured private registry) as keys along with the version as values.

Instead of the version string, it's equally possible to provide an inline table as a value that specifies optionality or other fields:

```
[dependencies]
hyper = "*"
rand = { version = "0.5", optional = true }
```

Interestingly, since this is an object, TOML allows us to use it like a section:

```
[dependencies]
hyper = "*"

[dependencies.rand]
version = "0.5"
features = ["stdweb"]
```

Since, in the 2018 edition, the `extern` crate declarations inside the `.rs` files are optional, renaming a dependency can be done inside the `Cargo.toml` specification by using the `package` property. Then, the specified key can become an alias for this `package`, like this:

```
[dependencies]
# import in Rust with "use web::*"
web = { version = "*", package = "hyper" }

[dependencies.random] # import in Rust with "use random::*"
version = "0.5"
package = "rand"
features = ["stdweb"]
```

Features are crate-specific strings that include or exclude certain features. In the case of rand (and some others), `stdweb` is a feature that allows us to use the crate in Wasm scenarios by leaving out things that would not compile otherwise. Note that these features might be automatically applied when they depend on toolchains.

Something that needs to be specified via those objects is the dependence on a remote Git repository or local path. This is useful for testing a patched version of a library locally without publishing it to `crates.io` (`https://crates.io/`) and having it built by `cargo` during the parent's build phase:

```
[dependencies]
hyper = "*"
rand = { git = "https://github.com/rust-lang-nursery/rand", branch = "0.4"
}
```

Specifying versions with `cargo` follows a pattern too. Since any crate is encouraged to follow a semantic versioning scheme (`<major>.<minor>.<patch>`), there are operators that include or exclude certain versions (and thereby APIs). For `cargo`, those operators are as follows:

- **Tilde** (~): Only patch increases are allowed.
- **Caret** (^): No major update will be done (2.0.1 to 2.1.0 is OK, to 3.0.1 is not!) .
- **Wildcard** (*): Allows any version, but it can be used to replace a position.

These operators avoid future dependency headaches and introduce a stable API without missing the required updates and fixes.

 It isn't possible to publish a crate with wildcard dependencies. After all, which version is the target computer supposed to use? This is why `cargo` enforces explicit version numbers when running `cargo publish`.

There are several ways to work with purpose-specific dependencies. They can either be declared by platform (`[target.wasm32-unknown-unknown]`) or by their intention: there is a dependency type, `[dev-dependencies]`, for compiling tests, examples, and benchmarks, but there is also a build-only dependency specification, `[build-dependencies]`, that will be separated from others.

Once the dependencies are specified, they are resolved and looked up to generate a dependency tree within the project. This is where the `Cargo.lock` file comes in.

Dependencies – Cargo.lock

Here is a great quote from the `cargo` FAQ (`https://doc.rust-lang.org/cargo/faq.html`) about what the purpose of this file is and what it does:

> *The purpose of a Cargo.lock is to describe the state of the world at the time of a successful build. It is then used to provide deterministic builds across whatever machine is building the project by ensuring that the exact same dependencies are being compiled.*

This serialized state can easily be transferred across teams or computers. Therefore, should a dependency introduce a bug with a patch update, your build should be largely unaffected unless you run `cargo update`. In fact, it's recommended for libraries to commit the `Cargo.lock` file to version control to retain a stable, working build. For debugging purposes, it's also quite handy to streamline the dependency tree.

Commands

`cargo` supports a wealth of commands that can be extended easily. It deeply integrates with the project and allows for additional build scripts, benchmarking, testing, and so on.

The compile and run commands

As the main build tool, `cargo` does compile and run by way of creating and then executing the output binary (usually found in `target/<profile>/<target-triple>/`).

What if a library written in a different language is required to precede the Rust build? This is where build scripts come in. As mentioned in the *Project configuration* section, the manifest provides a field called `build` which takes a path or name to a `build` script.

The script itself can be a regular Rust binary that generates output in a designated folder, and can even have dependencies specified in `Cargo.toml` (`[build-dependencies]`, but nothing else). Any required information (target architecture, output, and so on) is passed into the program using environment variables, and any output for `cargo` is required to have the `cargo:key=value` format. Those are picked up by `cargo` to configure further steps. While the most popular is building native dependencies, it's entirely possible to generate code (such as bindings, data access classes, and so on) as well. Read more in the `cargo` reference: `https://doc.rust-lang.org/cargo/reference/build-scripts.html`.

Larger projects will require a more complex structure than a simple `src/` folder to contain all the source code, which is why `cargo` provides the option to split projects into subprojects, called a workspace. This comes in handy for architectural patterns such as microservices (each service could be a project), or loosely coupling components (clean architecture). To set this up, place each subproject in a subdirectory and create a `Cargo.toml` in the workspace that declares its members:

```
[workspace]
members = [ "core", "web", "data"]
```

This applies any commands run at the top level to every crate in the workspace. Invoking `cargo test` will run all types of tests and that can take a long time.

Testing

As far as commands go, `cargo` supports test and bench to run a crate's tests. These tests are specified in the code by creating a "module" inside a module and annotating it with `#[cfg(test)]`. Furthermore, each test also has to be annotated with either `#[test]` or `#[bench]`, whereas the latter takes an argument to the `Bencher`, a benchmark runner class that allows us to collect stats on each run:

```
#![feature(test)]
extern crate test;

pub fn my_add(a: i32, b: i32) -> i32 {
    a + b
}

#[cfg(test)]
mod tests {
    use super::*;
    use test::Bencher;

    #[test]
```

```
        fn this_works() {
            assert_eq!(my_add(1, 1), 2);
        }
        #[test]
        #[should_panic(expected = "attempt to add with overflow")]
        fn this_does_not_work() {
            assert_eq!(my_add(std::i32::MAX, std::i32::MAX), 0);
        }
        #[bench]
        fn how_fast(b: &mut Bencher) {
            b.iter(|| my_add(42, 42))
        }
    }
```

After running `cargo test`, the output is as expected:

```
Finished dev [unoptimized + debuginfo] target(s) in 0.02s
    Running target/debug/deps/ch2-6372277a4cd95206

running 3 tests
test tests::how_fast ... ok
test tests::this_works ... ok
test tests::this_does_not_work ... ok

test result: ok. 3 passed; 0 failed; 0 ignored; 0 measured; 0 filtered out
```

In this example, the tests are importing and calling a function from its parent module, called `my_add`. One of the tests even expects a `panic!` (caused by an overflow) to be thrown, which is why the `#[should_panic]` annotation has been added.

On top of this, `cargo` supports doctests, which is a special form of testing. One of the most tedious things when refactoring is updating the examples in the documentation which is why they are frequently not working. Coming from Python, the doctest is a solution to this dilemma. By running the actual code in a denoted example, doctests makes sure that everything that's printed in the documentation can be executed—creating a black box test at the same time.

Every function in Rust can be annotated using a special docstring—which is used to generate the documentation at DOCS.RS (`https://docs.rs/`).

doctests are only available for crates of the library type.

This documentation has sections (indicated by a markdown header: #), and if a particular section is called `Examples`, any contained code will be compiled and run:

```
/// # A new Section
/// this [markdown](https://daringfireball.net/projects/markdown/) is
picked up by `Rustdoc`
```

We can now add another test to the preceding sample by creating a few lines of documentation:

```
/// # A Simple Addition
///
/// Adds two integers.
///
/// # Arguments
///
/// - *a* the first term, needs to be i32
/// - *b* the second term, also a i32
///
/// ## Returns
/// The sum of *a* and *b*.
///
/// # Panics
/// The addition is not done safely, overflows will panic!
///
/// # Examples
///
/// ```rust
/// assert_eq!(ch2::my_add(1, 1), 2);
/// ```
pub fn my_add(a: i32, b: i32) -> i32 {
    a + b
}
```

The `cargo test` command will now run the code in examples as well:

```
$ cargo test
   Compiling ch2 v0.1.0
(file:///home/cm/workspace/Mine/rust.algorithms.data.structures/code/ch2)
    Finished dev [unoptimized + debuginfo] target(s) in 0.58s
     Running target/debug/deps/ch1-8ed0f81f04655fe4

running 0 tests

test result: ok. 0 passed; 0 failed; 0 ignored; 0 measured; 0 filtered out

     Running target/debug/deps/ch2-3ddb7f7cbab6792d
```

```
running 3 tests
test tests::how_fast ... ok
test tests::this_does_not_work ... ok
test tests::this_works ... ok

test result: ok. 3 passed; 0 failed; 0 ignored; 0 measured; 0 filtered out

    Doc-tests ch2

running 1 test
test src/lib.rs - my_add (line 26) ... ok

test result: ok. 1 passed; 0 failed; 0 ignored; 0 measured; 0 filtered out
```

For larger tests or black-box tests, it's also possible (and recommended) to put the tests into a subfolder of the project, called `tests`. `cargo` will pick this up automatically and run the tests accordingly.

On top of tests, other commands are often required (code metrics, linting, and so on) and recommended. For that, `cargo` provides a third-party command interface.

Third-party subcommands

`cargo` allows the extension of its command-line interface with subcommands. These subcommands are binaries that are called when invoking `cargo <command>` (for example, `cargo clippy` for the popular linter).

In order to install a new command (for a particular toolchain), run `cargo +nightly install clippy`, which will download, compile, and install a crate called `cargo-clippy` and then put it into the `.cargo` directory in your home folder. In fact, this will work with any binary that is called `cargo-<something>` and is executable from any command line. The `cargo` project keeps an updated list of some useful subcommands in the repository at `https://github.com/rust-lang/cargo/wiki/Third-party-cargo-subcommands`.

Crates

Rust's modules (crates) can easily be packaged and distributed once all the compilation and testing is done, regardless of whether they are libraries or executables. First, let's take a look at Rust binaries in general.

Rust libraries and binaries

There are executable binaries and libraries in Rust. When these Rust programs use dependencies, they rely on the linker to integrate those so it will work on—at least—the current platform. There are two major types of linking: static and dynamic—both of which are somewhat dependent on the operating system.

Static and dynamic libraries

Generally, Rust dependencies have two types of linking:

- **Static**: Via the `rlib` format.
- **Dynamic**: Via shared libraries (`.so` or `.dll`).

The preference—if a corresponding `rlib` can be found—is to link statically and therefore include all dependencies into the output binary, making the file a lot larger (to the dismay of embedded programmers). Therefore, if multiple Rust programs use the same dependency, each comes with its own built-in version. It's all about the context though, since, as Go's success has shown, static linking can simplify complex deployments since only a single file has to be rolled out.

There are drawbacks to the static linking approach beyond size: for static libraries, all dependencies have to be of the `rlib` type, which is Rust's native package format, and cannot contain a dynamic library since the formats (for example, `.so` (dynamic) and `.a` (static) on ELF systems) aren't convertible.

For Rust, dynamic linking is commonly used for native dependencies, since they are usually available in the operating system and don't need to be included in the package. The Rust compiler can favor this with a `-C prefer-dynamic` flag, which will get the compiler to look for the corresponding dynamic libraries first.

Therein lies the current strategy of the compiler: depending on the output format (`--crate-format=` `rlib`, `dylib`, `staticlib`, `library`, or `bin`), it decides on the best linking type with your influence via flags. However, there is a rule that the output cannot statically link the same library twice, so it won't link two libraries with the same static dependency.

For more information on the topic, we recommend checking out `https://doc.rust-lang.org/reference/linkage.html`. That said, the compiler is usually trustworthy and, unless there is an interoperability goal, `rustc` will decide optimally.

Linking and interoperability

Rust compiles to native code like many other languages, which is great because it expands the available libraries and lets you choose the best technology to solve a problem. "Playing nice with others" has always been a major design goal of Rust.

Interoperability on that level is as simple as declaring the function that you want to import and dynamically linking a library that exports this function. This process is largely automated: the only thing required is to create and declare a build script that compiles the dependency and then tells the linker where the output is located. Depending on what type of library you built, the linker does what is necessary to include it into the Rust program: static or dynamic linking (the default).

If there is only one native library that is to be linked dynamically, the manifest file offers a `links` property to specify that. Programmatically, it's very easy to interact with these included libraries by using the Foreign Function Interface.

FFI

The **Foreign Function Interface (FFI)** is Rust's way of calling into other native libraries (and vice versa) using a simple keyword: `extern`. By declaring an `extern` function, the compiler knows that, either an outside interface needs to be bound via the linker (import) or, that the declared function is to be exported so other languages can make use of it (export).

In addition to the keyword, the compiler and linker have to get a hint of what type of binary layout is expected. That's why the usual `extern` declaration looks as follows:

```
extern "C" {
    fn imported_function() -> i32;
}

#[no_mangle]
pub extern "C" fn exported_function() -> i32 {
    42
}
```

This allows a C library function to be called from within Rust. However, there's one caveat: the calling part has to be wrapped in an `unsafe` section. The Rust compiler cannot guarantee the safety of an external library so it makes sense to be pessimistic about its memory management. The exported function is safe, and by adding the `#[no_mangle]` attribute, there is no name mangling, so it can be found using its name.

In order to use libraries for specialized algorithms available in a C/C++ library, there is a tool that generates suitable structures, `extern "C"` declarations, and data types, called `rust-bindgen`. Find out more at `https://github.com/rust-lang-nursery/rust-bindgen`. These interoperability capabilities make Rust code available to legacy software or for use in a vastly different context, such as web frontends.

Wasm

Wasm, which **WebAssembly** is now commonly called, is a binary format meant to complement JavaScript that Rust can be compiled to. The format is designed to run as a stack machine inside several sandboxed execution environments (such as web browsers, or the Node.js runtime) for performance-critical applications (`https://blog.x5ff.xyz/blog/azure-functions-wasm-rust/`). While this is—as of this writing—in its early stages, Rust and the Wasm target have been used in real-time frontend settings (such as browser games), and in 2018 there was a dedicated working group seeking to improve this integration.

Similar to other targets, such as ARM, the Wasm target is an LLVM (the compiler technology Rust is built on) backend so it has to be installed using `rustup target add wasm32-unknown-unknown`. Furthermore, it isn't necessary to declare the binary layout (the `"C"` in `extern "C"`) and a different bindgen tool does the rest: `wasm-bindgen`, available at `https://github.com/rustwasm/wasm-bindgen`. We highly recommend reading the documentation for more information.

The main repository – crates.io

The `crates.io` website (`https://crates.io/`) provides a huge repository of crates to be used with Rust. Along with discoverability functions, such as `tags` and `search`, it allows Rust programmers to offer their work to others.

The repository itself provides APIs to interact with and a wealth of documentation pointers for `cargo`, crates in general, and so on. The source code is available on GitHub—we recommend checking out the repository for more information: `https://github.com/rust-lang/crates.io`.

Publishing

For developers to get their crate into this repository, `cargo` harbors a command: `cargo publish`. The command is actually doing more things behind the scenes: first it runs the `cargo` package to create a `*.crate` file that contains everything that is uploaded. Then it verifies the contents of the package by essentially running `cargo test` and checks whether there are any uncommitted files in the local repository. Only if these checks pass does `cargo` upload the contents of the `*.crate` file to the repository. This requires a valid account on `crates.io` (available with your GitHub login) to acquire your personal secret API token, and the crate has to follow certain rules.

 With the previously-mentioned Wasm target, it's even possible to publish Rust packages to the famous JavaScript package repository: npm Keep in mind that Wasm support is still very new, but once a crate compiles to Wasm it can be packed into an npm package using Wasm-pack: `https://github.com/rustwasm/wasm-pack`.

`crates.io` aspires to be a permanent storage for Rust crates, so there is no "unpublish" button. Versions can be yanked with `cargo yank`, but this won't delete any code; it will just prohibit updates to this particular version. Additionally there can be team structures, colorful READMEs, badges, and so on, on your repository's site and we highly recommend you check out the docs on that as well: `https://doc.rust-lang.org/cargo/reference/publishing.html`.

Summary

`cargo` is Rust's package manager and build tool that is configurable with a manifest called `Cargo.toml`. The file is used by `cargo` to build the desired binary with the specified dependencies, profiles, workspaces, and package metadata. During this process, the package state is saved in a file called `Cargo.lock`. Thanks to its LLVM frontend, Rust compiles to native code on various platforms including the web (using Wasm)—thus keeping a high degree of interoperabilty. Successfully-built packages can be published on a repository called `crates.io`, a website that is a central hub for available Rust libraries and binaries.

Before we dive into data structures (starting with lists), the next chapter will introduce the ways Rust stores variables and data in memory, whether to copy or to clone, and what sized and unsized types are.

Questions

- What does `cargo` do?
- Does `cargo` provide linting support?
- In which cases is the `Cargo.lock` file important to publish?
- What are the requirements to publish to `crates.io`?
- What is Wasm and why should you care?
- How are tests organized in a Rust project?

Further reading

You can refer to the following links for more information on the topics covered in this chapter:

- `https://crates.io`
- `https://doc.rust-lang.org/cargo/`
- `https://github.com/rustwasm/team`
- `https://webassembly.org`
- `https://blog.x5ff.xyz/blog/azure-functions-wasm-rust/`

Storing Efficiently

3

With the foundation of the previous chapters in place, we can now move on to more architectural aspects of algorithms and data structures. Rust—with its ownership model—calls for considering lifetimes, memory placement, and mutability in their algorithmic design. In this chapter, you can look forward to learning about the following topics:

- Trade-offs considering speed and readability
- Accessing heap and stack variables
- How immutability influences design

Heaps and stacks

As we discussed in Chapter 1, *Hello Rust!*, stack variables are preferred thanks to their low overhead and speed compared to heap-allocated data, which automatically introduces overhead thanks to the necessary heap pointer. For stack variables, Rust's types even allow for zero overhead structures, so no additional metadata is stored. The following snippet asserts that there are no additional bytes being used for arrays or user-defined types:

```
use std::mem;

struct MyStruct {
    a: u8,
    b: u8,
    c: u8
}

fn main() {
    assert_eq!(mem::size_of::<MyStruct>(), 3 * mem::size_of::<u8>());
    assert_eq!(mem::size_of::<[MyStruct; 2]>(), 3 * mem::size_of::<u8>() *
2);
}
```

Consequently, the size of an instance of the `MyStruct` type is always going to be three bytes—perfectly suitable for placing it on the stack. Why is that good? In short, data locality. Instead of pointer dereferencing, the data is stored right at the point of execution, making it easy to cache and fast to access.

Types that don't have predictable sizes (such as `String` instances) require heap allocation, just like objects that are wrapped into `Rc`, `Cell`, `RefCell`, or `Box` instances. However, heap allocations and access come at a considerable cost, as minimizing those typically yields great performance improvements.

Sized and unsized

For the compiler to translate written code into a binary format, it's necessary to know each type's size. As we discussed earlier, the size is important so that we can put other types *on top* when working on the stack, something that is easy if the size doesn't change with respect to the data it contains (a sized type). The best example for this is `u32`: it uses 32 bits (or 4 bytes), regardless of whether you store `0` or `10000900`.

This isn't the case when the type is unsized or dynamically sized, the best example being a `str`. Depending on the number of characters, this type's size will vary considerably, and which is why instances are usually encountered in the form of slices.

 Slices are Rust's way of providing generic algorithms to all kinds of data types, and they will be discussed more in `Chapter 12`, *Algorithms of the Standard Library*.

Slices work around the size issue by storing a fixed-size reference (`&str`) to the heap-allocated value, along with its length in bytes. Similar to pointers, this is a fixed-size view into a previously-unsized value. Every time a pointer of some kind (`&`, `Rc`, `Box`, `Cell`, and so on) is created, the reference is stored alongside the length and some (fixed size) metadata. The knowledge of sized versus unsized is especially useful when the type is previously unknown—when working with Rust's generics, for example.

Generics

Rust supports generics and even allows us to enforce the implementation of certain traits. These constraints can either come as a where clause attached to the function definition or with a colon in the generic type declaration:

```
fn my_generic_func<T: MyTrait>(t: T) {
    // code
}

// ... is the same as

fn my_generic_func <T>(t: T) where T: MyTrait {
    // code
}

// but better use in 2018 and beyond

fn my_generic_func(t: impl MyTrait) {
    // code
}
```

Additionally, the 2018 `impl Trait` syntax simplifies single-trait requirements (to do static instead of dynamic dispatch) for input and return parameters, thereby eliminating the need for a `Box` or lengthy type constraints (such as `MyTrait` in the preceding snippet). Unless multiple trait implementations are required (for example, `fn f(x: T) where T: Clone + Debug + MyTrait {}`), the `impl Trait` syntax allows us to put them where they matter, which is into the parameter list:

```
fn my_generic_func<T>(t: T) {
    // code
}

// ... is the same as

fn my_generic_func <T: Sized>(t: T) {
    // code
}
```

When working with generics, the situation is a bit more complex. Type parameters are `Sized` by default (see the preceding snippet), which means that they will not match unsized types. To match those as well, the special `?Sized` type constraint can be used. This snippet also shows the required change to passing in a reference:

```
fn my_generic_func <T: ?Sized>(t: &T) {
    // code
}
```

However, any type of heap-allocated reference will incur an extra step to access the contained value.

Accessing the box

An extra step doesn't sound like much, but it has considerable consequences. This trade-off for easily sharing ownership across various functions or threads removes the ability to put as much data as possible into the CPU's cache, since the pointer makes any data locality difficult. Heap allocations themselves are expensive operations and reducing those will already provide a major speedup.

Furthermore, the compiler cannot deallocate a boxed value if it's still referenced in some places—a problem that occurs especially if the program is large and complex. Similar to orphaned objects in C# or Java, a saved `Rc` reference can easily be forgotten, creating a memory leak. Therefore, it's recommended to use heap memory only when required.

One principle piece of advice that requires a boxed value in Rust is to "favor object composition over class inheritance" (Gang of Four 1995:20). In the absence of class inheritance, the choice is obviously to use object composition. Considering that you should also "program to an interface not to an implementation" (ibid), there is often a strong wish to put a reference to a trait inside of a `struct` instead of directly working with the implementation.

To apply this architecture in Rust, the language requires us to put a trait's implementation into a `Box<dyn TheTrait>`, making it more difficult to handle, test, and reason about. This `trait` object requires the compiler to rely on dynamic dispatch, which is considerably slower than the default static dispatch.

Static and dynamic dispatch are the two major ways of calling functions in many programming languages, including Rust. While for static dispatch functions, locations are known at compile time, dynamic dispatch functions are only known at runtime and have to be looked up in a **vtable** that points to the actual address. Both have their merits, so be intentional with their use.

Other than generics, there is no default solution to this issue. The `impl Trait` addition of Rust 2018 alleviates this issue for function parameters and return values, but cannot be used for field types.

So far, it looks like the best choice is to use concrete types instead of traits to avoid multiple dereference operations—as long as refactoring on change seems to be doable. If you create a library, generics are a better way to go for performance and flexibility.

Copying and cloning

In `Chapter 1`, *Hello Rust!*, we discussed `Send`, a marker trait that allows a type to be "sent" across multiple threads. Something that's similar but less complex is local moving, which commonly occurs in a program—for example, when you pass a variable into a function.

Copying and cloning, on the other hand, happen on different occasions. When a variable is assigned to another variable, the compiler will typically copy the value implicitly, which can be done safely and cheaply for stack-allocated variables.

 `Copy` is an implicit, bitwise copy of the value of a variable. If that variable is a pointer, the memory responsibility becomes ambiguous (who takes care of freeing?) and compilation will fail. This is where `Clone` comes in. The trait requires an explicit implementation of the `clone()` function to provide an appropriate copy of the type.

Cloning is always a deep copy of a type—implemented either manually (with the `Clone` trait) or by using the `derive` macro. Then, cloning is only a matter of invoking the `clone()` function, an operation that is not necessarily cheap. The following snippet illustrates these two operations:

```
let y = 5;
let x = y;              // Copy

let a = Rc::new(5);
let b = a.clone();      // Clone
```

The regular usage of these traits and operations is usually intuitive and there isn't much that can go wrong. Usually the compiler clearly states the need for a `Copy` implementation.

 It's recommended to derive or implement `Copy` wherever possible, but be mindful of breaking changes. Adding the trait is a non-intrusive action, whereas removing the trait will potentially break other people's code.

While copying and cloning are great for providing ownership to multiple scopes, they are required when working with immutable storage.

Immutable storage

Garbage collectors simplified mutability considerably and, as a consequence, many of these languages don't need a specific modifier for mutability. While this garbage collection mechanism comes at the expense of runtime with frequent cleanups, not having to care about making variables mutable is very convenient. It lets developers focus on the logic they are implementing instead.

So why did Rust (and many functional languages) bring back this concept?

States and reasoning

The state of an object is essentially the current values that its fields have at any given time. Changing this state is done by the object itself via messages on defined behavior (called methods) according to object-orientation principles. These state changes require mutability.

Throughout their lifetimes, most objects change their states multiple times, and since this happens at runtime, we find ourselves often looking at an object's debug print in frustration, thinking, "How did this value get here?"

Immutable data structures remedy this by making it impossible to change their contents, so any time you would look at an object, it has exactly the right values. It's a known fact that the majority of variables don't need to be mutable, and unless there is a resource constraint, creating another instance of the object with its new state is recommended. This principle, called **copy-on-write**, improves readability for better maintenance.

A popular type that employs copy-on-write is the String—in almost any language. The type wraps a byte array and interprets it using a provided character set (usually UTF-8), and if you modify a character, this array is copied and saved with the changes made. This is done so often that String allocations are a common performance pitfall.

> In the Rust standard library, there is a Cow enumeration (std::borrow::Cow) that lazily clones a contained reference whenever mutation or ownership is requested. For a great example, check out the Cow documentation: https://doc.rust-lang.org/std/borrow/enum. Cow.html.

The principle of copy-on-write can also be found in filesystems to create snapshots (for example, in ZFS or BRTFS) and provides the benefits of both immutability and mutability at the cost of runtime resources. It's a trade-off between maintainability and absolute performance. A similar concept is employed by persistent data structures, which can be partially or fully persistent and still be immutable.

Concurrency and performance

Having code that is easier to reason about and where the state cannot be changed is even more important in multithreaded scenarios. This prevents so-called anomalies (or side effects) where the state of an object is changed outside a dependent thread.

Locks are generally made to change the state of a shared object—they secure critical sections, which only a single thread can modify at any given time. Other threads have to "line up" and wait for the lock to be released to access the part as well. In Rust, this is called a **mutex**.

Locks and mutex zones are bad for the following reasons:

- They have to be in the right order (acquired and released).
- What happens when a thread panics in a mutex zone?
- They are hard to integrate seamlessly into the part of the program that they protect.
- They are a bottleneck for performance.

Immutability is a simple way to avoid all of these, and there are many immutable data structure crates available, including one with persistent data structures called **Rust Persistent Data Structures (RPDS)** (`https://crates.io/crates/rpds`), that utilize a copy-on-write approach with versioning to capture state changes. Since these changes build on top of each other, threads can fully read one consistent object state at a time without having to wait or acquire a lock.

 Lock-free data structures are a specialized version of data structures that are very challenging to implement. These data structures use atomic operations to modify important parts (for example, the head pointer in a stack) and thereby achieve excellent performance without locking caveats. **Persistent data structures** are a take on creating data structures that are as efficient and mutable as their traditional counterparts, but better suited for concurrency. This is achieved by keeping the original data immutable and storing versioned change sets.

The idea of immutable data is best thought of in the context of functional programming. Functional programming is built on the principle of mathematical functions. A function is a relation of two sets of data (typically X and Y), where each element of X has exactly one element in Y that it maps to using the f function (in short: $f(x) = y$ where $x \in X, y \in Y$).

As a consequence, the input data, X, will not be changed to produce output data, Y, making it easy to run the f function in parallel. The downside is the increased cost at runtime: regardless of the operation, whether it's only to flip a bit on the input data or to overhaul everything, the result is always a full copy.

To reduce this inefficiency, the Gang of Four's decorator pattern on X's iterator can be used to stack up only the changes and execute them on every call, reducing runtime complexity and avoiding multiple copies of the output data. A problem that remains is that if the input and the output are large, a lot of memory is required. This is a tricky situation and can only be avoided by the programmer thinking thoroughly about decomposing the function better.

Summary

Moving one level above the details of code, this chapter discusses considerations when designing and using types. Rust's differentiation between stack- and heap-allocated variables in code provides a level of control that should be used to improve performance and API flexibility. `Sized`, a marker trait for mostly stack-allocated values, is the default for generic type parameters and can be relaxed by applying the `?Sized` constraint instead.

When working with more object-oriented architectures, trait objects become a way to "work with interfaces" instead of specific implementations. However, they come at a performance cost, that is, dynamic dispatch, another trade-off between maintainability and performance.

Other than moving, Rust can copy or clone variables when necessary. Copy performs a deep copy in the case of sized values; unsized values require a reference that has to be cloned instead. Using these operations is often encountered when working with immutable data types in a principle called copy-on-write. Choosing whether we are able to reason about the object's state at any given time and avoiding data race conditions, but having to create a copy for each change, is another important trade-off when designing data structures.

This trade-off will become apparent in the next chapter, where we will start working with lists, such as the singly-linked list, doubly-linked list, and the dynamic array.

Questions

- How are `Sized` types different from other types?
- How does `Clone` differ from `Copy`?
- What are the main drawbacks of immutable data structures?
- How can applications benefit from immutable data structures?
- Think about an immutable list that you want to work on—how would you distribute it across multiple threads?

Further reading

For more information on the topics that are covered in this chapter, check out the following links:

- http://cglab.ca/~abeinges/blah/too-many-lists/book/
- https://doc.rust-lang.org/std/mem/fn.size_of.html
- https://en.wikipedia.org/wiki/Functional_programming
- https://en.wikipedia.org/wiki/Persistent_data_structure

Lists, Lists, and More Lists

4

Lists are everywhere: shopping lists, to-do lists, recipes, street numbers in western countries... simply everywhere. Their defining characteristic, storing things in a linear, defined relationship with each other, helps us keep track of stuff and find it again later on. From a data structure perspective, they are also essential to almost any program and come in various shapes and forms. While some lists are tricky to implement in Rust, the general principles can be found here as well, along with some valuable lessons on the borrow checker! After this chapter, we want you to know more about the following:

- (Doubly) linked lists and when you should use them
- Array lists, better known as Rust's vector
- Skip lists and, ideally, the New York metro subway system
- Implementing a simple transaction log

 As a final note, this chapter will build *safe* implementations of various lists, even though unsafe versions could be faster and require less code. This decision is due to the fact that, when working on regular use cases, unsafe is almost never a solution. Check out the links in the *Further reading* section of this chapter for unsafe lists.

Linked lists

To keep track of a bunch of items, there is a simple solution: with each entry in the list, store a pointer to the next entry. If there is no next item, store null/nil/None and so on, and keep a pointer to the first item. This is called a **singly linked list**, where each item is connected with a single link to the next, as shown in the following diagram—but you already knew that:

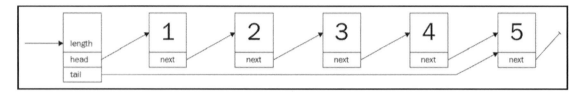

What are the real use cases for a linked list though? Doesn't everyone just use a dynamic array for everything?

Consider a transaction log, a typical append-only structure. Any new command (such as a SQL statement) is simply appended to the existing chain and is eventually written to a persistent storage. Thus, the initial requirements are simple:

- Append a command to an existing list
- Replay every command from the beginning to the end—in that order

In other words, its a queue (or **LIFO**—short for **Last In First Out**) structure.

A transaction log

First, a list has to be defined—in Rust, lacking a null type, each item is chained to the next by an Option property. The Option instances are enumerations that wrap either the value, in this case a heap reference (such as a Box, Rc, and so on), or none—Rust's typed null equivalent. Why? Let's find out!

Creating a prototypical implementation to explore a certain aspect is always a good idea, especially since the compiler often provides excellent feedback. Accordingly, an implementation of an integer list is the first step. How about this struct for each list element?

Have a look at the following code snippet:

```
struct Node {
    value: i32,
    next: Option<Node>
}
```

For practical considerations, it needs a way to know where to start and the length of the list. Considering the planned `append` operation, a reference to the end (tail) would be useful too:

```
struct TransactionLog {
    head: Option<Node>,
    tail: Option<Node>,
    pub length: u64
}
```

That looks great! Does it work though?

```
error[E0072]: recursive type `Node` has infinite size
  --> ch4/src/lib.rs:5:1
   |
5  | struct Node {
   | ^^^^^^^^^^^^ recursive type has infinite size
6  | value: i32,
7  | next: Option<Node>
   | ------------------ recursive without indirection
   |
   = help: insert indirection (e.g., a `Box`, `Rc`, or `&`) at some point to
make `Node` representable
```

Unfortunately, it doesn't work—and, thinking back to the previous chapters, it becomes clear why: the compiler cannot be certain of the data structure's size, since the entire list would have to be nested into the first element. However, as we know, the compiler cannot compute and therefore allocate the required amount of memory this way—which is why reference types are required.

Reference types (such as `Box`, `Rc`, and so on) are a good fit, since they allocate space on the heap and therefore allow for larger lists. Here's an updated version:

```
use std::cell::RefCell;
use std::rc::Rc;

struct Node {
    value: i32,
    next: Option<Rc<RefCell<Node>>>
}
```

```
struct TransactionLog {
    head: Option<Rc<RefCell<Node>>>,
    tail: Option<Rc<RefCell<Node>>>,
    pub length: u64
}
```

Storing each node item in a `Rc<RefCell<T>>` provides the ability to retrieve and replace data as needed (the internal mutability pattern)—crucial when executing operations on the list. Another good practice is to alias types, especially if there are a lot of generics in play. This makes it easy to replace type implementations and provides a more readable definition:

```
type SingleLink = Option<Rc<RefCell<Node>>>;

#[derive(Clone)]
struct Node {
    value: i32,
    next: SingleLink,
}
```

Perfect! This is the base definition of the transaction log, but to use it there are many things missing. First of all, the value type has to be `String`:

```
#[derive(Clone)]
struct Node {
    value: String,
    next: SingleLink,
}

impl Node {
    // A nice and short way of creating a new node
    fn new(value: String) -> Rc<RefCell<Node>> {
        Rc::new(RefCell::new(Node {
            value: value,
            next: None,
        }))
    }
}
```

In addition to that, it is going to be useful to create an empty list, so the `impl` block of the list has a single function for now—`new_empty()`:

```
impl TransactionLog {
    pub fn new_empty() -> TransactionLog {
        TransactionLog { head: None, tail: None, length: 0 }
```

```
        }
    }
```

Still, there is a lot missing. To recap, the transaction log has two requirements:

- `Append` entries at the end
- `Remove` entries from the front

Let's start with the first requirement: appending items to the back of the list!

Adding entries

The transaction log can now be created and hold entries, but there is no way to add anything to the list. Typically, a list has the ability to add elements to either end—as long as there is a pointer to that end. If that was not the case, any operation would become computationally expensive, since every item has to be looked at to find its successor. With a pointer to the end (tail) of the list, this won't be the case for the append operation; however, to access a random index on the list, it would require some time to go through everything.

 Naming is—especially if English is your second language—often tricky. Operations have different names by the language or library used. For example, common names for adding items to a list include `push` (can add to the front or back), `push_back`, `add`, `insert` (usually comes with a positional parameter), or `append`. On top of being able to guess method names, some imply completely different processes than others! If you design an interface or library, find the most descriptive and simple name possible and reuse whenever you can!

This is one of the things that a linked list does really well—adding items to either end. There are a few critical things that should not be overlooked, though:

- Creating the `Node` object within the method makes for a nicer API and better ownership handling.
- Edge cases such as empty lists.
- Incrementing the length is a good idea.
- The `RefCell` is used to retrieve mutable ownership for setting a new successor using its `borrow_mut()` function (interior mutability).

Once that is thought of, the actual implementation is not too bad. Rust's `Option` type offers a method to retrieve ownership of a value it contains, replacing it with `None` (see also the documentations for `Option.take()`—https://doc.rust-lang.org/std/option/enum. `Option.html#method.take` and `mem::replace()`—https://doc.rust-lang.org/stable/ `std/mem/fn.replace.html`), which conveniently shortens the code required to append a new node:

```
pub fn append(&mut self, value: String) {
    let new = Node::new(value);
    match self.tail.take() {
        Some(old) => old.borrow_mut().next = Some(new.clone()),
        None => self.head = Some(new.clone())
    };
    self.length += 1;
    self.tail = Some(new);
}
```

With that, it's now possible to create a log of any string commands passing through. However, there is something important missing here as well: log replay.

Log replay

Typically in databases, transaction logs are a resilience measure if something bad happens that the database must be restored—or to keep a replica up to date. The principle is fairly simple: the log represents a timeline of commands that have been executed in this exact order. Thus, to recreate that final state of a database, it is necessary to start with the oldest entry and apply every transaction that follows in that very order.

You may have caught how that fits the capabilities of a linked list nicely. So, what is missing from the current implementation?

The ability to remove elements starting at the front.

Since the entire data structure resembles a queue, this function is going to be called `pop`, as it's the typical name for this kind of operation. Additionally, `pop` will consume the item that was returned, making the list a single-use structure. This makes sense, to avoid replaying anything twice!

This looks a lot more complex than it is: the interior mutability pattern certainly adds complexity to the implementation. However, it makes the whole thing safe—thanks to RefCells checking borrowing rules at runtime. This also leads to the chain of functions in the last part—it retrieves the value from within its wrappers:

```
pub fn pop(&mut self) -> Option<String> {
    self.head.take().map(|head| {
        if let Some(next) = head.borrow_mut().next.take() {
            self.head = Some(next);
        } else {
            self.tail.take();
        }
        self.length -= 1;
        Rc::try_unwrap(head)
            .ok()
            .expect("Something is terribly wrong")
            .into_inner()
            .value
    })
}
```

Calling this function in sequence returns the commands in the order they were inserted, providing a nice replay feature. For a real-world usage, it's important to provide the ability to serialize this state to disk as well, especially since this operation consumes the list entirely. Additionally, handling errors gracefully (instead of panicking and crashing) is recommended.

After use

Whenever the list needs to be disposed of, Rust calls a drop() method that is automatically implemented. However, since this is an automated process, each member is dropped recursively—which works OK until the level of nested next pointers exceeds the stack for executing the drop() method and crashes the program with an unexpected stack overflow message.

As a consequence, it is a good idea for production usage to also implement the Drop trait and dispose of the list elements iteratively. By the way, a stack overflow also happens while using the derived Debug implementation to print a Node—for the same reason.

Wrap up

A (transaction) log is a great use case for a linked list: They often grow to unexpected sizes, and indexing is not required. While a linked list is often a very simple type in other languages, it harbors a surprising amount of challenges in Rust. This is mostly due to the borrowing and ownership concepts which require a programmer to think about what goes where in great detail. For real-world use cases, however, it's better to use Rust's standard library linked list (`std::collections::LinkedList`). From a performance perspective, finding a particular item in the singly linked list requires looking at the entire list in the worst case, resulting in a runtime complexity of `O(n)`, with n being the number of items in the list (more on the topic of runtime complexity in `Chapter 8`, *Algorithm Evaluation*).

Upsides

The main benefits of a linked list are the abilities to grow very large in size cheaply, always maintain a certain direction, and allow to access items individually. What makes this data structure unique?

There are a few points:

- Low overhead allocation per item.
- Item count is only limited by heap memory.
- Mutation while iterating is possible.
- A direction is strictly enforced—there is no going back.
- Implementation is fairly simple (even in Rust).
- Efficient append, prepend, delete, and insert operations—compared to an array (no shifting required).

Generally, the linked list performs well in an environment where limited memory does not allow overhead allocation (as dynamic arrays do), or as a basis for an exotic lock-free data structure.

Downsides

The linked list has some obvious shortcomings:

- Indexing is inefficient, since every node has to be looked at.
- Iteration in general involves a lot of jumping around on the heap, which takes more time and makes the operation hard to cache.
- Reversing a list is *very* inefficient.

The last point is important, so, commonly, a linked-list implementation will have a link back as well, which makes it a doubly linked list.

Doubly linked list

The transaction log of the previous section is due for an upgrade. The product team wants to enable users to be able to examine the log by going through it **forward and backward** to see what each step does. This is bad news for the regular linked list, as it's really inefficient to go anywhere other than forward. So, how is this rectified?

It is rectified using the doubly linked list. The doubly linked list introduces the link back. While this sounds like a minor change, it allows to work on that list backward as well as forward, which significantly improves the ability to look up items. By augmenting the previous singly linked list item with a back pointer, the doubly linked list is almost created:

```
#[derive(Debug, Clone)]
struct Node {
    value: String,
    next: Link,
    prev: Link,
}

type Link = Option<Rc<RefCell<Node>>>;

#[derive(Debug, Clone)]
pub struct BetterTransactionLog {
    head: Link,
    tail: Link,
    pub length: u64,
}
```

Similar to the singly linked list, the list itself only consists of a head and a tail pointer, which makes accessing either end of the list cheap and easy. Additionally, the nodes now also feature a pointer back to the preceding node, making the list look like this:

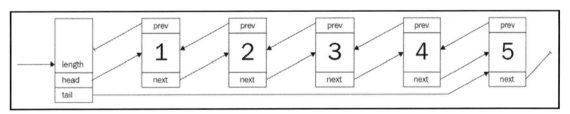

This is also the point that makes the doubly linked list tricky in Rust. The ownership principle is great if there is a hierarchy of ownership: a customer has an address, a text file has several lines of text, and so on. However, a node in a doubly linked list doesn't have clear ownership of either of its neighbors.

A better transaction log

So, the list of requirements got expanded:

- Move forward through the log
- Move backward through the log
- Moves don't consume the log

A nice fit for the doubly linked list, so the existing transaction log can be upgraded! With the pointers to both neighbors of a node, it can solve the problem. However, what about moving through the list without removing elements?

For that, another concept is required: **iterators**. Rust's iterators are leaning on the functional side of programming and provide a versatile interface for integrating with all kinds of other data structures and commands across the language. For example, `for` loops will pick up on the iterator and behave as expected.

Iterators are pointers to the current item with a method called `next()` that produces the next item while moving the pointer forward! This concept is applied a lot when using a more functional approach to working with collections: by chaining them together and applying a function after invoking `next()`, going through a list can be very efficient. Check the *Further reading* section and the last chapter of this book for more information!

The data model is going to look like the singly linked list, so most of the operations can be used as they are—they only need to be upgraded to work with the back-pointer as well.

Examining the log

Looking at the list without consuming it is an iterator's job (see the info box), which—in Rust as well as in most other languages—is a simple implementation of an interface or trait. In fact, this is so common that the Rust docs have a great article (`https://doc.rust-lang.org/std/iter/index.html#implementing-iterator`), which is exactly what's required.

Since we are already working with heap references, the iterator can simply save an optional reference to a node and it's easy to move it forward and backward:

```
pub struct ListIterator {
    current: Link,
}

impl ListIterator {
    fn new(start_at: Link) -> ListIterator {
        ListIterator {
            current: start_at,
        }
    }
}
```

As the documentation states, a `for` loop uses two traits: `Iterator` and `IntoIterator`. Implementing the former is usually a good idea, as it provides access to the powerful methods in `Iterator`, such as `map`, `fold`, and so on, and nicely chains together with other—compatible—iterators:

```
impl Iterator for ListIterator {
    type Item = String;
    fn next(&mut self) -> Option<String> {
        let current = &self.current;
        let mut result = None;
        self.current = match current {
            Some(ref current) => {
                let current = current.borrow();
                result = Some(current.value.clone());
                current.next.clone()
            },
            None => None
        };
        result
    }
}
```

This iterator is responsible for moving one direction: forward. How can we walk back too?

Reverse

Now, since the requirement was also to go back, the iterator needs to go both ways. One easy way is to simply add a function to the structure that is called `reverse()`, but that would not integrate well and would require developers to read up on this API, and it creates additional work, since the forward/backward iterators are separate.

Rust's standard library offers an interesting concept for this: `DoubleEndedIterator`. Implementing this trait will provide the ability to reverse an iterator in a standardized way by offering a `next_back()` function to get the previous value—with the doubly linked list, this is only a matter of which property gets set to the current item! Therefore, both iterators share a large chunk of the code:

```
impl DoubleEndedIterator for ListIterator {
    fn next_back(&mut self) -> Option<String> {
        let current = &self.current;
        let mut result = None;
        self.current = match current {
            Some(ref current) => {
                let current = current.borrow();
                result = Some(current.value.clone());
                current.prev.clone()
            },
            None => None
        };
        result
    }
}
```

With this in place, an iterator can be created by calling the `iter()` function on the list type, and by calling `iter().rev()`, the iterator will be reversed, providing the ability to go back as well as forward.

Wrap up

Doubly linked lists are in many cases improved versions (and the default) over regular linked lists, thanks to the better flexibility at the cost of a single pointer per node and slightly more complex operations.

In particular, by keeping the code safe (in Rust terms, so no `unsafe {}` was used), the code gets riddled with `RefCells` and `borrow()` to create a data structure that the borrow checker is auditing at runtime. Looking at the Rust source code for `LinkedList`, this is not the case there (more on that in Chapter 7, *Collections in Rust*). The basic structure is similar, but the operations use a bunch of unsafe code underneath—something that requires a good experience writing Rust.

 `PhantomData<T>` is a zero-size type that informs the compiler about a range of things, such as drop behavior, sizes, and so on, when generics are involved.

As a quick preview, here is the Rust standard library's `LinkedList<T>` definition and implementation. It's a doubly linked list! Additionally, the `push_front_node` (prepend) function shows the use of an unsafe area to speed up inserts. For more information on that, check out the link to the online book *Learning Rust With Entirely Too Many Linked Lists* in the *Further reading* section at the end of the chapter:

```
pub struct LinkedList<T> {
    head: Option<Shared<Node<T>>>,
    tail: Option<Shared<Node<T>>>,
    len: usize,
    marker: PhantomData<Box<Node<T>>>,
}

struct Node<T> {
    next: Option<Shared<Node<T>>>,
    prev: Option<Shared<Node<T>>>,
    element: T,
}

[...]

impl<T> LinkedList<T> {
    /// Adds the given node to the front of the list.
    #[inline]
    fn push_front_node(&mut self, mut node: Box<Node<T>>) {
        unsafe {
            node.next = self.head;
            node.prev = None;
            let node = Some(Shared::from(Box::into_unique(node)));

            match self.head {
                None => self.tail = node,
                Some(mut head) => head.as_mut().prev = node,
            }

            self.head = node;
            self.len += 1;
        }
    }

// [...]  The remaining code was left out.

}
```

Whatever the implementation, there are general upsides and downsides to the doubly linked list.

Upsides

As a linked list, the principles are the same but slightly different. However, the major points of when the list is a good choice are shared with the singly linked list:

- Low overhead allocation per item (but more than the singly linked list).
- Item count is only limited by heap memory.
- Mutation while iterating is possible.
- Implementation is more complex but still fairly simple.
- Inserts, deletes, append, and prepend remain efficient.
- Efficient reversion.

This makes the doubly linked list a superior version of the two versions of linked lists, which is why it's usually the default LinkedList type.

Downsides

The doubly linked list shares a lot of the downsides of its less complex sibling and replaces the "no going back" with "more memory overhead" and "more complex implementation". Here's the list again:

- Indexing is still inefficient.
- Nodes are also allocated on the heap, which requires a lot of jumping around too.
- An additional pointer has to be stored per node.
- Implementation is more complex.

Inefficient indexing and iteration is something that a lot of developers wanted to get rid of, so they invented a more exotic version of a linked list: the **skip list**.

Skip lists

A lot of people love New York—and so do we. It has many qualities that are hard to describe; it is a crazy (in a good way), lively city that brings together many cultures, backgrounds, ethnicities, activities, and opportunities. New York also features a large public transport network, almost like cities in Europe.

What does any of this have to do with skip lists? A subway system can be expressed as a simple list of stops (expressed in street numbers, a common thing in the USA): 14 -> 23 -> 28 -> 33 -> 42 -> 51 -> 59 -> 68 . However, the New York subway system has something called **express trains** which reduce the number of stops to cover larger distances faster.

Suppose someone wants to go from stop 14 to stop 51. Instead of seeing the doors open and close five times, they can go there getting off at the third stop. In fact, this is how New Yorkers use the trains 4, 5, and 6 between 14th Street (Union Square) and 51st Street. Turned on its side, the subway plan looks roughly like this:

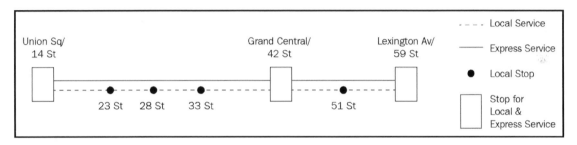

The local service trains stop at every stop along the way, but the express service trains skip certain smaller stops only to halt at shared stations where travelers can switch between the two. The skipping happens quite literally on some stops where trains simply drive through, sometimes confusing tourists and locals alike.

Expressed as a data structure, the list is essentially several lists, each at a different level. The lowest level contains *all* nodes, where the upper levels are their "express services" that can skip a number of nodes to get further ahead quicker. This results in a multilayered list, fused together only at certain nodes that have a connection on these particular levels:

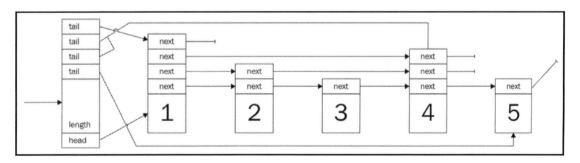

Ideally, each level has half the number of nodes that the previous level has, which means that there needs to be a decision-making algorithm that can work with a growing list and still maintain this constraint. If this constraint is not kept, search times get worse, and in the worst-case scenario it's a regular linked list with a lot of overhead.

 A node's level is decided using a probabilistic approach: increment the level as long as a coin flip comes out on the same side. While this produces the desired distribution, that's only meaningful if the higher-level nodes are evenly distributed. There are a few posts on improved versions in the *Further reading* section.

In addition to that, the skip list has to be ordered to function properly. After all, if the elements of the list are in a random order, how would the list know what it is skipping? In general, however, a node type for this—basic—skip list looks like this:

```
type Link = Option<Rc<RefCell<Node>>>;

struct Node {
    next: Vec<Link>,
    pub value: u64,
}
```

And to chain them together, a list type is also required:

```
struct SkipList {
    head: Link,
    tails: Vec<Link>,
    max_level: usize,
    pub length: u64,
}
```

What stands out is that the `struct` is very similar to the previous lists. Indeed—the relationship is undeniable, since they share almost all the properties. However, there are two differences: the `tails` is a `Vec<Link>` and the `max_level` is a property of the list.

The `tails` property being a vector is due to the fact that every level will have a tail end, meaning that whenever an append occurs, all tails may need to be updated. Additionally, the developer is responsible for providing an appropriate `max_level` value, since changing `max_level` would result in constructing a new list!

Going back to the previous example, the product team has requested more features! Users are confused by the lack of a clear direction in the list, and they are annoyed that there is no way to quickly skip the verbose but less-than-interesting parts in the beginning.

As a consequence, the product team wants the following:

- A time associated with the logged transaction
- To be able to quickly jump to an arbitrary time
- To start iterating from there

Doesn't this sound a lot like a skip list?

The best transaction log

To improve the transaction log in the way the product team describes, it's a perfect fit for a skip list. How about ordering the commands by a u32 number—a millisecond offset from the initial timestamp. The commands it contains are going to be stored as strings associated with the offset.

Nevertheless, the list and its nodes need to be implemented.

Compared to previous implementations (especially since the singly linked list is a close relative), there are two major differences in this declaration. Firstly, the next pointer is an array, which is due to the node having a different successor at every level.

Secondly, the content was previously named value, but to differentiate between the timestamp offset and the actual content, value has been replaced by offset and command:

```
#[derive(Clone)]
struct Node {
    next: Vec<Link>,
    pub offset: u64,
    pub command: String,
}
```

These nodes form the basis of this—improved—transaction log. As previously, with the singly linked list, this is done by creating a type that has a head pointer.

The list

Other than a simple pointer to the head, the list best stores the length as well as the maximum level that elements can have. This user-supplied parameter is critical, since if it's chosen too low, searching will approximate the search performance of a singly linked list ($O(n)$).

In contrast, choosing a maximum level that is too high will also result in an uneven distribution that could see as many vertical (levels down) as horizontal iterations (O(n + h)), none of which are good. The Big O notation (O(n) and so on) will be discussed in Chapter 8, *Algorithm Evaluation*.

Consequently, this parameter has to be set to somewhat reflect the future size of the list and the highest level only contains two or three nodes at most:

```
#[derive(Clone)]
pub struct BestTransactionLog {
    head: Link,
    tails: Vec<Link>,
    max_level: usize,
    pub length: u64,
}
```

The `tails` property is a vector pointing to the tail of each level. When adding data, this is the primary place to update this transaction log, thanks to the append-only nature of our skip list.

Adding data

Having the basic data structures ready, a function to insert data is required. As previously stated, a skip list can only work if the values are somehow comparable and follow an ascending order. This makes sense: skipping ahead is only useful if you know where you are going!

A very efficient way to create a sorted list is by doing a **sorted insert** (sometimes called an **insertion sort**). Commonly, this would add some complexity to the insert logic to find the correct place for the node. However, since a timestamp is naturally ascending and a comparable value, this version of the transaction log works without a sophisticated insert, thereby requiring fewer tests and fewer headaches when reading it a year down the road.

In fact, this means reusing some code from earlier sections is entirely possible:

```
pub fn append(&mut self, offset: u64, value: String) {
    let level = 1 + if self.head.is_none() {
        self.max_level   // use the maximum level for the first node
    } else {
        self.get_level() // determine the level by coin flips
    };

    let new = Node::new(vec![None; level], offset, value);
```

```
    // update the tails for each level
    for i in 0..level {
        if let Some(old) = self.tails[i].take() {
            let next = &mut old.borrow_mut().next;
            next[i] = Some(new.clone());
        }
        self.tails[i] = Some(new.clone());
    }

    // this is the first node in the list
    if self.head.is_none() {
        self.head = Some(new.clone());
    }
    self.length += 1;
}
```

Yet, there is an important addition: deciding on the level a node should (also) be present at. This is what makes the list powerful and is done just before the node is created:

```
let level = 1 + if self.head.is_none() {
    self.max_level
} else {
    self.get_level()
};
let new = Node::new(vec![None; level], offset, value);
```

This snippet shows some important details:

- The first node is always present on all levels, which makes search considerably easier, since the algorithm only needs to descend. However, this is only possible thanks to the append-only approach!
- Each node's `next` vector has to store succeeding pointers at the level's index, which means that the actual length needs to be `highest level + 1`.

How do you decide on the level, though? This is a great question, since this is the heart of a well-performing skip list.

Leveling up

Since `search` in a skip list is very much like `search` in a binary search tree (the first section in `Chapter 5`, *Robust Trees*, will get more into those), it has to retain a certain distribution of nodes to be effective. The original paper by William Pugh proposes a way to create the desired distribution of nodes on a certain level by repeatedly flipping a coin (assuming $p = 0.5$).

This is the proposed algorithm (*William Pugh, Skip Lists: A Probabilistic Alternative to Balanced Trees, Figure 5*):

```
randomLevel()
    lvl := 1
    -- random() that returns a random value in [0...1)
    while random() < p and lvl < MaxLevel do
        lvl := lvl + 1
    return lvl
```

Since this is a simple and understandable implementation, the skip list in this chapter will use this as well. However, there are better ways to generate the required distribution, and this is left for you to explore further. For this task, the first external crate is going to be used: rand.

 rand is provided by the Rust project but published in its own repository. There certainly are discussions about why this is not part of the default standard library; however, it's not too bad having the choice of crates to import if it needs to be replaced by something more lightweight, or if the target platform is not supported.

This Rust code should do just fine and generate the required level on call:

```
fn get_level(&self) -> usize {
    let mut n = 0;
    // bool = p(true) = 0.5
    while rand::random::<bool>() && n < self.max_level {
        n += 1;
    }
    n
}
```

Regarding the algorithm, bear this in mind: a range of levels that come out are [0, max_level], including the level. Each time a value is inserted, this function is called to acquire the level for the resultant node, so jumps can actually make search faster.

Jumping around

The skip list only resembles a binary search tree, but it is able to achieve the same runtime complexity (O(log n)) without the need for expensive rebalancing. This is due to the jumps the skip list allows. Logically, it makes sense: by jumping over several nodes, these nodes don't need to be looked at to find out whether those are the values that are being searched for. Fewer nodes means fewer comparisons, leading to a reduced runtime.

The jumps are quickly implemented too and can be implemented in a function using a few loops:

```rust
pub fn find(&self, offset: u64) -> Option<String> {
    match self.head {
        Some(ref head) => {
            let mut start_level = self.max_level;
            let node = head.clone();
            let mut result = None;
            loop {
                if node.borrow().next[start_level].is_some() {
                    break;
                }
                start_level -= 1;
            }
            let mut n = node;
            for level in (0..=start_level).rev() {
                loop {
                    let next = n.clone();
                    match next.borrow().next[level] {
                        Some(ref next)
                            if next.borrow().offset <= offset =>
                                n = next.clone(),
                        _ => break
                    };
                }
                if n.borrow().offset == offset {
                    let tmp = n.borrow();
                    result = Some(tmp.command.clone());
                    break;
                }
            }
            result
        }
        None => None,
    }
}
```

These 30 lines of code allow you to search the list quickly within a few steps. First, a sensible starting level has to be found by starting at the highest possible level, to see which has a valid node that follows it. The following happens in this part:

```rust
let mut start_level = self.max_level;
let node = head.clone();
loop {
    if node.borrow().next[start_level].is_some() {
        break;
    }
}
```

```
                    start_level -= 1;
        }
```

Once this level is figured out, the next step is to move vertically toward the desired node and move lower, as the potential next node is greater than the value we are looking for:

```
let mut n = node;
for level in (0..=start_level).rev() {
    loop {
        let next = n.clone();
        match next.borrow().next[level] {
            Some(ref next)
                if next.borrow().offset <= offset =>
                    n = next.clone(),
            _ => break
        };
    }
    if n.borrow().offset == offset {
        let tmp = n.borrow();
        result = Some(tmp.command.clone());
        break;
    }
}
result
```

Finally, the result of the search is returned as an Option that contains the command that was issued at the specified time—or None. Depending on the semantics of failure, it could be a better choice to use a Result with the appropriate message that informs the user about why there was no result (the list was empty, no value has been found, and so on).

Thoughts and discussion

skip list is a fascinating data structure, as it is fairly simple to implement and combines the benefits of tree-like structures within a list without the need for expensive inserts or rebalancing. To visualize the power of this data structure, here is a chart that compares the find() operation of skip lists and (std::collections::) LinkedList:

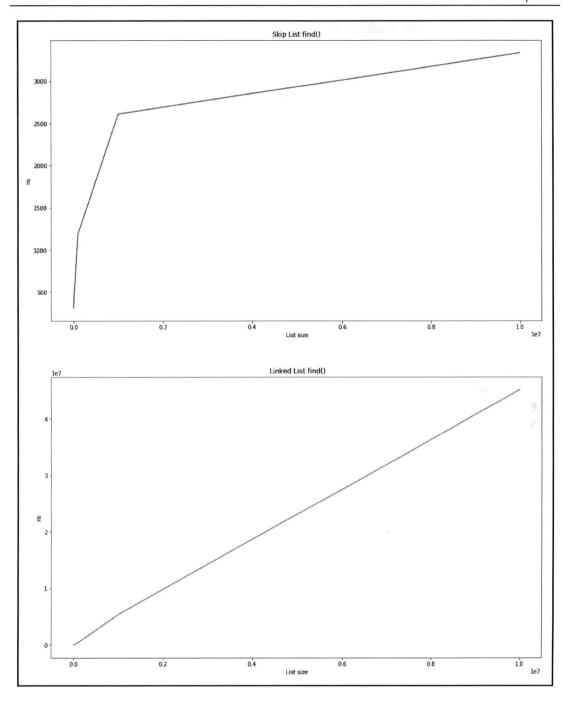

The graph output for Skip List find () and Linked List find ()

The first chart (higher) shows how the skip list behaves according to an O(log n) type function, which proves that the implementation works! The second (lower) chart shows the linear search in LinkedList, with the time required growing in O(n). The raw numbers are even more impressive:

Size	Skip list [avg ns]	Linked list [avg ns]
1,000	311	825
10,000	438	17,574
100,000	1,190	428,259
1,000,000	2,609	5,440,420
10,000,000	3,334	45,157,562

These numbers reflect the **nanoseconds (ns)** required for a single call to the find() method averaged over a number of trials. This is truly a great data structure for search.

Upsides

In a word: search. The number of steps required to retrieve a single item is linear (it will take as many steps to find an item as there are items in the list), in the *worst case*. Commonly, the time would be at the level of a binary search tree!

In more practical terms, this would provide the ability to store large amounts of data in a list and quickly find the items that you were looking for. However, there is more; here is a list of upsides:

- The item count is only limited by heap memory
- The search is really efficient
- It is less complex to implement than many trees

Yet, there are downsides to this list.

Downsides

The memory efficiency of a skip list and its complexity can be an issue. With the append-only approach, the list implemented in this book avoids a few complexities such as sorted insert (we'll get there later). Other points include the following:

- Memory efficiency: lots and lots of pointers create overhead
- Implementation complexity
- Sorting required

- Updates are expensive
- Probabilistic approach to elevating nodes onto certain levels

Depending on the type of project, these might be prohibitive issues. However, there are other types of lists that might be suitable, one of them being the dynamic array.

Dynamic arrays

Arrays are another common way to store sequences of data. However, they lack a fundamental feature of lists: expansion. Arrays are efficient because they are a fixed-size container of length *n*, where every element has an equal size. Thus, any element can be reached by calculating the address to jump to using the simple formula start_address + n * element_size, making the entire process really fast. Additionally, this is very CPU cache-friendly, since the data is always at least one hop away.

The idea of using arrays to emulate list behavior has been around for a long time (Java 1.2 included an ArrayList class in 1998, but the idea is likely much older) and it is still a great way to achieve high performance in lists. Rust's Vec<T> uses the same technique. To start off, this is how an array list is built:

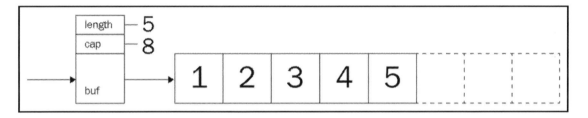

Consequently, this Rust implementation will have an array (actually a slice, but more on that later) as the main storage facility as well:

```
pub struct DynamicArray {
    buf: Box<[Option<u64>]>,
    cap: usize,
    pub length: usize,
}
```

The idea is that, dynamic list sizes can be emulated at the cost of memory and potentially excessive overallocation. Consequently, the critical point is when the currently allocated size is exceeded and the list needs to grow. The question becomes this: how much memory is going to be needed?

The consequence of too little memory is that reallocation is going to happen again quickly—which will remove any performance gains over regular lists. If the resizing was too large, a lot of memory would go to waste, and, depending on the program's target platform, this might be a huge issue. Thus, the strategy of acquiring more memory is essential. Rust's Vec follows a smart implementation and allows either an exact allocation and an amortized allocation of simply double (or more) the size of the current internal array.

Java's implementation grows the vector by simply creating a new array with the old capacity added to a bit-shifted version (to the right by one) of the old capacity. That is, of course, only if that is enough. Typically, that leads to adding half of the current capacity or more to the number of possible elements. Naturally, all existing elements are (shallow) copied to the new array before disposing of the original memory. In code, it looks as follows (from OpenJDK 8, class ArrayList, lines 237 to 247; new lines added for readability):

```
private void grow(int minCapacity) {
    // overflow-conscious code
    int oldCapacity = elementData.length;
    int newCapacity = oldCapacity + (oldCapacity >> 1);

    if (newCapacity - minCapacity < 0)
        newCapacity = minCapacity;

    if (newCapacity - MAX_ARRAY_SIZE > 0)
        newCapacity = hugeCapacity(minCapacity);

    // minCapacity is usually close to size, so this is a win:
    elementData = Arrays.copyOf(elementData, newCapacity);
}
```

This code has a fascinating simplicity, and it's used by billions of programs worldwide, and the implementation of this book's dynamic array will use the same strategy.

Again, the product team has another feature request. Users liked the going-back-and-forth feature a lot, so they want to save a few noteworthy timestamps in a separate list.

Often, these kinds of requirements send developers straight to a hash table or dictionary type. However, these usually do not retain the order of the items that were inserted and, if iteration is a primary concern, they are perhaps not the most efficient way to do this.

Favorite transactions

To clean up the product team's demands, here is a list of the required features:

- Save a transaction's timestamp in a list
- Access the elements quickly by index, in any order
- Iterate the items in the order they were saved

A dynamic array utilizes an expanding array underneath and works really quickly, for accessing indices directly while still supporting iteration—great for saving a numbered list of noteworthy timestamps. The direct index access provides a way to fetch the stored data without having to go through the entire list, and since transaction timestamps are basically u64 numbers (milliseconds), the data structure can be a dynamic array of multiple u64.

Other than previous lists, this time, a node only stores data and can therefore be a type alias as well:

```
type Node = Option<u64>;
```

Making the node an Option type is necessary, since the capacity and actual length of the internal slice may differ—which means that an "empty" marker is needed:

```
pub struct TimestampSaver {
    buf: Box<[Node]>,
    cap: usize,
    pub length: usize,
}
```

Once the node type is declared, it can be used inside the new list's internal buffer. This construct is called a **boxed slice** (see the following section) and stores nodes in an array-like fashion.

Internal arrays

Arrays are defined as data structures that have a known size at compile time. Rust takes this very seriously, and the array constructor will only take constants to denominate size in an array. [0u8; 4] will work, but let my_array_size = 2 * 2; [0u8; my_array_size] won't.

So, how do you dynamically reallocate a new array then? In Rust, there is also something called `slices`, which are views into a sequence data structure, akin to an array. These are a great fit when stored inside a `Box` pointer: allocated on the heap, it has all the benefits of an array with a dynamic size.

As previously mentioned, this implementation goes with Java's `ArrayList` growth strategy and increases its size by at least 50% each time more capacity is required. While this has the unfortunate effect of exponential growth, it has worked for Java—a *very* popular language—for decades.

The Rust implementation is close to its Java pendant; in fact, only the oversized variety is missing:

```
fn grow(&mut self, min_cap: usize) {
    let old_cap = self.buf.len();
    let mut new_cap = old_cap + (old_cap >> 1);

    new_cap = cmp::max(new_cap, min_cap);
    new_cap = cmp::min(new_cap, usize::max_value());
    let current = self.buf.clone();
    self.cap = new_cap;
    self.buf = vec![None; new_cap].into_boxed_slice();
    self.buf[..current.len()].clone_from_slice(&current);
}
```

You will quickly see that the `vec![]` macro has been used—*"why is that?"* you might ask. Unfortunately, there is no great and safe way outside the `vec![]` macro to allocate this boxed slice. This use of the macro, however, allows to create an empty vector with the appropriate size and convert it into a boxed slice—a slice stored in a `Box`. This slice can afterward clone data from the previous slice.

This code works well up to the length of `usize`, which depends on the platform the program has been compiled for.

Quick access

Due to the underlying slice, accessing an index is cheap. In fact, it always takes the same amount of time, regardless of the index (which makes it different to previously discussed lists). A call to the `at()` function will therefore simply forward it accordingly:

```
pub fn at(&mut self, index: usize) -> Option<u64> {
    if self.length > index {
        self.buf[index]
```

```
        } else {
            None
        }
}
```

Here, again, the Rust implementation has to deal with sharing borrowed content or clone the data structure which might require more memory. Under the hood, a u64 is implicitly cloned.

To fulfill all requirements, the Iterator trait has to be implemented as well. Unlike the doubly linked list, the iterator cannot store a single node and go forward or backward from there. It has to store a pointer to the entire list, along with the current index:

```
pub struct ListIterator {
    current: usize,
    data: Box<[Node]>,
}
```

This struct makes the implementation already obvious. Move the current pointer back and forth as needed:

```
impl Iterator for ListIterator {
    type Item = u64;

    fn next(&mut self) -> Option<u64> {
        if self.current < self.data.len() {
            let item = self.data[self.current];
            self.current += 1;
            item
        } else {
            None
        }
    }
}

impl DoubleEndedIterator for ListIterator {
    fn next_back(&mut self) -> Option<u64> {
        if self.current < self.data.len() {
            let item = self.data[self.current];
            if self.current == 0 {
                self.current = self.data.len() - 1;
            } else {
                self.current -= 1;
            }
            item
        } else {
            None
```

```
            }
        }
    }
```

This is a simple and clear iterator: no unpacking, explicit borrowing, and so on, just a simple counter that is incremented or decremented as it moves through the list.

Wrap up

The dynamic array is a very flexible way of using array-like structures as a list—and it's surprisingly easy to implement and use. In fact, adding other features (`prepend`, insert at a specified position, and so on) is only a matter of a few lines of code.

For Rust, the difference from the other list types is the clearly defined hierarchical ownership: the list `struct` owns the internal structure, which in turn owns the data in its elements. There are no links among the elements that could create ambiguity in who owns what, making the dynamic array a great example for how productive Rust code can be.

Upsides

Other than it being only a few lines of code, the dynamic array has quite a few upsides:

- Speed: arrays/slices make things really fast
- Simple and fast element access
- Clear ownership structures
- Fast append and iteration
- Very CPU cache-friendly

One thing is clear: it's fast in many cases. When is the dynamic array not the best choice, though?

Downsides

However, this type of list is also quite memory-inefficient, and its rigid structure can be a downside as well:

- Operations other than append will require to shift elements
- Growth strategy is not memory-efficient

- A single large chunk of memory is required
- Size is limited by `usize` type, which differs from platform to platform
- Growth speed decreases with list size

This concludes this journey into the realm of lists, hopefully in a successful manner. Before the next chapter begins, a quick summary highlights all the important parts.

Summary

Lists are everywhere! While this is true, it's a fact that makes everything harder. Which list is the right tool for the job? How well will it do at certain sizes to add and later find elements? What's the overhead if my payload size is really small?

These are all questions that programmers are faced with today, and the author hopes to provide some guidance on these decisions. To recap: the least complex is the singly linked list, upon which the doubly linked list is built. Skip lists are in essence multilayered singly linked lists that provide excellent search performance at the cost of memory overhead. Last, but not least, there is the dynamic array—a type of list that wraps and manages an array for storing data just like a list.

Implementing these structures in Rust requires many pointers to the heap, especially `Rc` and `RefCells`, which were companions from the beginning to the end of the chapter. When you consider the structure of a singly linked list, each item required access to the next—but with a predictable size. This fact requires programmers to work with references, but how would this work if the list gets passed around the program, possibly living on the heap itself? The consequence is to simplify things and put them on to the heap from the beginning and use an interior mutable `Rc` and `RefCell` construct to do that.

Similarly, is the doubly linked list. Other than the forward (next) pointer that the singly linked sibling provides, a doubly linked node has to point backward as well. Therefore, each item has two pointers in addition to the payload, enabling a set of powerful features such as instant list reversal.

Skip lists, on the other hand, have been implemented as singly linked lists in this chapter (but certainly can be doubly linked as well). Their main improvement is the great ability to search the contained data quickly—just like a binary search tree. This means that, almost regardless of the size, the look-up performance is vastly better than that of a regular list, both in absolute and relative terms. Unfortunately, this comes at the cost of many more pointers per node.

The most popular data structure is probably the dynamic array. Often dubbed `Vec<T>` (Rust), `ArrayList` (Java), `List<T>` (C#), or simply `list()` (Python), these are wrappers around an array that is allocated and reallocated intelligently as required. By doing this, they can accommodate the need for fast element access and quick iteration at the cost of a shallow copy on resize, as well as having a large chunk of memory available. These are the best choice for storing a limited amount of small- to medium-sized items.

The next chapter is going to delve deeper into less linear data structures: trees. These constructs provide interesting capabilities by the way they are built and are a great choice for read-heavy undertakings.

Questions

- Why is a linked list tricky to implement in Rust?
- How does Rust's standard library `LinkedList` work?
- What is the difference between a doubly linked list and a skip list?
- Does a dynamic array outperform a skip list for element access?
- How is a dynamic array a great choice for CPU caching?
- What is another growth strategy for dynamic arrays?
- Rust takes arrays seriously, so what does the dynamic array use internally?

Further reading

You can refer to the following links for more information:

- *Learning Rust With Entirely Too Many Linked Lists* (http://cglab.ca/~abeinges/blah/too-many-lists/book/README.html)
- Implementing the `Iterator` trait (https://doc.rust-lang.org/std/iter/index.html#implementing-iterator)
- *Skip Lists: Done Right* (https://doc.rust-lang.org/std/iter/index.html#implementing-iterator)
- *Skip Lists: A Probabilistic Alternative to Balanced Trees*, William Pugh (https://www.epaperpress.com/sortsearch/download/skiplist.pdf)

5
Robust Trees

Lists are great for storing a bunch of items, but what about looking up specific elements? In the previous chapter, a skip list greatly outperformed a regular linked list when simply finding an item. Why? Because it was utilizing an iteration strategy that resembles that of a balanced tree structure: there, the internal order lets the algorithm strategically skip items. However, that's only the beginning. Many libraries, databases, and search engines are built on trees; in fact, whenever a program is compiled, the compiler creates an abstract syntax tree.

Tree-based data structures incorporate all kinds of smart ideas that we will explore in this chapter, so you can look forward to the following:

- Implementing and understanding a binary search tree
- Learning about self-balancing trees
- How prefix or suffix trees work
- What a priority queue uses internally
- Graphs, the most general tree structure

Binary search tree

A tree structure is almost like a linked list: each node has branches—in the case of a binary tree, there are two—which represent children of that node. Since these children have children of their own, the node count grows exponentially, building a hierarchical structure that looks like a regular tree turned on its head.

Binary trees are a subset of these structures with only two branches, typically called left and right. However, that does not inherently help the tree's performance. This is why using a *binary search tree*, where left represents the smaller or equal value to its parent, and right anything that's greater than that parent node, was established!

If that was confusing, don't worry; there will be code. First, some vocabulary though: what would you call the far ends of the tree? Leaves. Cutting off branches? Pruning. The number of branches per node? Branching factor (binary trees have a branching factor of 2).

Great, with that out of the way, the nodes can be shown—although they look a lot like the doubly linked list from the previous chapter:

```
type Tree = Option<Box<Node>>;

struct Node {
    pub value: u64,
    left: Tree,
    right: Tree,
}
```

Similarly, the tree structure itself is only a pointer to the root node:

```
pub struct BinarySearchTree {
    root: Tree,
    pub length: u64,
}
```

Yet before you can get comfortable with the new data structure, the product team from the previous chapter is back! You did a great job improving the transaction log and they want to continue that progress and build an **Internet of Things (IoT)** device management platform so users can register a device with a numerical name and later search for it. However, the search has to be fast or really fast, which is especially critical since many customers have announced the incorporation of more than 10,000 devices into the new system!

Isn't this a great opportunity to get more experience with a binary search tree?

IoT device management

Device management in the IoT space is mostly about storing and retrieving specific devices or device twins. These objects typically store addresses, configuration values, encryption keys, or other things for small devices so nobody has to connect manually. Consequently, keeping an inventory is critical!

For now, the product team settled on a numerical "name", to be available faster than the competition, and to keep the requirements short:

- Store IoT device objects (containing the IP address, numerical name, and type)
- Retrieve IoT objects by numerical name
- Iterate over IoT objects

A great use for a tree: the numerical name can be used to create a tree and search for it nice and quickly. The basic object for storing this IoT device information looks like this:

```
#[derive(Clone, Debug)]
pub struct IoTDevice {
    pub numerical_id: u64,
    pub address: String,
}
```

For simplicity, this object will be used in the code directly (adding generics isn't too tricky, but would go beyond the scope of this book):

```
type Tree = Option<Box<Node>>;
struct Node {
    pub dev: IoTDevice,
    left: Tree,
    right: Tree,
}
```

Starting with this basic implementation, the requisite operations, `add` and `find`, can be implemented.

More devices

Unlike lists, trees make a major decision on insert: which side does the new element go to? Starting at the root node, each node's value is compared to the value that is going to be inserted: is this greater than or less than that? Either decision will lead down a different subtree (left or right).

This process is (usually recursively) repeated until the targeted subtree is `None`, which is exactly where the new value is inserted—as a leaf of the tree. If this is the first value going into the tree, it becomes the root node. There are some problems with this, and the more experienced programmers will have had a strange feeling already: what happens if you insert numbers in ascending order?

These feelings are justified. Inserting in ascending order (for example, 1, 2, 3, 4) will lead to a tree that is basically a list in disguise! This is also called a (very) unbalanced tree and won't have any of the benefits of other trees:

During this chapter, we are going to go a lot more things on balancing trees and why that is important in order to achieve high performance. In order to avoid this pitfall associated with binary search trees, the first value to insert should ideally be the median of all elements since it will be used as the root node, as is visible in the following code snippet:

```rust
pub fn add(&mut self, device: IoTDevice) {
    self.length += 1;
    let root = mem::replace(&mut self.root, None);
    self.root = self.add_rec(root, device);
}

fn add_rec(&mut self, node: Tree, device: IoTDevice) -> Tree {
    match node {
        Some(mut n) => {
            if n.dev.numerical_id <= device.numerical_id {
                n.left = self.add_rec(n.left, device);
                Some(n)
            } else {
                n.right = self.add_rec(n.right, device);
                Some(n)
            }
        }
        _ => Node::new(device),
    }
}
```

Split into two parts, this code walks the tree recursively to find the appropriate position and attaches the new value as a leaf there. Actually, the insert is not that different from a regular tree walk in search or iteration.

Recursion is when a function calls itself. Think of the movie Inception—having a dream inside a dream inside a dream. it's the same concept. There are a few implications in programming: the original function is disposed of last since it's only finished after all recursive calls return. This also means that everything lives on the much smaller stack, which may result in a stack overflow when there are too many calls! Typically, recursive algorithms can also be implemented iteratively, but they are much harder to understand—so choose wisely!

Finding the right one

Having the ability to add devices to the tree, it's even more important to retrieve them again. Just like the skip list in the previous chapter, this retrieval ideally runs in *O(log n)* time, meaning that the majority of elements are going to be skipped when searching.

Consequently, if the tree is skewed in one direction, the performance approaches *O(n)* and more elements are looked at, thereby making the search slower. Since a skewed tree is more like a list, the recursive insert algorithm can overflow the stack quickly thanks to the high number of "levels" with only a single item. Otherwise, the recursive algorithm is only called as many times as the tree's height, a considerably lower number in a balanced tree. The algorithm itself resembles the previously shown insert algorithm:

```
pub fn find(&self, numerical_id: u64) -> Option<IoTDevice> {
    self.find_r(&self.root, numerical_id)
}

fn find_r(&self, node: &Tree, numerical_id: u64) -> Option<IoTDevice> {
    match node {
        Some(n) => {
            if n.dev.numerical_id == numerical_id {
                Some(n.dev.clone())
            } else if n.dev.numerical_id < numerical_id {
                self.find_r(&n.left, numerical_id)
            } else {
                self.find_r(&n.right, numerical_id)
            }
        }
        _ => None,
    }
}
```

Although this snippet's purpose is to find a specific node, there is a close relationship to enumerating every device—something that the users of this service certainly will want to have.

Finding all devices

Walking a tree and executing a callback when visiting each node can be done in three ways:

- Pre-order, executing the callback *before descending*
- In-order, which executes the callback *after descending left, but before descending into the right subtree*
- Post-order, where the callback is executed *after descending*

Each of these traversal strategies yields a different order of tree elements, with in-order producing a sorted output, while pre- and post-order create a more structurally oriented sorting. For our users, the in-order walk will provide the best experience, since it also lets them reason better regarding the expected outcome, and, if displayed in a list, it's easier to navigate.

While implementing this walk is very easy to do recursively, providing an iterator is more user-friendly (just like the lists in the previous chapter) and it enables a number of added functions, such as map() and filter(). However, this implementation has to be iterative, which makes it more complex and removes some of the efficiency of the tree.

Therefore, this tree supports a walk() function which calls a provided function each time it encounters a node, which can be used to fill a vector for the iterator:

```
pub fn walk(&self, callback: impl Fn(&IoTDevice) -> ()) {
    self.walk_in_order(&self.root, &callback);
}

fn walk_in_order(&self, node: &Tree, callback: &impl Fn(&IoTDevice) -> ())
{
    if let Some(n) = node {
        self.walk_in_order(&n.left, callback);
        callback(&n.dev);
        self.walk_in_order(&n.right, callback);
    }
}
```

An example of how to build a vector using this walk method is shown here:

```
let my_devices: RefCell<Vec<IoTDevice>> = RefCell::new(vec![]);
tree.walk(|n| my_devices.borrow_mut().push(n.clone()));
```

With this walking ability, all requirements are satisfied for now.

Wrap up

Thanks to their simplicity, binary search trees are beautifully efficient. In fact, the entire tree implementation for this section was done in fewer than 90 lines of Rust code, with functions of about 10 lines each.

A binary tree's efficiency allows for recursion to be used a lot, which typically results in functions that are easier to understand compared to their iterative counterparts. In the ideal case, that is, when a tree is perfectly balanced, a function only has to process $log2(n)$ nodes (*n* being the total number of nodes)—19 in a tree of 1,000,000 elements!

Unbalanced trees will decrease performance significantly and they are easily created by accident. The most unbalanced tree is created by inserting values that are already sorted, creating a very large difference in search performance:

```
test tests::bench_sorted_insert_bst_find ... bench: 16,376 ns/iter (+/-
6,525)
test tests::bench_unsorted_insert_bst_find ... bench: 398 ns/iter (+/- 182)
```

These results reflect the differences between a skip list and a doubly linked list from the previous chapter.

Upsides

To recap, a binary search tree has a number of great benefits for its users:

- Simple implementation
- Efficient and fast search
- Traversal allows for different orderings
- Great for large amounts of unsorted data

Downsides

By using a binary search tree, its drawbacks become obvious quickly:

- Worst-case performance is that of a linked list
- Unbalanced trees are easy to create by accident
- Unbalanced trees cannot be "repaired"
- Recursive algorithms can overflow on unbalanced trees

Obviously, a lot of the deeper issues result from the tree being unbalanced in some way—for which there is a solution: self-balancing binary search trees.

Red-black tree

With the previous tree structure, there was a major downside: a previously unknown sequence of keys that is inserted into the tree cannot be sorted. Think of how most identifiers are generated; they are typically ascending numbers. Shuffling these numbers won't always work, especially when they are gradually added. Since this leads to an unbalanced tree (the extreme case behaves just like a list), Rudolf Bayer came up with the idea of a special, self-balancing tree: the red-black tree.

This tree is a binary search tree that adds logic to rebalance after inserts. Within this operation, it is crucial to know when to stop "balancing"—which is where the inventor thought to use two colors: red and black.

In literature, the red-black tree is described as a binary search tree that satisfies a set of rules:

- The root node is always black
- Each other node is either red or black
- All leaves (often `null/NIL` values) are considered black
- A red node can only have black children
- Any path from the root to its leaves has the same number of black nodes

By enforcing these rules, a tree can be programmatically verified to be balanced. How are these rules doing that? Rules 4 and 5 provide the answer: if each branch has to have the same number of black nodes, neither side can be significantly longer than the other unless there were lots of red nodes.

How many of those can there be? At most, as many as there are black nodes—because they cannot have red children. Thus, one branch cannot significantly exceed the other, making this tree balanced. The code of the validation function illustrates this very well:

```
pub fn is_a_valid_red_black_tree(&self) -> bool {
    let result = self.validate(&self.root, Color::Red, 0);
    let red_red = result.0;
    let black_height_min = result.1;
    let black_height_max = result.2;
    red_red == 0 && black_height_min == black_height_max
}

// red-red violations, min black-height, max-black-height
fn validate(
    &self,
    node: &Tree,
    parent_color: Color,
    black_height: usize,
) -> (usize, usize, usize) {
    if let Some(n) = node {
        let n = n.borrow();
        let red_red = if parent_color == Color::Red && n.color ==
Color::Red {
            1
        } else {
            0
        };
        let black_height = black_height + match n.color {
            Color::Black => 1,
            _ => 0,
        };
        let l = self.validate(&n.left, n.color.clone(), black_height);
        let r = self.validate(&n.right, n.color.clone(), black_height);
        (red_red + l.0 + r.0, cmp::min(l.1, r.1), cmp::max(l.2, r.2))
    } else {
        (0, black_height, black_height)
    }
}
```

Like the binary search tree, each node in a tree has two children, with a key either greater than, equal to, or less than that of the current node. In addition to the key (as in a key-value pair), the nodes store a color that is red on insert, and a pointer back to its parent. Why? This is due to the required rebalancing, which will be described later. First, this can be a typical node:

```
type BareTree = Rc<RefCell<Node>>;
type Tree = Option<BareTree>;
```

```
struct Node {
    pub color: Color,
    pub key: u32,
    pub parent: Tree,
    left: Tree,
    right: Tree,
}
```

Using these nodes, a tree can be created just like a binary search tree. In fact, the insert mechanism is exactly the same except for setting the parent pointer. Newly inserted nodes are always colored red and, once in place, the tree might violate the rules. Only then is it time to find and fix these issues.

After an insert, the tree is in an invalid state that requires a series of steps to restore the red-black tree's properties. This series, comprised of rotation and recolor, starts at the inserted node and goes up the tree until the root node is considered valid. In summary, a red-black tree is a binary search tree that is rotated and recolored until balance is restored.

Recolor is simply changing the color of a specified node to a specific color, which happens as a final step when doing tree rebalancing. **Rotation** is an operation of a set of three nodes: the current node, its parent, and its grandparent. It is employed to fold list-like chains into trees by rotating either left or right around a specified node. The result is a changed hierarchy, with either the left or right child of the center node on top, and its children adjusted accordingly:

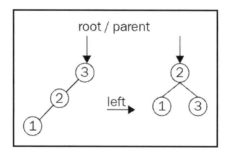

Clearly, this example is too simple and it can only happen within the first few inserts. Rotations require recolors after redefining the hierarchy of a set of nodes. To add further complexity, rotations regularly happen in succession:

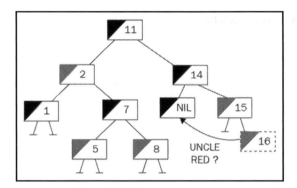

The preceding tree has had a node inserted and is now violating rule 4: *no red children on a red node*. The next step is to determine which steps are required to establish balance. For that, the parent's sibling's color (that is, the uncle's color) is examined. Red means that a simple recoloring of both siblings to black and their parent to red won't invalidate the tree and will fix the condition. This is not the case here (the uncle is None, which means black), and some rotation is required:

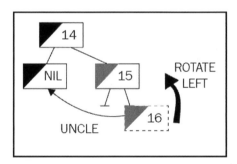

The first move is to align the nodes into a chain of left children (in this case), which is done by rotating around the center node, the insertee's parent:

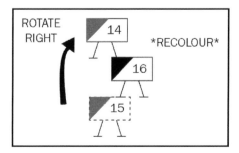

Once the chain is aligned, a right rotation of the third node (grandparent) creates a valid subtree by elevating the middle node (the "youngest" node/insertee), with the former parent and grandparent to the left and right, respectively. Then, the new constellation is recolored and the procedure begins anew, centered around the root of the new subtree (in this example, though, the tree is already valid):

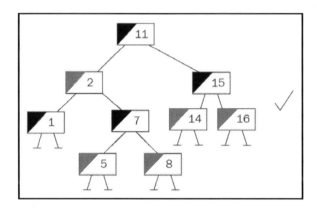

These steps can be repeated until the tree is valid and the root is reached (which might be different from what you started off with). This root node is heuristically painted black as well, which cannot violate the rules but shortcuts a potential red-red violation. For code on the fixing operation, see the following subsections.

The product team has even called this time to put emphasis on their new product ideas. The IoT platform is quite popular and customers have been using it a lot—and recognized a major slowdown when they kept adding their sequentially numbered devices. This resulted in angry calls to customer services, which then turned to the product team for help—and now it's time to implement the solution and replace the current tree for device management.

Better IoT device management

The problem that our users face is clear: if a binary search tree encounters sorted data (such as incremental IDs), it can only ever append to one side, creating an unbalanced tree. A red-black tree is able to handle this at the cost of more operations being executed during insert (such as rotating subtrees), which is acceptable for the users.

This tree has similar nodes to the binary search tree, with the addition of a color field and a parent field, the latter of which triggers a wider change compared to the binary search tree. Thanks to the pointer back, the tree nodes cannot exclusively own the pointers to the children and parent (because, who owns this value, the parent or the child?), which requires a well-known pattern in Rust: interior mutability. As discussed in an earlier chapter, RefCell owns the data's portion of the memory and handles borrow-checking at runtime so that mutable and immutable references can be obtained:

```
type BareTree = Rc<RefCell<Node>>;
type Tree = Option<BareTree>;

struct Node {
    pub color: Color,
    pub dev: IoTDevice,
    pub parent: Tree,
    left: Tree,
    right: Tree,
}

impl Node {
    pub fn new(dev: IoTDevice) -> Tree {
        Some(Rc::new(RefCell::new(Node {
            color: Color::Red,
            dev: dev,
            parent: None,
            left: None,
            right: None,
        })))
    }
}
```

With that in place, devices can be added.

Even more devices

Once the tree is created, an add() function lets the user add a device. The tree then proceeds to insert the new key just as if it were a binary search tree—only to check and fix any errors immediately afterward. Where a binary search tree could use a simple if condition to decide the direction it proceeds in, in the red-black tree, the direction has a larger impact, and nesting if conditions will result in chaotic, unreadable code.

Thus, let's create `enum` first, so any time the direction (example, insert, position of a node relative to another node, and so on) has to be decided, we can rely on that `enum`. The same goes for the tree's color:

```
#[derive(Clone, Debug, PartialEq)]
enum Color {
    Red,
    Black,
}

#[derive(PartialEq)]
enum RBOperation {
    LeftNode,
    RightNode,
}
```

Now, the `add()` function can use Rust's match clause to nicely structure the two branches:

```
pub fn add(&mut self, device: IoTDevice) {
    self.length += 1;
    let root = mem::replace(&mut self.root, None);
    let new_tree = self.add_r(root, device);
    self.root = self.fix_tree(new_tree.1);
}

fn add_r(&mut self, mut node: Tree, device: IoTDevice) -> (Tree, BareTree)
{
    if let Some(n) = node.take() {
        let new: BareTree;
        let current_device = n.borrow().dev.clone();

        match self.check(&current_device, &device) {
            RBOperation::LeftNode => {
                let left = n.borrow().left.clone();
                let new_tree = self.add_r(left, device);
                new = new_tree.1;
                let new_tree = new_tree.0.unwrap();
                new_tree.borrow_mut().parent = Some(n.clone());
                n.borrow_mut().left = Some(new_tree);
            }

            RBOperation::RightNode => {
                let right = n.borrow().right.clone();
                let new_tree = self.add_r(right, device);
                new = new_tree.1;
                let new_tree = new_tree.0.unwrap();

                new_tree.borrow_mut().parent = Some(n.clone());
```

```
                n.borrow_mut().right = Some(new_tree);
            }
        }
        (Some(n), new)
    } else {
        let new = Node::new(device);
        (new.clone(), new.unwrap())
    }
}
```

One of the primary parts of the code is "checking" two devices, that is, comparing them in order to provide a direction that they should be appended to. This comparison is done in a separate function to improve maintainability:

```
fn check(&self, a: &IoTDevice, b: &IoTDevice) -> RBOperation {
    if a.numerical_id <= b.numerical_id {
        RBOperation::LeftNode
    } else {
        RBOperation::RightNode
    }
}
```

While this tree will append every larger item to the left (which seems unusual), the algorithms don't care; they will work regardless—and, by wrapping this into its own function, change is quick and easy.

Balancing the tree

After the node is added properly, fix_tree() takes care of restoring the red-black tree's properties—iteratively. While this is nicely descriptive and demonstrative it is long, so let's break it up into parts. Initially, the function determines whether it should stop (or not even start)—which only happens in two cases:

- When it's already the root node
- When the parent of the currently inspected node is red

Clearly, the former is the regular exit criterion as well, as the loop optimizes and moves the current pointer (n as in node) from the bottom toward the root of the tree to stop there:

```
fn fix_tree(&mut self, inserted: BareTree) -> Tree {
    let mut not_root = inserted.borrow().parent.is_some();

    let root = if not_root {
        let mut parent_is_red = self.parent_color(&inserted) == Color::Red;
        let mut n = inserted.clone();
```

```
while parent_is_red && not_root {
    if let Some(uncle) = self.uncle(n.clone()) {
```

Once started, the loop immediately goes for the uncle of a particular node (that is, the grandparent's second child) and its color. The uncle node can either be black (or None) or red, which are the two cases covered next. It is also important to find out *which* uncle it is, and therefore which node the current pointer points to: a left node or a right node. Let's take a look at the following code snippet:

```
if let Some(uncle) = self.uncle(n.clone()) {
    let which = uncle.1;
    let uncle = uncle.0;

    match which {
        RBOperation::LeftNode => {
            // uncle is on the left
            // ...

        RBOperation::RightNode => {
            // uncle is on the right
            // ...
```

This information is critical in determining the rotation order in this area of the tree. In fact, the two branches will execute the same steps, but mirrored:

```
// uncle is on the left
let mut parent = n.borrow().parent
                    .as_ref().unwrap().clone();
if uncle.is_some()
    && uncle.as_ref().unwrap().borrow()
        .color == Color::Red
{
    let uncle = uncle.unwrap();
    parent.borrow_mut().color = Color::Black;
    uncle.borrow_mut().color = Color::Black;
    parent.borrow().parent.as_ref()
      .unwrap().borrow_mut().color =
                            Color::Red;

    n = parent.borrow().parent.as_ref()
            .unwrap().clone();
} else {
    if self.check(&parent.borrow().dev,
            &n.borrow().dev)
                == RBOperation::LeftNode
    {
        // do only if it's a right child
```

```
            let tmp = n.borrow().parent.as_ref()
                        .unwrap().clone();
            n = tmp;
            self.rotate(n.clone(),
            Rotation::Right);
            parent = n.borrow().parent.as_ref()
                        .unwrap().clone();
        }
        // until here. then for all black uncles
        parent.borrow_mut().color = Color::Black;
        parent.borrow().parent.as_ref()
          .unwrap().borrow_mut().color =
                                Color::Red;
        let grandparent = n
            .borrow()
            .parent
            .as_ref()
            .unwrap()
            .borrow()
            .parent
            .as_ref()
            .unwrap()
            .clone();
        self.rotate(grandparent, Rotation::Left);
    }
```

This code contains a large amount of `unwrap()`, `clone()`, and `borrow()` instances, a consequence of the interior mutability pattern. In this case, macros could help to reduce the code's verbosity.

Once the operations for one part of the tree finishes, the next iteration is prepared by checking for a red-red violation to see whether the loop needs to continue.

After the main loop exits, the pointer to the current node is moved up the tree to the root node (which is the function's return value, after all) and colored black. Why? This is a shortcut solution that would otherwise result in another iteration requiring many more expensive steps to be executed, and the rules of a red-black tree mandate a black root anyway:

```
    not_root = n.borrow().parent.is_some();
    if not_root {
        parent_is_red = self.parent_color(&n) == Color::Red;
    }
}
while n.borrow().parent.is_some() {
    let t = n.borrow().parent.as_ref().unwrap().clone();
    n = t;
```

```
        }
        Some(n)
    } else {
        Some(inserted)
    };
    root.map(|r| {
        r.borrow_mut().color = Color::Black;
        r
    })
```

With that shortcut, a valid tree is returned that can be set as the new root. However, the main purpose of the tree is to find stuff, which is not that different from a regular binary search tree.

Finding the right one, now

This piece of code can almost be reused from the binary search tree. Other than the borrow() calls (instead of a simple dereference or * operator) adding some amount of processing time, they provides a consistent search speed. For greater reuse of existing functions, the value to be found is wrapped into a dummy node. This way, no additional interface has to be created for comparing nodes:

```
pub fn find(&self, numerical_id: u64) -> Option<IoTDevice> {
    self.find_r(
        &self.root,
        &IoTDevice::new(numerical_id, "".to_owned(), "".to_owned()),
    )
}

fn find_r(&self, node: &Tree, dev: &IoTDevice) -> Option<IoTDevice> {
    match node {
        Some(n) => {
            let n = n.borrow();
            if n.dev.numerical_id == dev.numerical_id {
                Some(n.dev.clone())
            } else {
                match self.check(&n.dev, &dev) {
                    RBOperation::LeftNode => self.find_r(&n.left, dev),
                    RBOperation::RightNode => self.find_r(&n.right, dev),
                }
            }
        }
        _ => None,
    }
}
```

This is, again, a recursive walk of the tree until the specified value is found. Additionally, the "regular" tree walk was also added to the red-black tree variant:

```
pub fn walk(&self, callback: impl Fn(&IoTDevice) -> ()) {
    self.walk_in_order(&self.root, &callback);
}

fn walk_in_order(&self, node: &Tree, callback: &impl Fn(&IoTDevice) -> ())
{
    if let Some(n) = node {
        let n = n.borrow();

        self.walk_in_order(&n.left, callback);
        callback(&n.dev);
        self.walk_in_order(&n.right, callback);
    }
}
```

With these parts fixed, the platform performs consistently fast!

Wrap up

Red-black trees are great self-balancing binary trees, similar to **AVL** (short for **Adelson-Velsky and Landis**) trees. Both appeared around the same time, yet AVL trees are considered to be superior thanks to a lower height difference between the branches. Regardless of which tree structure is used, both are significantly faster than their less complex sibling, the binary search tree. Benchmarks using sorted data on insert (100,000 elements in this case) show how significant the difference between a balanced and unbalanced tree is:

```
test tests::bench_sorted_insert_bst_find ... bench: 370,185 ns/iter (+/-
265,997)
test tests::bench_sorted_insert_rbt_find ... bench: 900 ns/iter (+/- 423)
```

Another variation of a balanced tree is the 2-3-4 tree, a data structure that the red-black tree can be converted into. However, the 2-3-4 tree is, like the B-Tree (coming up later in this chapter), non-binary. Therefore, it is briefly discussed later in this chapter, but we encourage you to find other sources for details.

One major upside to implementing a red-black tree in Rust is the deep understanding of borrowing and ownership that follows the reference juggling when rotating, or "unpacking", a node's grandfather. It is highly recommended as a programming exercise to implement your own version!

Upsides

A red-black tree has a few desirable properties over a regular binary search tree:

- Balance makes searches consistently fast
- Predictable, low-memory usage
- Inserts are reasonably fast
- Simplicity of a binary tree
- Easy to validate

However, the data structure has some significant downsides as well, especially when planning to implement it!

Downsides

Speed is great, but can your implementation achieve it? Let's have a look at the downsides of red-black trees:

- Complex implementation, especially in Rust
- Concurrent writes require the entire tree to be locked
- Performance is great compared to binary search trees, but other trees perform better at the same complexity
- Skip lists (from the previous chapter) perform similarly with better concurrency and simpler implementations

In any case, the red-black tree is a great journey into sophisticated binary tree structures. A more exotic binary tree structure is the heap (not to be confused with the portion of main memory).

Heaps

Since binary trees are the most basic forms of trees, there are several variations designed for a specific purpose. Where the red-black tree is an advanced version of the initial tree, the binary heap is a version of the binary tree that does not facilitate search.

In fact, it has a specified purpose: finding the maximum or minimum value of a node. These heaps (min-heap or max-heap) are built in a way that the root node is always the value with the desired property (min or max) so it can be retrieved in constant time—that is, it always takes the same number of operations to fetch. Once fetched, the tree is restored in a way that the next operation works the same. How is this done though?

Heaps work, irrespective of whether they are min-heaps or max-heaps, because a node's children always have the same property as the entire tree. In a max-heap, this means that the root node is the maximum value of the sequence, so it has to be the greatest value of its children (it's the same with min-heaps, just in reverse). While there is no specific order to this (such as the left node being greater than the right node), there is a convention to prefer the right node for max-heaps and the left for min-heaps.

Upon inserting a new node, it is added last and then a place in the tree has to be determined. The strategy to do that is simple: look at the parent node; if it's greater (in a max-heap), swap the two, and repeat until this doesn't work or it becomes the root node. We call this operation **upheap**.

Similarly, this is how removals work. Once removed, the now-empty slot is replaced by a leaf of the tree—which is either the smallest (max-heap) or greatest (min-heap) value. Then, the same comparisons as with the insert are implemented, but in reverse. Comparing and swapping this node with the children restores the heap's properties and is called **downheap**.

If you paid attention to a node's journey, there is one detail that will be obvious to you: the tree is always "filled". This means that each level is fully populated (that is, every node has both children), making it a **complete binary tree** that maintains total order. This is a property that lets us implement this tree in an array (dynamic or not), making jumps cheap. It will all become clear once you see some diagram:

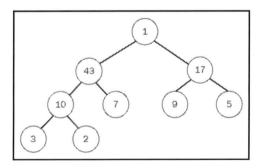

Commonly, the heap is used to create a priority queue of some kind, thanks to the ability to quickly retrieve the highest- or lowest-valued items. A very basic heap can be implemented in Rust as an array, which will provide everything necessary to make it work, but won't be as convenient as a `Vec`.

After the great success of the IoT device platform, an add-on has been planned. The product team is asking for a way to efficiently process messages that come from the devices, so that customers only have to deal with the actual handling of the message and skip the "plumbing" code. Since processing can be executed at (short) intervals, they require a way to order them quickly—ideally so that the device with the most messages can come first.

This sounds like the heap data structure, doesn't it? In fact, it can be a max-heap.

A huge inbox

Typically, heaps are used as priority queues of all kinds. Queues like that exist in any resource-constrained environment (and everywhere else, probably), but their purpose is to output things in an ordered fashion. By using the number of messages to determine the priority of a message notification, the heap can do the heavy lifting of this feature. Before jumping into the hard stuff, though, here are the bits containing the information:

```
#[derive(Clone, Debug)]
pub struct MessageNotification {
    pub no_messages: u64,
    pub device: IoTDevice,
}
```

The idea is to use the number of messages as an indicator of which device to poll first, which is why the device is required. Using this type, the heap does not require any specific node or link types to work:

```
pub struct MessageChecker {
    pub length: usize,
    heap: Vec<Box<MessageNotification>>,
}
```

There are two interesting points here: the underlying structure is a regular `Vec<T>`, which was chosen for its expansion capabilities (Rust's arrays are sized at compile time), and the functionality of `push` or `pop`.

Another noteworthy modification is that no `Option` is needed, which removes a check from the code and makes it easier to read. However, since many of the heap's operations work well with a direct, 1-index-based access, indices have to be translated before hitting `Vec<T>`.

So how does data get in?

Getting messages in

Once a message arrives, it is pushed to the back of the array when the upheap operation "bubbles up" the item until it finds its proper place. In Rust code, this is what that looks like:

```rust
pub fn add(&mut self, notification: MessageNotification) {
    self.heap.push(Box::new(notification));
    self.length = self.heap.len();
    if self.length > 1 {
        let mut i = self.length;
        while i / 2 > 0 && self.has_more_messages(i, i / 2) {
            self.swap(i, i / 2);
            i /= 2;
        }
    }
}
```

Initially, the new notification lives in a `Box` at the back of the `Vec<T>`, inserted via `push()`. A simple `while` loop then bubbles up the new addition by repeatedly swapping it whenever the `has_more_messages()` function is true. When is it true? Let's see the code:

```rust
fn has_more_messages(&self, pos1: usize, pos2: usize) -> bool {
    let a = &self.heap[pos1 - 1];
    let b = &self.heap[pos2 - 1];
    a.no_messages >= b.no_messages
}
```

By encapsulating this function, it's easily possible to change the heap into a min-heap should that be required—and the index translations are wrapped away here as well.

Getting data out requires doing this process in reverse in a function called `pop()`.

Taking messages out

Removing the first item in a Vec<T> is not difficult—in fact, Vec<T> ships with a swap_remove() function that does exactly what a heap needs: removing the first element of a Vec<T> by replacing it with the last element! This makes the code significantly shorter and therefore easier to reason about:

```
pub fn pop(&mut self) -> Option<MessageNotification> {
    if self.length > 0 {
        let elem = self.heap.swap_remove(0);
        self.length = self.heap.len();
        let mut i = 1;
        while i * 2 < self.length {
            let children = (i * 2, i * 2 + 1);
            i = if self.has_more_messages(children.0, children.1) {
                if self.has_more_messages(children.0, i) {
                    self.swap(i, children.0);
                    children.0
                } else {
                    break;
                }
            } else {
                if self.has_more_messages(children.1, i) {
                self.swap(i, children.1);
                children.1
                } else {
                    break;
                }
            }
        }
        Some(*elem)
    } else {
        None
    }
}
```

Obviously, this code is not short though—so what's amiss? The bubbling down. Swapping downward requires to look at the children (which are at the positions i * 2 and i * 2 + 1) to find out where (or if) the next iteration should proceed.

Wrap up

The heap data structure is surprisingly simple to implement. There are no lengthy unwraps, borrows, or other calls, and the pointer is owned by the Vec and can easily be swapped. Other than that, the upheap operation is only a while loop, just like the (slightly more complex) downheap function.

There is another typical use case for a heap though: sorting! Consider a bunch of numbers going into the heap instead of MessageNotification objects—they would come out sorted. Thanks to the efficiency of the upheap/downheap operations, the worst-case runtime of that sorting algorithm is great—but more on that in Chapter 9, *Ordering Things*.

Upsides

Compact and low-complexity implementation make the binary heap a great candidate for requiring any kind of sorting data structure. Other benefits include the following:

- An efficient way to sort lists
- Works well in concurrent situations
- A very efficient way to store a sorted array

Yet there are also downsides.

Downsides

Heaps are generally great, but have two caveats that limit their use:

- Use cases outside of queuing or sorting are rare
- There are better ways to sort

The binary heap was the last of the binary trees, and the next section will cover another rather exotic variation of a tree: the trie.

Trie

The trie is another interesting data structure—in particular, the way in which it is pronounced! Depending on your mother tongue, intuition might dictate a way, but—according to Wikipedia—the name was selected thanks to Edward Fredkin, who pronounced this type of tree differently, namely like **trie** in re**trie**val. Many English speakers resort to saying something along the lines of "try" though.

With that out of the way, what does the trie actually do for it to deserve a different name? It transpires that using retrieval was not a bad idea: tries store strings.

Imagine having to store the entire vocabulary of this book in a way to find out whether certain words are contained within the book. How can this be done efficiently?

After the previous sections, you should already have an answer, but if you think about strings—they are stored as arrays or lists of `char` instances—it would use a good amount of memory. Since each word has to use letters from the English alphabet, can't we use that?

Tries do something similar. They use characters as nodes in a tree where the parent node is the preceding character and all children (limited only by the size of the alphabet) are what follows. A trie storing the strings ABB, ABC, CAACB, CAACA, BBB, and BBA can be seen in the following trie diagram:

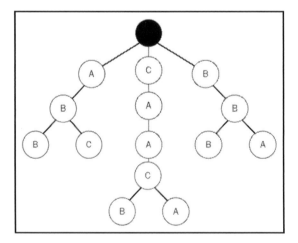

Storing strings like this enables a very efficient search. You only have to walk through the letters in the key that is to be stored to find out (or store) whether that string is contained in—for example—a set. In fact, if a string can only have a certain size, then the retrieval time is constant and it does not matter whether the trie stores 10 or 10 million words. Typically, this is useful for set data structures or key-value stores with string keys (such as hashes, but more on that later). Just like the binary search tree, this structure has a strong hierarchical memory management (that is, no pointers "back up"), making it a perfect fit for Rust.

Lately, the product team has looked into the user's device keys once again and found that the typical IoT device uses keys that represent a path, and they would often look like `countryA/cityB/factoryC/machine1/positionX/sensorY`. Reminded of the trees that worked so well earlier, they thought that you could use those to improve the directory as well. But you already have a better idea!

More realistic IoT device management

Paths like that tend to have a huge overlap, since there are countless sensors and devices in a single location. Additionally, they are unique thanks to the hierarchical properties and are human-readable in case the sensor needs to be found. A great fit for a trie!

The basis for this trie will be a node type that stores the children, current character, and, if it's a node that concludes a full key, the `IoTDevice` object from earlier in this chapter. This is what this looks like in Rust:

```
struct Node {
    pub key: char,
    next: HashMap<char, Link>,
    pub value: Option<IoTDevice>,
}
```

This time, the children is a different data structure as well: a `HashMap`. Maps (also called dictionaries, associative arrays) explicitly store a key alongside a value and the word "hash" hints at the method, which will be discussed in the next chapter. For now, the `HashMap` guarantees a single character to be associated with a Node type, leading the way for iteration. On top of that, this data structure allows for a get-or-add type operation, which significantly improves code readability.

Since the number of possible word beginnings is similar, the root is a `HashMap` as well, giving the trie multiple roots:

```
pub struct BestDeviceRegistry {
    pub length: u64,
    root: HashMap<char, Link>,
}
```

In order to fill up these maps with data, a method to add paths is required.

Adding paths

The algorithm for inserting a string into a trie can be described in only a few sentences: go through each character of the word and trace it down the trie. If a node does not yet exist, create it, and add the object with the last entry.

Of course, there are special cases that need to be decided as well: what happens when a string already exists? Overwrite or ignore? In the case of this implementation, the last write will win—that is, it's overwriting whatever existed previously:

```
pub fn add(&mut self, device: IoTDevice) {
    let p = device.path.clone();
    let mut path = p.chars();
    if let Some(start) = path.next() {
        self.length += 1;
        let mut n = self.root
                .entry(start)
                .or_insert(Node::new(start, None));
        for c in path {
            let tmp = n.next
                    .entry(c)
                    .or_insert(Node::new(c, None));
            n = tmp;
        }
        n.value = Some(device);
    }
}
```

Another special case is the root node, since it's not a real node but a `HashMap` right away. Once a trie is set up, the most important thing is to get stuff out again!

Walking

Add and search work in a very similar manner: follow the links to the characters of the key and return the "value" in the end:

```
pub fn find(&mut self, path: &str) -> Option<IoTDevice> {
    let mut path = path.chars();
    if let Some(start) = path.next() {
        self.root.get(&start).map_or(None, |mut n| {
            for c in path {
                match n.next.get(&c) {
                    Some(ref tmp) => n = tmp,
                    None => break,
                }
            }
            n.value.clone()
        })
    } else {
        None
    }
}
```

Since the trie does not store strings in any particular order (or even consistently), getting the same data out in a predictable way is tricky! Walking it like a binary tree works well enough, but will only be deterministic with respect to the insertion order, something that should be kept in mind when testing the implementation:

```
pub fn walk(&self, callback: impl Fn(&IoTDevice) -> ()) {
    for r in self.root.values() {
        self.walk_r(&r, &callback);
    }
}

fn walk_r(&self, node: &Link, callback: &impl Fn(&IoTDevice) -> ()) {
    for n in node.next.values() {
        self.walk_r(&n, callback);
    }
    if let Some(ref dev) = node.value {
        callback(dev);
    }
}
```

As previously mentioned, this walk is called a breadth-first traversal.

Wrap up

The trie data structure is a very efficient way of storing and finding strings by storing common prefixes, and they are often used in practice. One use case is the popular Java search engine Lucene, which uses this structure to store words in the search index, but there are plenty of other examples across different fields. Additionally, the simplicity is great for implementing a custom trie to store entire words or other objects instead of characters.

Upsides

The inherent prefix is great for efficient storage and, apart from that, there are the following benefits:

- Easy implementation facilitates customizing
- Minimal memory requirements for sets of strings
- Constant-time retrieval for strings with a known maximum length
- Exotic algorithms are available (for example, Burst Sort)

While the trie is great, it is also fairly simple, which comes with a number of downsides.

Downsides

Tries can work in a lot of shapes and forms, but can't handle every use case, unfortunately. Other disadvantages include the following:

- It has a name that's strange to pronounce
- There is no deterministic order on walking
- There are no duplicate keys

This concludes the more exotic tree varieties. Next up is the B-Tree, which is essentially a universal tree!

B-Tree

As you have noticed, restricting the number of children to 2 (like the binary trees earlier) yields a tree that only lets the algorithm decide whether to go left or right, and it's easily hardcoded. Additionally, storing only a single key-value pair in a node can be seen as a waste of space—after all, the pointers can be a lot larger than the actual payload!

B-Trees generally store multiple keys and values per node, which can make them more space-efficient (the payload-to-pointer ratio is higher). As a tree, each of these (key-value) pairs has children, which hold the values between the nodes they are located at. Therefore, a B-Tree stores triples of key, value, and child, with an additional child pointer to cover any "other" values. The following diagram shows a simple B-Tree. Note the additional pointer to a node holding smaller keys:

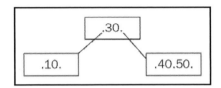

As depicted here, a B-Tree can have varying amounts of those key-value pairs (only the keys are visible), but they will have a maximum number of children—defined by the *order* parameter. Consequently, a binary search tree can be considered an order-2 B-Tree, without the added benefit of being self-balancing.

In order to achieve the self-balancing nature, a B-Tree has certain properties (as defined by Donald Knuth):

1. Each node can only have *order* children
2. Each node that is not a leaf node or root has at least *order/2* children
3. The root node has at least two children
4. All nodes hold *order - 1* keys when they have *order* children
5. All leaf nodes appear on the same level

How does self-balancing work? It is way simpler than a red-black tree. Firstly, new keys can only be inserted at the leaf level. Secondly, once the new key has found a node, the node is evaluated to the preceding rules—in particular, if there are now more than *order - 1* keys. If that is the case, the node has to be split, moving the center key to the parent node, as shown in the following diagram:

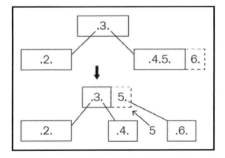

Next, the children are put in their intended position (especially important if the elevated node had children) and then the process is repeated up the tree until the root node is valid.

This process creates something that is called a **fat tree** (as opposed to a high tree), which means that adding height is only possible through splitting, which doesn't happen very often. In order to work with the nodes, they contain additional information about themselves:

```
type Tree = Box<Node>;

#[derive(Clone, PartialEq, Debug)]
enum NodeType {
    Leaf,
    Regular,
}

#[derive(Clone)]
struct Node {
    keys: Vec<Option<(u64, String, Option<Tree>)>>,
    left_child: Option<Tree>,
    pub node_type: NodeType,
}
```

In this case, the type of node is determined by a property, node_type, but the entire node could be wrapped into an enumeration as well. Furthermore, a special variable holding the "left child" has been attached in order to deal with keys lower than what is associated with the triples in the keys vector.

Like binary trees, the B-Tree exhibits logarithmic runtime complexity on search and insert ($O(log2(n))$) and, with the the simplified rebalancing, they make for a great choice for database indices. In fact, many SQL databases (such as SQLite and SQL Server) use B-Trees to store those search indices, and B+ Trees to store tables thanks to their smart ways of accessing the disk.

The product team has also heard about this and, since the previous attempts at the IoT device management solution have been a huge success, they thought about replacing the red-black tree with something better! They want to reduce the number of bugs by creating a more simplified version of the original database, so the requirements actually stay the same.

An IoT database

As in the previous implementation, this tree builds on the `numerical_id` property of `IoTDevice` as keys, and the device object as value. In code, a node looks very similar to the previous example:

```
type Tree = Box<Node>;
type KeyType = u64;

type Data = (Option<IoTDevice>, Option<Tree>);

#[derive(Clone, PartialEq, Debug)]
enum NodeType {
    Leaf,
    Regular,
}

#[derive(Clone, PartialEq)]
enum Direction {
    Left,
    Right(usize),
}

#[derive(Clone)]
struct Node {
    devices: Vec<Option<IoTDevice>>,
    children: Vec<Option<Tree>>,
    left_child: Option<Tree>,
    pub node_type: NodeType,
}
```

Instead of triples, this node type uses a synchronized index to find the children associated with a specified key-value pair. These pairs are also created ad hoc by evaluating the `numerical_id` property of the contained device, thereby also simplifying the code and eventual updates to the keys. Something that is missing from the node is a parent pointer, which made the entire red-black tree code significantly more complex.

The tree itself is stored as an `Option` on a boxed node (aliased as `Tree`), along with the `order` and `length` properties:

```
pub struct DeviceDatabase {
    root: Option<Tree>,
    order: usize,
    pub length: u64,
}
```

Finally, to check the validity of the tree, here's a `validate` method that recursively finds the minimum and maximum leaf height and checks whether the number of children is within bounds (as mentioned in the rules indicated earlier):

```
pub fn is_a_valid_btree(&self) -> bool {
    if let Some(tree) = self.root.as_ref() {
        let total = self.validate(tree, 0);
        total.0 && total.1 == total.2
    } else {
        false // there is no tree
    }
}

fn validate(&self, node: &Tree, level: usize) -> (bool, usize, usize) {
    match node.node_type {
        NodeType::Leaf => (node.len() <= self.order, level, level),
        NodeType::Regular => {
            // Root node only requires two children,
            //  every other node at least half the
            // order
            let min_children = if level > 0 {
                self.order / 2usize } else { 2 };
            let key_rules = node.len() <= self.order &&
                node.len() >= min_children;

            let mut total = (key_rules, usize::max_value(), level);
            for n in node.children.iter().chain(vec![&node.left_child]) {
                if let Some(ref tree) = n {
                    let stats = self.validate(tree, level + 1);
                    total = (
                        total.0 && stats.0,
                        cmp::min(stats.1, total.1),
                        cmp::max(stats.2, total.2),
                    );
                }
            }
            total
        }
    }
}
```

Having established these basic structures, we can move on to how to add new devices to the tree.

Adding stuff

B-Trees add new entries to their leaves, which then bubble up as nodes grow too large. In order to efficiently find a spot, this is done recursively, removing and replacing ownership as needed. Here is the add() function, which takes care of retrieving ownership of the root node and calling the recursive call with an existing or new node:

```
type Data = (Option<IoTDevice>, Option<Tree>);

pub fn add(&mut self, device: IoTDevice) {
    let node = if self.root.is_some() {
        mem::replace(&mut self.root, None).unwrap()
    } else {
        Node::new_leaf()
    };

    let (root, _) = self.add_r(node, device, true);
    self.root = Some(root);
}
```

Except in the case of the root node, the add_r() function (the recursive call) returns two pieces of information: the key it descended into and—in case of a "promotion"—the device and child that are to be added to whichever node it returns to. In principle, this function works as follows:

1. Recursively find the appropriate leaf and perform a sorted insert.
2. Increment the length if it's not a duplicate.
3. If the node now has more keys than are allowed: split.
4. Return the original node and the key with its new value to the caller.
5. Place the new node where it came from.
6. Add the promoted key.
7. Repeat from step 3 until at the root level:

```
fn add_r(&mut self, node: Tree, device: IoTDevice, is_root: bool)
-> (Tree, Option<Data>) {
    let mut node = node;
    let id = device.numerical_id;

    match node.node_type {
        NodeType::Leaf => {                          // 1
            if node.add_key(id, (Some(device), None)) {
                self.length += 1;                    // 2
            }
        }
    }
```

```
            NodeType::Regular => {
                let (key, (dev, tree)) = node.remove_key(id).unwrap();
                let new = self.add_r(tree.unwrap(), device, false);
                if dev.is_none() {                    // 5
                    node.add_left_child(Some(new.0));
                } else {
                    node.add_key(key, (dev, Some(new.0)));
                }
                                                      // 6
                if let Some(split_result) = new.1 {
                    let new_id = &split_result.0.clone().unwrap();
                    node.add_key(new_id.numerical_id, split_result);
                }
            }
        }

        if node.len() > self.order {                  // 3
            let (new_parent, sibling) = node.split();

            // Check if the root node is "full" and add a new level
            if is_root {
                let mut parent = Node::new_regular();
                // Add the former root to the left
                parent.add_left_child(Some(node));
                // Add the new right part as well
                parent.add_key(new_parent.numerical_id,
                            (Some(new_parent), Some(sibling)));
                (parent, None)
            } else {
                                                      // 4
                (node, Some((Some(new_parent), Some(sibling))))
            }
        } else {
            (node, None)
        }
    }
```

Since the root node is a special case where a new level is added to the tree, this has to be taken care of where the last split is happening—in the add_r() function. This is as simple as creating a new non-leaf node and adding the former root to the left and its sibling to the right, placing the new parent on top as the root node.

In this implementation, a lot of the heavy lifting is done by the node's implementation of several functions, including `split()`. While this is complex, it encapsulates the inner workings of the tree—something that should not be exposed too much so as to facilitate change:

```
pub fn split(&mut self) -> (IoTDevice, Tree) {
    let mut sibling = Node::new(self.node_type.clone());

    let no_of_devices = self.devices.len();
    let split_at = no_of_devices / 2usize;

    let dev = self.devices.remove(split_at);
    let node = self.children.remove(split_at);

    for _ in split_at..self.devices.len() {
        let device = self.devices.pop().unwrap();
        let child = self.children.pop().unwrap();
        sibling.add_key(device.as_ref().unwrap()
                    .numerical_id, (device, child));
    }

    sibling.add_left_child(node);
    (dev.unwrap(), sibling)
}
```

As described previously, splitting yields a new sibling to the original node and a new parent to both of them. The sibling will receive the upper half of the keys, the original node remains with the lower half, and the one in the center becomes the new parent.

Having added several devices, let's talk about how to get them back out.

Searching for stuff

A B-Tree's search works just the way binary tree searches do: recursively checking each node for the path to follow. In B-Trees, this becomes very convenient since it can be done in a loop, in this case, by the `get_device()` function:

```
pub fn get_device(&self, key: KeyType) -> Option<&IoTDevice> {
    let mut result = None;
    for d in self.devices.iter() {
        if let Some(device) = d {
            if device.numerical_id == key {
                result = Some(device);
                break;
            }
        }
```

```
            }
        }
        result
    }
```

This function is implemented at the node structure and does a regular linear search for the key itself. If it is unable to find that key, the `find_r()` function has to decide whether to continue, which it does by evaluating the node type. Since leaf nodes don't have any children, not finding the desired key will end the search, returning `None`. Regular nodes allow the search to continue on a deeper level of the tree:

```
pub fn find(&self, id: KeyType) -> Option<IoTDevice> {
    match self.root.as_ref() {
        Some(tree) => self.find_r(tree, id),
        _ => None,
    }
}

fn find_r(&self, node: &Tree, id: KeyType) -> Option<IoTDevice> {
    match node.get_device(id) {
        Some(device) => Some(device.clone()),
        None if node.node_type != NodeType::Leaf => {
            if let Some(tree) = node.get_child(id) {
                self.find_r(tree, id)
            } else {
                None
            }
        }
        _ => None,
    }
}
```

Another method for finding something within the tree's values is walking the tree.

Walking the tree

Similarly to the binary trees earlier in this chapter, walking can be done with different strategies, even if there are many more branches to walk. The following code shows an in-order tree walking algorithm, where the callback is executed between the left child and before descending into the child that is currently looked at:

```
pub fn walk(&self, callback: impl Fn(&IoTDevice) -> ()) {
    if let Some(ref root) = self.root {
        self.walk_in_order(root, &callback);
    }
}
```

```
fn walk_in_order(&self, node: &Tree, callback: &impl Fn(&IoTDevice) -> ())
{
    if let Some(ref left) = node.left_child {
        self.walk_in_order(left, callback);
    }

    for i in 0..node.devices.len() {
        if let Some(ref k) = node.devices[i] {
            callback(k);
        }

        if let Some(ref c) = node.children[i] {
            self.walk_in_order(&c, callback);
        }
    }
}
```

Thanks to the internal sorting, this walk retrieves the keys in an ascending order.

Wrap up

B-Trees are awesome. They are widely used in real-world applications, their implementation in Rust is not all that complex, and they maintain a great performance regardless of insertion order. Furthermore, the tree's order can dramatically improve performance by decreasing the tree's height. It is recommended to estimate the number of key-value pairs beforehand and adjust the order accordingly.

As a benchmark, let's evaluate the trees by inserting 100,000 unsorted, unique elements, and retrieving them using find(). Dot size represents the variance, while the values shown along the *y* axis are nanoseconds:

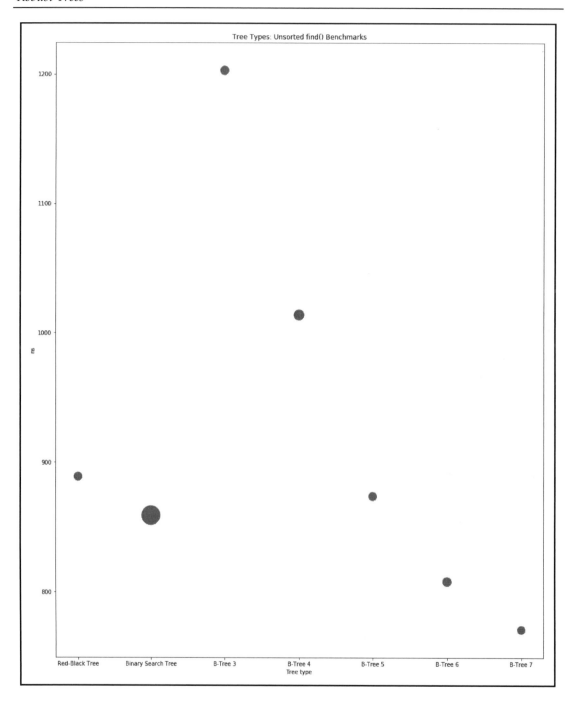

The chart output of Unsorted find ()

Other than that, it performs at the level of other trees, with vastly fewer lines of code and less code complexity, both of which impact readability and maintainability for other developers.

Upsides

This type of tree achieves great performance with the order parameter set accordingly:

- Less complex to implement than other self-balancing trees
- Widely used in database technology
- Predictable performance thanks to self-balancing
- Range queries are possible
- Variants that minimize disk access (B+ Tree)

The tree's downsides are few.

Downsides

Absolute performance depends significantly on the tree's order; other than that, this tree does not have many downsides.

Graphs

In their most generic form, trees are graphs—directed, acyclic graphs. A general graph can be described as a collection of connected nodes, sometimes referred to as vertices, with certain properties such as whether cycles are allowed. The connections between those also have their own name: edges. These edges can have certain properties as well, in particular, weights and directions (like one-way streets).

By enforcing these constraints, a model can be built that, just like trees, reflects a certain reality very well. There is one particular thing that is typically represented as a weighted graph: the internet. While, nowadays, this might be an oversimplification, with various versions of the Internet Protocol (IPv4 and IPv6) and **Network Address Translation** (**NAT**) technologies hiding large numbers of participants online, in its earlier days, the internet could be drawn as a collection of routers, computers, and servers (nodes) interconnected with links (edges) defined by speed and latency (weights).

The following diagram shows a random, undirected, unweighted graph:

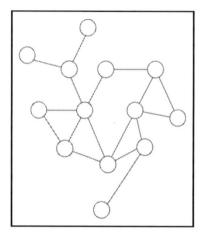

Other than humans, who can typically see and follow a reasonably efficient path through this mesh of interconnected nodes, computers require specific instructions to find anything in there! This called for new algorithms that allow for dealing with this complexity—which is especially tricky once the number of nodes in the mesh exceeds the number of nodes that can be looked at in time. This led to the development of many routing algorithms, techniques to finding cycles and segmenting the network, or popular NP-hard problems, such as the traveling salesman problem or the graph-coloring problem. The traveling salesman problem is defined as follows.

Find the optimal (shortest) path between cities without visiting one twice. On the left are some cities in Europe; on the right, two possible solutions (dotted versus solid lines):

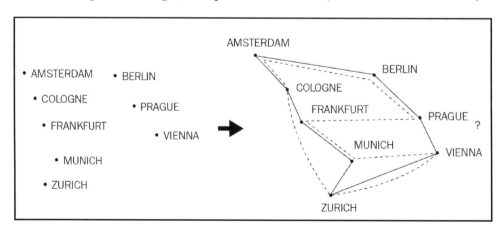

Today, there are many examples of graphs, the most obvious being a social graph (in social networks), but also as part of TensorFlow's deep learning API, state machines, and the rise of graph databases that offer a generic query language to traverse graphs. Even some less obvious use cases can be found, such as storing genetic sequences (nodes being the small parts of the DNA)!

To get out of theoretical constructs, how would you represent a graph in a program *efficiently*? As a node structure with a list of outbound vertices? How would you find a particular node then? A tricky problem! Graphs also have the habit of growing quite large, as anyone who ever wanted to serialize object graphs to JSON can testify: they run out of memory quite easily.

The best way to work with this data structure is surprisingly simple: a matrix. This matrix can either be sparse (that is, a list of lists with varying sizes), called an **adjacency list**, or a full-blown matrix (adjacency matrix). Especially for a matrix, the size is typically the number of nodes on either side and the weights (or Boolean values representing "connected" or "not connected") at each crossing. Many implementations will also keep the "real" nodes in its own list, using the indices as IDs. The following diagram shows how to display a graph as a matrix:

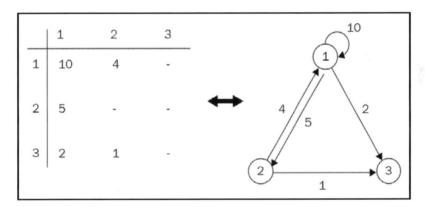

Rust provides many great tools for implementing really complex graph structures: enumerations and pattern-matching provide ways to operate on types of nodes and edges with low overhead, while iterators and functional approaches remove the need for verbose loops. Let's look at a generic graph structure in Rust:

```
struct ASimpleGraph {
    adjacency_list: Vec<Vec<usize>>,
}
```

This adjacency list can store nodes and whether they are connected, making this a finite, undirected, unweighted graph—great for storing simple relationships between objects. Already, a data structure such as this has the ability to implement sophisticated routing algorithms or run out of resources on a backtracking algorithm. In an adjacency list, each index in the list represents the origin of an edge and the contained elements (also lists) are any outbound edges. To traverse the graph, start at an origin index and find the next index by searching its edges. Then repeat until arriving at the destination node!

When the product team heard of this amazing data structure—and they are now well aware of your abilities—they came up with a new product: the literal Internet of Things (it's a working title). Their idea is to provide customers with a way to model complex sensor placements that would have distance built in! Customers can then go and evaluate all sensors that are within a certain range of each other, find single points of failure, or plan a route to inspect them quickly.

To summarize, customers should be able to do the following:

- Create or add a list of nodes
- Connect nodes with their physical distance to each other
- Find the shortest path between two nodes with respect to the distance provided
- Retrieve a list of neighbors of a specified node, up to a certain degree

Great idea, right? A great fit for graphs as well.

The literal Internet of Things

In order to get a head start on these requirements, the decision for a graph representation has to be made: list or matrix? Both work well, but for explanatory reasons, the examples will go with an adjacency list built on top of a vector of vectors:

```
pub struct InternetOfThings {
    adjacency_list: Vec<Vec<Edge>>,
    nodes: Vec<KeyType>,
}
```

As previously mentioned, it makes sense to keep the actual values, identifiers, or even entire objects in their own list and simply work with indices of the `usize` type. The edge structure in this example could be represented as a tuple just as well, but it's way more readable this way:

```
#[derive(Clone, Debug)]
struct Edge {
```

```
        weight: u32,
          node: usize,
    }
```

Having those two structures in place, adding nodes (or... things) to the graph can be done with only a few lines:

```
fn get_node_index(&self, node: KeyType) -> Option<usize> {
    self.nodes.iter().position(|n| n == &node)
}

pub fn set_edges(&mut self, from: KeyType, edges: Vec<(u32, KeyType)>) {
    let edges: Vec<Edge> = edges.into_iter().filter_map(|e| {
        if let Some(to) = self.get_node_index(e.1) {
            Some(Edge { weight: e.0, node: to })
        } else {
            None
        }}).collect();
    match self.nodes.iter().position(|n| n == &from) {
        Some(i) => self.adjacency_list[i] = edges,
        None => {
            self.nodes.push(from);
            self.adjacency_list.push(edges)
        }
    }
}
```

Within that function, there is a crucial check that's made: every edge has to connect to a valid node, otherwise it will not be added to the graph. To achieve this, the code looks up the IDs provided in the `edges` parameter in its internal node storage to find the index it's at, something that is done by the `position()` function of Rust's iterator trait. It returns the position of when the provided predicate returns true! Similarly, the `filter_map()` function of the iterator will only include elements that evaluate to `Some()` (as opposed to `None`) in its result set. Therefore, the nodes have to have a setter that also initializes the adjacency list:

```
pub fn set_nodes(&mut self, nodes: Vec<KeyType>) {
    self.nodes = nodes;
    self.adjacency_list = vec![vec![]; self.nodes.len()]
}
```

Once that's done, the graph is ready to use. How about we go looking for neighbors first?

Neighborhood search

Neighborhood search is a very trivial algorithm: starting from the node provided, follow every edge and return what you find. In our case, the degree of the relationship is important.

Just like for the tree algorithms shown previously, recursion is a great choice for solving this problem. While an iterative solution will often be more memory-efficient (no stack overflows), recursion is way more descriptive once you get the hang of it. Additionally, some compilers (and partly rustc, but not guaranteed) will expand the recursion into a loop, providing the best of both worlds (look for tail call optimization)! Obviously, the most important thing is to have a projected growth in mind; 100,000 recursive calls are likely to fill up the stack.

However, the function to run the neighborhood is implemented two-fold. First, the public-facing function takes care of validating input data and sees whether the node actually exists:

```
pub fn connected(&self, from: KeyType, degree: usize) ->
Option<HashSet<KeyType>> {
    self.nodes.iter().position(|n| n == &from).map(|i| {
        self.connected_r(i, degree).into_iter().map(|n|
        self.nodes[n].clone()).collect()
    })
}
```

With that out of the way, the recursive call can create a list of all its neighbors and run the same call on each of them. Returning a set of nodes eliminates the duplicates as well:

```
fn connected_r(&self, from: usize, degree: usize) -> HashSet<usize> {
    if degree > 0 {
        self.adjacency_list[from]
            .iter()
            .flat_map(|e| {
                let mut set = self.connected_r(e.node, degree - 1);
                set.insert(e.node);
                set
            }).collect()
    } else {
        HashSet::new()
    }
}
```

Since the recursive call returns the internal representation (that is, indices), the outer function translates those back into data the user can understand. This function can serve as a basis for other features, such as intersecting the neighborhoods of two nodes, and vicinity search. Or, to make it more real, on a sensor outage, the company can check whether there is a common device that's responsible (intersection), or if other close-by sensors are reporting similar measurements to rule out malfunctions (neighborhood search). Now, let's move on to something more complex: finding the shortest path.

The shortest path

This algorithm has its roots in early networking: routers had to decide where to forward packets to, without having any knowledge of what's beyond. They simply had to make the best decision without having perfect information! Edsger Dijkstra, one of the pioneers of computer science, then came up with a graph-routing algorithm that has been named after him: Dijkstra's algorithm.

The algorithm works iteratively and goes over each node to add up their weights, thereby finding the distance (or cost) of reaching this node. It will then continue at the node with the lowest cost, which makes this algorithm a "greedy" algorithm. This continues until the desired node is reached or there are no more nodes to evaluate.

Algorithms that immediately converge toward what's best right now (**local optimum**) in order to find the best overall solution (**global optimum**) are called **greedy algorithms**. This, of course, is tricky, since the path to a global optimum might require the acceptance of an increased cost! There is no guaranteed way to finding the global optimum, so it's about reducing the probability of getting stuck in a local optimum. A well-known greedy algorithm in 2018 is stochastic gradient descent, which is used to train neural networks.

In code, this is what that looks like:

```
pub fn shortest_path(&self, from: KeyType, to: KeyType) -> Option<(u32,
Vec<KeyType>)> {
    let mut src = None;
    let mut dest = None;

    for (i, n) in self.nodes.iter().enumerate() {
        if n == &from {
            src = Some(i);
        }
        if n == &to {
            dest = Some(i);
```

```
        }
        if src.is_some() && dest.is_some() {
            break;
        }
    }
    if src.is_some() && dest.is_some() {
        let (src, dest) = (src.unwrap(), dest.unwrap());

        let mut distance: Vec<TentativeWeight> =
            vec![TentativeWeight::Infinite; self.nodes.len()];
        distance[src] = TentativeWeight::Number(0);

        let mut open: Vec<usize> =
                (0..self.nodes.len()).into_iter().collect();
        let mut parent = vec![None; self.nodes.len()];
        let mut found = false;
        while !open.is_empty() {
            let u = min_index(&distance, &open);
            let u = open.remove(u);

            if u == dest {
                found = true;
                break;
            }

            let dist = distance[u].clone();

            for e in &self.adjacency_list[u] {
                let new_distance = match dist {
                    TentativeWeight::Number(n) =>
                        TentativeWeight::Number(n + e.weight),
                    _ => TentativeWeight::Infinite,
                };
                let old_distance = distance[e.node].clone();

                if new_distance < old_distance {
                    distance[e.node] = new_distance;
                    parent[e.node] = Some(u);
                }
            }
        }
        if found {
            let mut path = vec![];
            let mut p = parent[dest].unwrap();
            path.push(self.nodes[dest].clone());
            while p != src {
                path.push(self.nodes[p].clone());
                p = parent[p].unwrap();
```

```
        }
        path.push(self.nodes[src].clone());

        path.reverse();
        let cost = match distance[dest] {
            TentativeWeight::Number(n) => n,
            _ => 0,
        };
        Some((cost, path))
    } else {
        None
    }
} else {
    None
}
}
```

Since this is a long one, let's break it down. This is boiler-plate code to ensure that both source and destination nodes are nodes in the graph:

```
pub fn shortest_path(&self, from: KeyType, to: KeyType) -> Option<(u32,
Vec<KeyType>)> {
    let mut src = None;
    let mut dest = None;

    for (i, n) in self.nodes.iter().enumerate() {
        if n == &from {
            src = Some(i);
        }
        if n == &to {
            dest = Some(i);
        }
        if src.is_some() && dest.is_some() {
            break;
        }
    }
    if src.is_some() && dest.is_some() {
        let (src, dest) = (src.unwrap(), dest.unwrap());
```

Then, each node gets a tentative weight assigned, which is infinite in the beginning, except for the origin node, which has zero cost to reach. The "open" list, which contains all the nodes yet to be processed, is conveniently created using Rust's range—as it corresponds to the indices we are working with.

The parent array keeps track of each node's parent once the lower cost is established, which provides a way to trace back the best possible path!

```
let mut distance: Vec<TentativeWeight> =
    vec![TentativeWeight::Infinite; self.nodes.len()];
distance[src] = TentativeWeight::Number(0);

let mut open: Vec<usize> =
            (0..self.nodes.len()).into_iter().collect();
let mut parent = vec![None; self.nodes.len()];
let mut found = false;
```

Now, let's plunge into the path-finding. The helper function, `min_index()`, takes the current distances and returns the index of the node that is easiest (as in lowest distance) to reach next. This node will then be removed from the open list. Here's a good point at which to also stop if the destination has been reached. For more thoughts on this, see the preceding information box on greedy algorithms. Setting `found` to `true` will help distinguish between no result and early stopping.

For each edge of this node, the new distance is computed and, if lower, inserted into a distance list (as seen from the source node). There are a lot of clones going on as well, which is due to ensuring not borrowing while updating the vector. With `u64` (or `u32`) types, this should not create a large overhead (pointers are typically that large too), but for other types, this can be a performance pitfall:

```
while !open.is_empty() {
    let u = min_index(&distance, &open);
    let u = open.remove(u);

    if u == dest {
        found = true;
        break;
    }

    let dist = distance[u].clone();

    for e in &self.adjacency_list[u] {
        let new_distance = match dist {
            TentativeWeight::Number(n) =>
                TentativeWeight::Number(n + e.weight),
            _ => TentativeWeight::Infinite,
        };
        let old_distance = distance[e.node].clone();

        if new_distance < old_distance {
            distance[e.node] = new_distance;
```

```
                    parent[e.node] = Some(u);
                }
            }
        }
```

After this loop exits, there is a distance array and a parent array to be prepared for returning to the caller. First, trace back the path from the destination to the origin node in the parent array, which leads to the reverse optimal path between the two nodes:

```
        if found {
            let mut path = vec![];
            let mut p = parent[dest].unwrap();
            path.push(self.nodes[dest].clone());
            while p != src {
                path.push(self.nodes[p].clone());
                p = parent[p].unwrap();
            }
            path.push(self.nodes[src].clone());
            path.reverse();
            let cost = match distance[dest] {
                TentativeWeight::Number(n) => n,
                _ => 0,
            };
            Some((cost, path))
        } else {
            None
        }
    } else {
        None
    }
}
```

By strictly following the node with the lowest distance, Dijkstra's algorithm achieves a great runtime when stopping early, and runtime can even be improved by using more efficient data structures (such as a heap) to fetch the next node efficiently.

Modern approaches to shortest paths in a graph typically use the *A** (pronounced "a star") algorithm. While it operates on the same principles, it is also a bit more complex and would therefore go beyond the scope of this book.

Wrap up

A graph is surprisingly straightforward to implement: clear ownership in adjacency lists or matrices makes them almost effortless to work with! On top of that, there are two additional aspects that weren't yet covered in this implementation: an enumeration with an implementation, and using regular operations (here: comparison) with this implementation.

This shows how conforming to standard interfaces provides great ways to interface with the standard library or well-known operations in addition to the flexibility enumerations provide. With a few lines of code, infinity can be represented and worked with in a readable way. It was also a step toward more algorithmic aspects, which will be covered later in the book. For now, let's focus on graphs again.

Upsides

Graph structures are unique and there are rarely other ways of achieving the same outcome. Working in this environment enables you to focus deeply on relationships and think about problems differently. Following are some upsides of using graphs:

- Are amazing in modeling relationships
- Efficient retrieval of dependencies of a specific node
- Simplify complex abstractions
- Enable certain problems to be solved at all

Whether you choose a matrix or list representation is often a subjective choice and, for example, while the matrix provides easy deletes, a list stores edges more efficiently in the first place. It's all a trade-off.

Downsides

This leads us to the downsides of this particular data structure:

- Unable to solve certain problems efficiently (for example, a list of all nodes that have a certain property)
- More resource-inefficient

- Unsolved problems exist (for example, the traveling salesman problem with a high number of cities)
- Typically requires a problem to be reconsidered

With this, we can conclude this chapter about trees and their relatives after a summary.

Summary

This chapter went deep into trees, starting off with the simplest form: the binary search tree. This tree prepares the inserted data for search by creating a left and a right branch which hold smaller or greater values. A search algorithm can therefore just pick the direction based on the current node and the value coming in, thereby skipping a majority of the other nodes.

The regular binary search tree has a major drawback, however: it can become unbalanced. Red-black trees provide a solution for that: by rotating subtrees, a balanced tree structure is maintained and search performance is guaranteed.

Heaps are a more exotic use of the tree structure. With their primary use as a priority queue, they efficiently produce the lowest or highest number of an array in constant time. The upheap and downheap operations repair the structure upon insert or removal so that the root is again the lowest (min-heap) or highest (max-heap) number.

Another very exotic structure is the trie. They are specialized in holding strings and very efficiently find the data associated with a certain string by combining the characters as nodes with words "branching off" as required.

To go up in the generalization level, B-Trees are a generic form of a tree. They hold several values, with the ranges between them leading to a child node. Similar to red-black trees, they are balanced, and adding nodes only happens at the leaves where they may be "promoted" to a higher level. Typically, these are used in database indices.

Last but not least, the most generic form of a tree: the graph. Graphs are a flexible way to express constrained relationships, such as no cycles, and directionality. Typically, each node has weighted connections (edges) that provide some notion of cost of transitioning between the nodes.

With some of the essential data structures covered, the next chapter will explore sets and maps (sometimes called dictionaries). In fact, some of those have already been used in this chapter, so the next chapter will focus on implementing our own.

Questions

- How does a binary search tree skip several nodes when searching?
- What are self-balancing trees?
- Why is balance in a tree important?
- Is a heap a binary tree?
- What are good use cases for tries?
- What is a B-Tree?
- What are the fundamental components of a graph?

6

Exploring Maps and Sets

Up until this chapter, data structures have only become faster for searching, and this chapter is no different. What makes it different is why and how data can be found in two higher-level data structures: maps and sets. While the former is also known as dictionary, associative array, object, or hash table, the latter commonly crosses people's minds as a mathematical concept. Both can rely on hashing, a technique that allows for constant (or close to constant) time retrieval of items, checking whether they are contained in a set, or routing requests in distributed hash tables.

These data structures are also one level higher than the previous ones, since all of them build on existing structures, such as dynamic arrays or trees, and to top things off, the chapter starts with an algorithm. Understanding this chapter will be great preparation heading into the second part of the book, where algorithms are the main focus. Topics learned in this chapter include the following:

- Hashing functions and what they are good for
- How to implement a set based on different data structures
- What makes maps special

Hashing

The birthday paradox is a well-known phenomenon; two people share this special day that year, seemingly often, and we still get excited when it happens. Statistically speaking, the probability of meeting someone like this is really high, since in a room of just 23 people, the probability is already at 50%. While this may be an interesting fact, why is this introducing a section about hashing?

Birthdays can be considered a hash function—although a bad one. Hash functions are functions that map one value onto another value of a fixed size, like combining the day and month of a birthday into u64, shown as follows:

```
fn bd_hash(p: &Person) -> u64 {
    format!("{}{}", p.day, p.month) as u64
}
```

This function will prove very ineffective indeed, shown as follows:

- It is very hard to find out someone's birthday deterministically without asking them
- The space is limited to 366 unique values, which also makes collisions very likely
- They are not evenly distributed across the year

What makes a good hash function? It depends on the use case. There are many properties that can be associated with a hash function, such as the following:

- One way or two way (that is, given a hash, can one get the original value back?)
- Deterministic
- Uniform
- Fixed or variable range

Designing good hash functions is a *very* hard task in any field; there are countless algorithms that have been shown to be too weak for their designed purpose after several years of use, with SHA-1 being the latest prominent victim.

There is a wide variety of hashing algorithms for all kinds of use cases available, ranging from cryptographically secure to something akin to a parity bit to mitigate tampering. This section will focus on a few areas that we deemed interesting; for a wider picture, Wikipedia (https://en.wikipedia.org/wiki/List_of_hash_functions) provides a list that shows a number of available hashing algorithms and their articles.

Signatures are one of the most important fields for hashing algorithms and they can be as simple as the last digit on a credit card number (to validate the number) to 512-bit strong cryptographic digest functions, where a single collision is the end of that particular algorithm.

Outside of cryptography, hashing is used in completely different areas as well, such as peer-to-peer routing or encoding information in a tree-like structure. **GeoHashes** are a great example; instead of comparing longitude and latitude, these GeoHashes allow to quickly check if an area is located close to (or within) another area by comparing the first few characters of the hash. The algorithm was put into the public domain and can be found under http://geohash.org/. Collisions in this space can be ruled out since the entire space of possible input variations (coordinates on planet Earth) is known beforehand.

What are **collisions**? A collision occurs when two different input parameters lead to the same output, making the hash ambiguous. In cryptography, this fact will lead to a large scale crisis, just like it would if you found another key that matches your door lock. The main difference being that in the physical world, trying every door in your neighborhood is highly impractical, but with fully connected computers, this can be done in a matter of seconds. This means that the potential inputs are just as important as the quality of the hashing function itself—be it time and practicality (like physical items), or the applicable range (Earth coordinates, maximum number of nodes in a cluster)—transferring a function to a domain with a larger range leads to unexpected outcomes.

To summarize, collisions appear when the potential space of a key is either not large enough to withstand a full enumeration (brute force), or the outputs of the hash function are unevenly distributed.

Create your own

For the purpose of representing an object as a number (for use in a hash map or for comparison), most languages' built-in types come with a solid hash function for exactly that purpose, so building your own is almost never a good idea, unless a lot of time and effort goes into it. The better choice is to use what's built-in, or use a library that provides tested and proven methods.

It is important though to know how those functions are built, so let's create a trivial implementation to analyze the basic principles. The following example is one that uses the XOR operation on the previous and current byte to save their binary differences, then shifts it to the left up to four times (to fill up the u32 type):

```
pub fn hashcode(bytes: &[u8]) -> u32 {
    let mut a = 0_u32;
    for (i, b) in bytes.iter().enumerate() {
        a ^= *b as u32;
        a <<= i % 4;
```

```
        }
        a
    }
```

When this function is applied to a range of repeated letter strings, how are the values distributed? A histogram and a scatter plot tell the story, shown as follows:

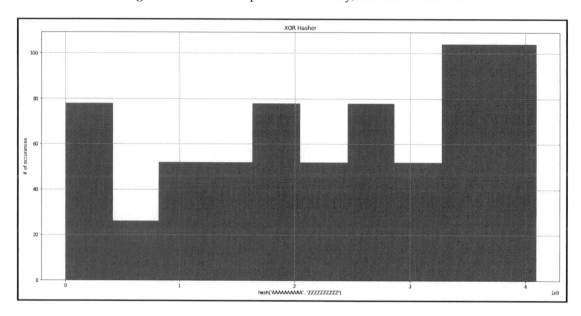

The output chart of the XOR Hasher

This histogram shows the distribution of the hash output, when the function is applied to all combinations of ten AA-ZZ, but each letter repeated ten times, so the first string is AAAAAAAAAAAAAAAAAAAA (20 letters), the last string is ZZZZZZZZZZZZZZZZZZZZ, yielding 675 combinations of 20 letter "words." This leads to a less optimal distribution, where the highest frequency is five times as high as the lowest. While speed can be a factor in using that function, it will clearly produce suboptimal results for cryptography.

In a scatter plot, this looks like the following:

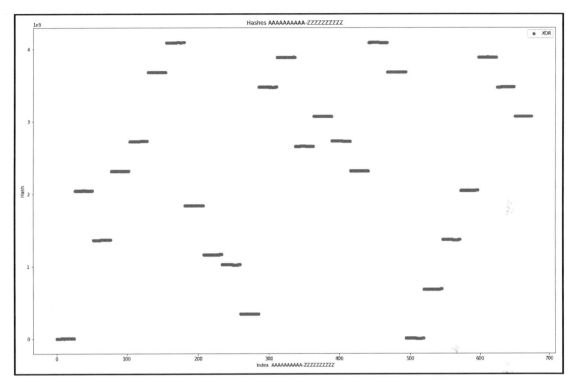

The output graph of the scatter plot

The scatter plot shows a different story. On the *x* axis, the index of each combination is shown, the *y* axis shows the hash output. Therefore, horizontal lines mean collisions, and they are all over the place! It can be interesting to explore further properties of a function like this, but the first results look quite dire, and searching for a better algorithm is the best use of anyone's time. Let's move on to checksums and digests.

Message digestion

Message digests are created as a way to guarantee authenticity; if a message was sent, a digest or signature of this message provides an ability to check whether the message has been tampered with. Typically, the signature will therefore be transmitted differently than the original message.

Obviously, this requires the hashing function to adhere to some basic rules to be considered good, listed as follows:

- A signature has to be quick and easy to obtain regardless of message size
- The signature can only have a fixed length
- The function has to minimize collisions

The hash functions contained in this group are the most popular ones and are the objective of many security researchers: MD5, SHA-1/2/3, or Adler 32. Adler 32 is prominently used in the zlib library to ensure the file's integrity, but should not be used to authenticate messages, thanks to the limited output space of 32-bit. However, it is easy to implement and understand, which makes it great for the purposes of this book:

```
const MOD_ADLER: u32 = 65521;

pub fn adler32(bytes: &[u8]) -> u32 {
    let mut a = 1_u32;
    let mut b = 0_u32;

    for byte in bytes {
        a = (a + byte as u32) % MOD_ADLER;
        b = (b + a) % MOD_ADLER;
    }

    (b << 16) | a
}
```

The algorithm sums up the bytes of any byte stream, and avoids an overflow by applying the modulo operation, using a large prime number (65521), which makes it harder for a byte to change without changing the final result. The algorithm has considerable weaknesses since there are many ways to change the operands of a sum without affecting the outcome!

Additionally, rolling over (after the modulo is applied) gives some weight to the order of bytes, so if the sum of bytes is not large enough, the algorithm is expected to produce even more collisions. Generally, this algorithm primarily protects against random transmission errors that cause bits to change, and is not useful in authenticating messages.

Wrap up

Hashing is a very useful tool that developers use every day—knowingly or unknowingly. Integer comparisons are fast, so checking the equality of two strings can be improved by comparing their hashes. Diverse keys can be made comparable by hashing—a method that is used in distributed databases to assign a partition to a row.

 Modulo hashing is a technique that lets a distributed database assign a row to a partition deterministically. Hash the row's key, then use the modulo operator with the maximum number of partitions to receive a destination to store the row.

Earlier, we explored some hash functions (XOR-based and Adler 32), but we never compared them. Additionally, Rust's standard library offers a hash function (built for `HashSet<K,V>`/`HashMap<K,V>`, and implemented for all standard types), which is a good baseline.

First, histograms—to show how many occurrences each hash has. As mentioned before, the XOR-based approach yields a very strange distribution, where some hashes clearly appear more often than others, shown as follows:

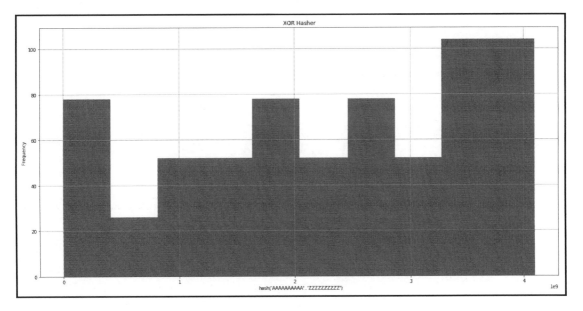

The output chart of the XOR Hasher

The Adler checksum creates a normal distribution in this case, which is probably due to the repetitive content, and the commutative nature of summing up numbers (*2 + 1 = 1 + 2*). Considering that transmission errors in compressed files are probably creating repetition, it looks like a solid choice for that use case. It would not do well in most other scenarios though:

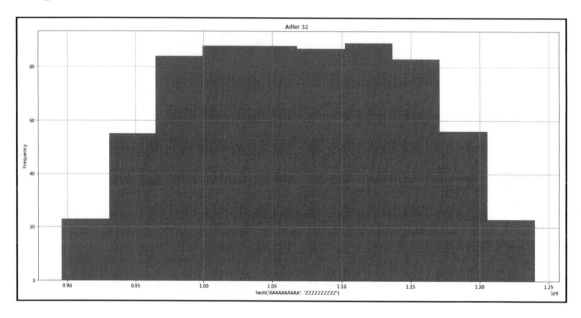

The output chart of Adler 32

The following is Rust's default choice, the `SipHash` based `DefaultHasher`:

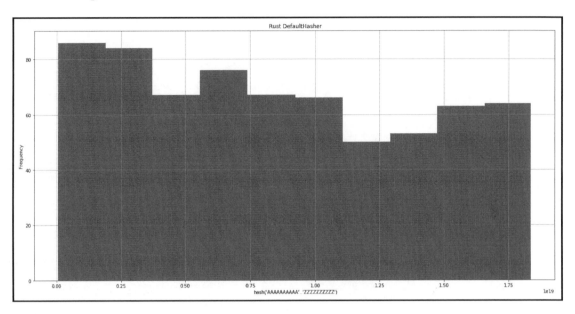

The output chart of the Rust DefaultHasher

Seeing the three distributions, their use in a hash table, where the frequency directly translates to the length of the lists at each bucket, becomes obvious. While it's best to have a length of one, lists of the same length at least yield the best performance if there is *any* collision. The Rust standard library clearly made a great choice with the `SipHash` based (`https://link.springer.com/chapter/10.1007/978-3-642-34931-7_28`) implementation.

A comparative scatter plot also sheds some light on the behavior of hash functions. Be aware that it is log-scaled to fit the results into a manageable plot, shown as follows:

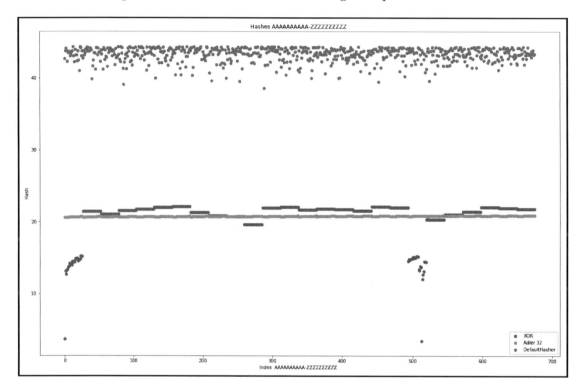

The comparison plot for XOR, Adler 32, and DefaultHasher

While the scale does not allow for a detailed judgment, what appears to be a line is always a collision-heavy behavior. As expected from the histograms, the Adler 32 and XOR-based approach both do not show a cloud. Since the y axis shows the actual hash (log-scaled), the more vertically spread it is, the better the distribution. Ideally, there would be a unique hash for each x value, but roughly the same number of dots for each y value predict a uniform hash function. Again, Rust's `DefaultHasher` looks very good in this plot, while both contenders show less optimal behaviors when used in similar cases.

A word of caution in the end. This is a software developer's perspective on hashing: security researchers and professionals know *a lot* more about hashing. It should be left to them to come up with new ways to create message signatures, so we can focus on building great software and use the best possible components to do that. In short: *do not build your own hash function for any production system.*

Now, for some practical application of hashing in a data structure: the map.

Maps

Index operations in arrays are fast, simple, and easy to understand, with one drawback: they only work with integers. Since an **array** is a continuous portion in memory that can be accessed by dividing it evenly, which makes the jumps between the elements easy, can this work with arbitrary keys as well? Yes! Enter maps.

Maps (also called dictionaries or associative arrays), are data structures that store and manage unique key-value pairs in an efficient way. These structures aim to quickly provide access to the values associated with the keys that are typically stored in one of the following two ways:

- A hashtable
- A tree

When key-value pairs are stored in a tree, the result is very similar to what was discussed in the previous chapter: self-balancing trees will provide consistent performance, avoiding the worst-case cost of a hash map.

Since trees have been discussed extensively in the previous chapter, the hash map is the main focus in this section. It uses a hashing function to translate the provided key into a number of some sort, which is in turn "mapped" on array buckets. This is where the entire pair is typically stored as a list (or tree) to deal with collisions effectively. Whenever a key is looked up, the map can search the associated bucket for the exact key. A key-value pair is inserted by hashing the key, using the modulo operation to find a spot in the array, and appending the pair to the list at the bucket.

If two or more elements are in that list, one or more collisions have occurred:

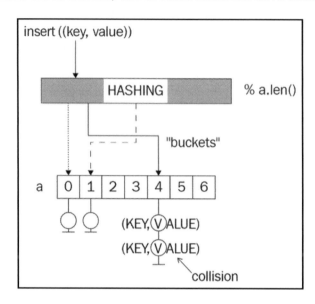

While this usually results in great access times, whenever similar hashes have to be stored (due to a bad hash function), the worst case scenario will be a search through an unordered list—with linear performance. This results in a boxed slice that holds all the data in the form of an Entry type, a vector of tuples. In this case, the implementation is even using generics:

```
type Entry<K, V> = Vec<(K, V)>;

pub struct HashMap<K, V>
where
  K: PartialEq + Clone,
  V: Clone,
{
    hash_fn: Box<dyn (Fn(&K) -> usize)>,
    store: Box<[Entry<K, V>]>,
    pub length: usize,
}
```

Additionally, the hash function can be freely chosen and is stored as a boxed function, which makes it handy to store within the object, and call whenever required. This also lets users customize the type of hashing for a particular use case.

By associating an index with a certain hash, a map lacks the ability to traverse its content in any kind of order. Therefore, keys and values cannot be iterated over in any kind of order, requiring sorting before any operation happens.

Once again, the product team is innovating and another feature would really add a lot of value to customers: associating postcodes with their factual data about the location. This way, a web service can cache commonly used data and reduce the load on the database, while serving customers a lot quicker! Since these locations are updated manually, an expiration is not required and the map can be filled on startup.

Customers provided a list of concise requirements as well to assist, shown as follows:

- Insert location information under their unique name
- Quickly retrieve information using their name
- Fetch all location names and associated information
- Update locations using their name

A hash table would do a great job here, would it not?

A location cache

Caching values is a typical use case for maps because even a large number of items won't affect the performance much, since the keys are always distinct. These keys can even carry information themselves!

For the use case defined in the last section, each customer uses postcodes within a country to identify locations; they typically cover an area that only holds a single office. Postal codes are stored as strings to cover the real world's wide variety of systems, and they are unique per country.

Thanks to a previous generic implementation, the entire `LocationCache` type can be an alias to a specialized `HashMap`, only requiring the hash function to be supplied on creation, shown as follows:

```
pub type LocationCache = HashMap<String, LocationInformation>;
```

The `HashMap` itself is a custom implementation that contains a key of type `K`, which has to also implement `PartialEq` (for comparing key instances directly), and `Clone` (for practical reasons).

The hash function

In addition to providing a generic data structure, the implementation lets the user supply a custom hash function that only maps a reference to the key type to a `usize` return type. The choice for the return type is arbitrary, and was chosen to avoid overflows.

Since the previously implemented hash function performed better than the Adler 32 checksum algorithm, the location cache will use this. To recall, the algorithm applies XOR between a byte and its predecessor and then bit shifts to the left, based on the byte's index. Alternatively, Rust's `DefaultHasher` is available as well:

```
pub fn hashcode(bytes: &[u8]) -> u32 {
    let mut a = 0_u32;
    for (i, b) in bytes.iter().enumerate() {
        a ^= *b as u32;
        a <<= i % 4;
    }
    a
}
```

Choosing a hashing algorithm is an important decision, as we will see in the *Wrap up* section. But first, locations need to be added!

Adding locations

In order to add a location, there are two important steps:

1. Compute the hash
2. Choose a bucket

Further operations, such as doing a sorted insert, will improve performance too, but they can be omitted by using a tree instead of a list within each bucket.

The location cache implementation uses a simple modulo operation between the hash and the length of the array to choose a bucket, which means that on top of regular hash collisions, choosing the size of the internal storage has a major influence on the performance as well. Choose a size too small and the buckets will overlap, regardless of the hash function!

In Rust code, the first part is done in the first line using the provided boxed `hashcode` function to create a hash. What follows is finding a bucket by applying something akin to the modulo operation (a binary AND operation between the hash and the highest index of the storage array) and a linear search of the attached list. If the key is found, the attached pair is updated and if not, it is added to the vector:

```
pub fn insert(&mut self, key: K, value: V) {
    let h = (self.hash_fn)(&key);
    let idx = h & (self.store.len() - 1);
    match self.store[idx].iter().position(|e| e.0 == key) {
        Some(pos) => self.store[idx][pos] = (key, value),
        None => {
            self.store[idx].push((key, value));
            self.length += 1
        }
    }
}
```

Once a location and the matching hash is stored, it can be retrieved again.

Fetching locations

Just like inserting, the retrieval process has the same steps. Whether the `get()` function to return a value or the `remove()` function, both go through the same steps: hash, match a bucket, do a linear search, and lastly, match with the expected return type. The `get()` function can utilize Rust's powerful iterators by using `find` to match the predicate within a bucket's vector and, since an `Option<Item>` is returned, its `map` function to extract the value instead of returning the entire pair:

```
pub fn get(&self, key: &K) -> Option<V> {
    let h = (self.hash_fn)(key);
    let idx = h & (self.store.len() - 1);
    self.store[idx]
        .iter()
        .find(|e| e.0 == *key)
        .map(|e| e.1.clone())
}

pub fn remove(&mut self, key: K) -> Option<V> {
    let h = (self.hash_fn)(&key);
    let idx = h & (self.store.len() - 1);
    match self.store[idx].iter().position(|e| e.0 == key) {
        Some(pos) => {
            self.length -= 1;
            Some(self.store[idx].remove(pos).1)
```

```
            }
            _ => None,
        }
    }
}
```

The `remove` function is literally the inversion of an `insert` function; instead of updating the key-value pair if found, it is removed from the bucket and returned to the caller.

Wrap up

Hash maps are a great data structure, and often their value cannot be overstated, especially in caching or to simplify code that would otherwise have to match labels (or keys) to values using array indices. Their key breaking points are the hash function itself, and the bucket selection and organization, all of which warrant entire PhD theses and papers in computer science.

While a hash map is quick and easy to implement, the real question is: how does it perform? This is a valid question! Software engineers are prone to prefer their own implementation over learning what others already created, and while this is the premise for this entire book, benchmarks keep us honest and help us to appreciate the work that others have done.

How did this `HashMap` do, especially compared to `std::collections::HashMap<K,V>`? We have seen the hash function is far from ideal in some histograms, but what are the performance implications? Here is a scatter plot to answer all of these questions; it shows the `HashMap` implemented here with different hashing functions (Adler 32, `DefaultHasher`, XOR-based) compared to the `HashMap<K,V>` from the standard library (which uses `DefaultHasher` exclusively). The following benchmarks were performed on the same 1,000 to 10,000 randomly permuted strings between A and Z of lengths of 10 to 26 characters. The y axis shows the time required for a `get()` operation in nanoseconds, the x axis shows the number of items in the map. The sizes represent the deviation of the result:

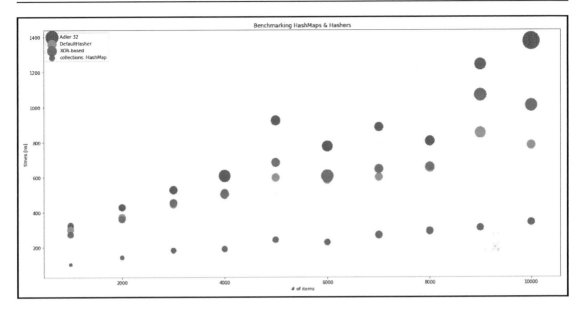

The scatter plot of the deviation of the result in Adler 32, DefaultHasher, XOR-based, collections-HashMap

This plot shows the real value and use of the particular hash functions, as they were all applied to this `HashMap`, and the work of the amazing Rust community with `std::collections::HashMap<K,V>`, which uses the `DefaultHasher`. Adler 32, as a checksum algorithm, did rather badly, which was expected, with even an increasing variance as the number of inserted items increased. Surprisingly, the XOR-based algorithm was not as bad as expected, but still had a high variance compared to the `DefaultHasher`, which performed consistently well.

All of them are a far cry off the `HashMap<K,V>` that comes with the standard library. This is great news, because the performance of this hash map implementation is also worse than the trees and skip lists presented in `Chapter 5`, *Robust Trees* and `Chapter 4`, *Lists, Lists, More Lists.*

This is proof that while the theory sounds great (constant time retrieval, best case)—implementation details can make or break a particular data structure, which is why we suspect that `collections::HashMap` sorts and inserts and use of traits instead of a boxed (hash) function to significantly improve performance.

Upsides

The hash map provides a great way to do key-value associations, which are highlighted as follows:

- Low overhead storage
- Hashed complex keys by default thanks to hashing
- Easy to understand
- Constant time retrieval

Yet, there are a few things that may be troublesome when compared to trees, or other efficient retrieval structures.

Downsides

Even though constant time retrieval sounds nice, the benchmarks show that it's not that simple. The downsides are as follows:

- Performance highly depends on the hash function and application
- Easy to implement naively, hard to get right
- Unordered storage

Some of these downsides could be mitigated by using a tree-based map, but that would be a tree as described in the previous chapter, and there is one data structure left to discuss here: the set.

Sets

Structured Query Language (SQL), is a declarative language invented to perform database operations. Its primary qualities are the ability to express *what* you want, rather than *how* you want it ("I want a set of items that conform to a predicate X" versus "Filter every item using predicate X"); this also allows non-programmers to work with databases, which is an aspect that today's NoSQL databases often lack.

You may think: how is that relevant? SQL allows us to think of the data as sets linked together with relations, which is what makes it so pleasant to work with. Understanding sets as a distinct collection of objects is sufficient to understand the language and how to manipulate the results. While this definition is also called the naive set theory, it is a useful definition for most purposes.

In general, a set has elements as members that can be described using a sentence or rule, like all positive integers, but it would contain every element only once and allow several basic operations: unions, intersections, differences, and the Cartesian product, which is the combination of two sets so that elements are combined in every possible way:

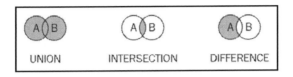

Since set elements are unique, any implementation of a set, therefore, has to make sure that each element is unique within the data structure, which is what makes the actual data structure special; it optimizes for uniqueness and retrieval.

What about using linear search on a vector to guarantee uniqueness? It works, but inserting in a populated set is going to take a lot longer than a new one. Additionally, the previous chapters talked about how trees are much better at finding things than lists, which is also why no good set implementation should use them.

The Rust collections in the standard library know two types of sets: BTreeSet<K, V> and HashSet<K, V>, both names that hint at their implementations. As mentioned in Chapter 5, *Robust Trees*, the B-Tree is a generic, self-balancing tree implementation that allows an arbitrary number of children per node, and makes search within its keys very efficient.

HashSet<K, V> is different. By storing a hash representation of the key, lookup can be done in constant time if the hashes are distributed uniformly. Since hash sets and hash maps have the same inner workings, this section will focus on a tree-based implementation and another section goes further into the depths of a hash map.

Other than inserting and checking whether a set contains a certain element, the main operations that a set should provide are union, intersect, and difference, as well as an iterator. Having these operations available will provide an efficient way to combine multiple sets in various ways, which is part of why they are useful.

In Rust code, a trie-based set could look like the following:

```
type Link<K> = Box<Node<K>>;

struct Node<K>
where
    K: PartialEq + Clone + Ord,
{
    pub key: K,
    next: BTreeMap<K, Link<K>>,
```

```
        ends_here: bool,
    }

    pub struct TrieSet<K>
    where
        K: PartialEq + Clone + Ord,
    {
        pub length: u64,
        root: BTreeMap<K, Link<K>>,
    }
```

This the trie implementation of `Chapter 5`, *Robust Trees,* with generics added and using a `BTreeMap<K, V>` root node to avoid creating too many trait dependencies. This allows arbitrary chains of simple data types to be stored as a trie, a highly efficient data structure where overlaps are kept together only to branch off once they diverge (read more on tries in `Chapter 5`, *Robust Trees*).

Can this store numbers? Yes, although they have to be converted to a byte array, but then anything can be stored in this set.

The product team has had an idea: they want to store network addresses for a network analysis software. They want to store these addresses in order to run some basic analysis on top of them: which network devices are in both networks, gathering all the addresses that are in either all or not in some specified networks. Since IP addresses are unique and consist of individual bytes that have to have common prefixes, wouldn't this be a great opportunity to use that trie set?

Storing network addresses

Storing network addresses is not a hard problem and there are many solutions out there. Their binary structure provides an opportunity to create something really specific—if time is not an issue.

In many cases, however, an off-the-shelf implementation of a data structure is enough to cover most basic use cases when that isn't your main concern. Hence, the network address storage can simple be a type alias that specifies the key type for the trie set, shown as follows:

```
    pub type NetworkDeviceStore = TrieSet<u8>;
```

Slight modifications to the `insert` (former `add`) function of the trie allows users to simply pass a slice of the key type into the function, shown in the following code:

```
    pub fn insert(&mut self, elements: &[K]) {
        let mut path = elements.into_iter();
```

```
if let Some(start) = path.next() {
    let mut n = self
        .root
        .entry(start.clone())
        .or_insert(Node::new(start.clone(), false));
    for c in path {
        let tmp = n
            .next
            .entry(c.clone())
            .or_insert(Node::new(c.clone(), false));
        n = tmp;
    }
    if !n.ends_here {
        self.length += 1;
    }
    n.ends_here = true;
}
}
```

This implementation differs only in a few details from what was done in the previous chapter. Firstly, it's important to avoid incrementing the length twice, which is avoided by checking if a key ends at the last node of the new key. This flag is also a new addition since the other implementation was specifically implemented to store instances of the IoTDevice type, and each node would have an optional device attached to it to signal the completion of a key.

A similar reasoning was applied to the walk and contains functions.

Networked operations

One key requirement of the product team was the ability to run simple analytics on top of this set. As a first step, these analytics can be comprised of set operations and comparing their lengths in order to create simple indicators.

One thing that is important, however, is to also get the addresses back out. For that, the implementation this time provides an iterator implementation that consumes the trie and stores it as a Vec<T>, shown as follows:

```
// [...] trie set implementation
pub fn into_iter(self) -> SetIterator<K> {
    let v: RefCell<Vec<Vec<K>>> = RefCell::new(vec![]);
    self.walk(|n| v.borrow_mut().push(n.to_vec()));
    SetIterator::new(v.into_inner(), 0)
}
}
```

```
pub struct SetIterator<K>
where
    K: PartialEq + Clone + Ord,
{
    data: Vec<Vec<K>>,
    last_index: usize,
}

impl<K> SetIterator<K>
where
    K: PartialEq + Clone + Ord,
{
    fn new(data: Vec<Vec<K>>, start_at: usize) -> SetIterator<K> {
        SetIterator {
            data: data,
            last_index: start_at,
        }
    }
}

impl<K> Iterator for SetIterator<K>
where
    K: PartialEq + Clone + Ord,
{
    type Item = Vec<K>;

    fn next(&mut self) -> Option<Vec<K>> {
        let result = self.data.get(self.last_index);
        self.last_index += 1;
        result.cloned()
    }
}
```

Once the vector is created, an index will do for keeping track of moving the iterator around. The set operations are actually not much more complex than that. However, all of them use the `walk()` function, which requires us to provide mutability in a lambda expression (or closure), and consequently a `RefCell` to take care of mutability management dynamically.

Union

The definition of a set union is that every element that occurs in either set is required to occur in the result. Therefore, the challenge is to insert elements from both sets into the resulting set, without creating duplicates.

Since this is handled by the `insert` process, a naive implementation could look like the following:

```
pub fn union(self, other: TrieSet<K>) -> TrieSet<K> {
    let new = RefCell::new(TrieSet::new_empty());
    self.walk(|k| new.borrow_mut().insert(k));
    other.walk(|k| new.borrow_mut().insert(k));
    new.into_inner()
}
```

This consumes both sets, returning only the result. The next operation, the intersection, looks very similar.

Intersection

To find the common elements of two sets, the intersection is a way of doing that. The definition also describes exactly that, which is why the naive implementation in Rust also follows that pattern, shown as follows:

```
pub fn intersection(self, other: TrieSet<K>) -> TrieSet<K> {
    let new = RefCell::new(TrieSet::new_empty());
    if self.length < other.length {
        self.walk(|k| {
            if other.contains(k) {
                new.borrow_mut().insert(k)
            }
        });
    } else {
        other.walk(|k| {
            if self.contains(k) {
                new.borrow_mut().insert(k)
            }
        });
    }
    new.into_inner()
}
```

As a last function, the difference is important, since it excludes common elements from the result set.

Difference

Instead of common elements, sometimes the opposite is required—removing elements that occur in both sets. This operation is also referred to as the complement of two sets, which only inserts elements into the result if they don't occur in the other set:

```
pub fn difference(self, other: TrieSet<K>) -> TrieSet<K> {
    let new = RefCell::new(TrieSet::new_empty());
    self.walk(|k| {
        if !other.contains(k) {
            new.borrow_mut().insert(k)
        }
    });
    new.into_inner()
}
```

With that, the set is finished, and all the desired functionality can be provided.

Wrap up

Sets are not complicated, but are useful. While database indices might be B-Trees, the result sets are the sets of primary keys that get moved around and operated on until the very last step, when the associated row information is fetched from disk. These are the moments when set data structures come in handy and provide a simple solution.

Similarly to everyday tasks, creating a list of unique elements can be very inefficient when a list is used; storing them in a set, however, requires no extra effort. In fact, most elements can then just be thrown into the set, which won't insert duplicates anyway.

Upsides

The set is a higher-level data structure that does the following:

- provides a simple interface for unique lists
- Implements a mathematical concept
- Has a very efficient way of storing and retrieving its elements

Downsides

The set has some downsides as well, primarily the following:

- Element order determinism depends on the implementation
- Does not always add a lot of value compared to maps
- Limited use cases

Since maps will be used a lot more often, let's dive into those.

Summary

Hashing is the art (and science) of creating a single representation (typically a number) from an arbitrary object, be it strings, `type` instances, or collections; there is a way to break them down into a number that should reflect a particular use case. The real question is what you want to achieve and what characteristics are expected from the outcome. Cryptographic hashing deals with minimizing collisions and creating signatures that create a very different hash from minor modifications, whereas GeoHashes are a way to hierarchically structure Earth's coordinates into a string. Whenever two (or more) inputs to a hash function lead to the same output, this is called a collision—a bad sign for any cryptographic hashing, but fine if it's mostly about storing something in a hash map, as long as the collisions are evenly distributed. Most importantly, however, software engineers should *never* come up with their own hash functions, especially if security is a concern.

Maps store and manage key-value pairs in an underlying data structure, which is typically either a tree or an array that maps hashes to key-value pairs called hash maps. By using a hash function to describe the key and sort the pair into buckets (array elements), hash maps are a great use case for hashing. These buckets are basically indices on an array that stores a list (or tree) for whenever different inputs lead to the same bucket. Consequently, the best case performance of a hash map is constant time ($O(1)$) to retrieve any value, whereas the worst case is linear time ($O(n)$) if the hash function returns a constant number. In reality, there are other uses that might be beneficial, such as caching, where the use case limits the potential inputs, and best case performance is always achieved.

Contrary to maps, **sets** are great data structures to store a unique collection of elements to perform set operations on. They can be implemented just like a hash map, using a hash function or a tree. In this chapter, we implemented a set based on a modified trie data structure from the previous chapter (*Robust Trees*), as well as the basic three operations: union, intersection, and difference.

In the next chapter, we will continue to explore Rust's `std::collections` library and its contents. This will include some benchmarking and looking into more implementation details, since these are the best implementations of all the concepts discussed in the book so far.

Questions

- What makes a good hash function?
- How can you estimate the suitability of a hash function for a particular task?
- Is a checksum hash useful in other ways?
- What are two ways to implement a map?
- What are buckets?
- Can a set replace a list?
- What makes a set useful?

Further reading

Refer to the following links for more information:

- `http://geohash.org/`
- *Fletcher's checksum* (`https://en.wikipedia.org/wiki/Fletcher%27s_checksum`)
- Rust's `HashMap` implementation reasoning (`https://www.reddit.com/r/rust/comments/52grcl/rusts_stdcollections_is_absolutely_horrible/d7kcei2`)
- `https://doc.rust-lang.org/std/hash/`
- Wikipedia's list of hash functions (`https://en.wikipedia.org/wiki/List_of_hash_functions`)

7
Collections in Rust

In the previous chapters, we implemented a range of data structures, something that rarely happens in reality. Especially in Rust, the excellent Vec<T> covers a lot of cases, and if a map type structure is required, the HashMap<T> covers most of these too. So what else is there? How are they implemented? Why were they implemented if they won't be used? These are all great questions, and they'll get answered in this chapter. You can look forward to learning about the following:

- Sequence data types such as LinkedList<T>, Vec<T>, or VecDeque<T>
- Rust's BinaryHeap<T> implementation
- HashSet<T> and BTreeSet<T>
- How to map things with the BTreeMap<T> and HashMap<T>

Sequences

Lists of any kind are the most essential data structure in a typical program; they provide flexibility and can be used as a queue, as a stack, as well as a searchable structure. Yet the limitations and the operations make a huge of difference between different data structures, which is why the documentation for std::collections offers a decision tree to find out the collection type that is actually required to solve a particular problem.

The following were discussed in Chapter 4, *Lists, Lists, More Lists*:

- **Dynamic arrays** (Vec<T>) are the most universal and straightforward to use sequential data structure. They capture the speed and accessibility of an array, the dynamic sizing of a list, and they are the fundamental building block for higher order structures (such as stacks, heaps, or even trees). So, when in doubt a Vec<T> is always a good choice.

- `VecDeque<T>` is a close relative of the `Vec<T>`, implemented as a **ring buffer**—a dynamic array that wraps around the ends end, making it look like a circular structure. Since the underlying structure is still the same as `Vec<T>`, many of its aspects also apply here.
- The `LinkedList<T>` is very limited in its functionality in Rust. Direct index access will be inefficient (it's a counted iteration), which is probably why it can only iterate, merge and split, and insert or retrieve from the back and front.

This was a nice primer, so let's look deeper into each of Rust's data structures in `std::collections`!

Vec<T> and VecDeque<T>

Just like the dynamic array in `Chapter 4`, *Lists, Lists, More Lists*, `Vec<T>` and `VecDeque<T>` are growable, list-like data structures with support for indexing and based on a heap-allocated array. Other than the previously implemented dynamic array, it is generic by default without any constraints for the generic type, allowing literally any type to be used.

`Vec<T>` aims to have as little overhead as possible, while providing a few guarantees. At its core, it is a triple of (`pointer`, `length`, `capacity`) that provides an API to modify these elements. The `capacity` is the amount of memory that is allocated to hold items, which means that it fundamentally differs from `length`, the number of elements currently held. In case a zero-sized type or no initial length is provided, `Vec<T>` won't actually allocate any memory. The `pointer` only points to the reserved area in memory that is encapsulated as a `RawVec<T>` structure.

The main drawback of `Vec<T>` is its lack of efficient insertion at the front, which is what `VecDeque<T>` aims to provide. It is implemented as a ring, which wraps around the edges of the array, creating a more complex situation when the memory has to be expanded, or an element is to be inserted at a specified position. Since the implementations of `Vec<T>` and `VecDeque<T>` are quite similar, they can be used in similar contexts. This can be shown in their architecture.

Architecture

Both structures, Vec<T> and RawVec<T>, allocate memory in the same way: by using the RawVec<T> type. This structure is a wrapper around lower level functions to allocate, reallocate, or deallocate an array in the heap part of the memory, built for use in higher level data structures. Its primary goal is to avoid capacity overflows, out-of-memory errors, and general overflows, which saves the developer a lot of boilerplate code.

The use of this buffer by Vec<T> is straightforward. Whenever the length threatens to exceed capacity, allocate more memory and transfer all elements, shown in the following code:

```
#[stable(feature = "rust1", since = "1.0.0")]
pub fn reserve(&mut self, additional: usize) {
    self.buf.reserve(self.len, additional);
}
```

So this goes on to call the reserve() function, followed by the try_reserve(), followed by the amortized_new_size() of RawVec<T>, which also makes the decision about the size:

```
fn amortized_new_size(&self, used_cap: usize, needed_extra_cap: usize)
    -> Result<usize, CollectionAllocErr> {

    // Nothing we can really do about these checks :(
    let required_cap =
used_cap.checked_add(needed_extra_cap).ok_or(CapacityOverflow)?;
    // Cannot overflow, because `cap <= isize::MAX`, and type of `cap` is
`usize`.
    let double_cap = self.cap * 2;
    // `double_cap` guarantees exponential growth.
    Ok(cmp::max(double_cap, required_cap))
}
```

Let's take a look at VecDeque<T>. On top of memory allocation, VecDeque<T> has to deal with wrapping the data around the ring, which adds considerable complexity to inserting an element at a specified position, or when the capacity has to increase. Then, the old elements need to be copied to the new memory area, starting with the shortest part of a wrapped list.

Like the Vec<T>, the VecDeque<T> doubles its buffer in size if it is full, but uses the double() function to do so. *Be aware that doubling is not a guaranteed strategy and might change.*

However, whatever replaces it will have to retain the runtime complexities of the operations. The following are the functions used to determine whether the data structure is full and if it needs to grow in size:

```
#[inline]
fn is_full(&self) -> bool {
    self.cap() - self.len() == 1
}

#[inline]
fn grow_if_necessary(&mut self) {
    if self.is_full() {
        let old_cap = self.cap();
        self.buf.double();
        unsafe {
            self.handle_cap_increase(old_cap);
        }
        debug_assert!(!self.is_full());
    }
}
```

The `handle_cap_increase()` function will then decide where the new ring should live and how the copying into the new buffer is handled, prioritizing copying as little data as possible. Other than `Vec<T>`, calling the `new()` function on `VecDeque<T>` allocates at `RawVec<T>` with enough space for seven elements, which then can be inserted without growing the underlying memory, therefore it is not a zero-size structure when empty.

Insert

There are two ways to add elements to `Vec<T>`: `insert()` and `push()`. The former takes two parameters: an index of where to insert the element and the data. Before inserting, the position on the index will be freed by moving all succeeding elements towards the end (to the right). Therefore, if an element is inserted at the front, every element has to be shifted by one. `Vec<T>` code shows the following:

```
#[stable(feature = "rust1", since = "1.0.0")]
pub fn insert(&mut self, index: usize, element: T) {
    let len = self.len();
    assert!(index <= len);

    // space for the new element
    if len == self.buf.cap() {
        self.reserve(1);
    }
```

```
    unsafe {
        // infallible
        // The spot to put the new value
        {
            let p = self.as_mut_ptr().add(index);
            // Shift everything over to make space. (Duplicating the
            // `index`th element into two consecutive places.)
            ptr::copy(p, p.offset(1), len - index);
            // Write it in, overwriting the first copy of the `index`th
            // element.
            ptr::write(p, element);
        }
        self.set_len(len + 1);
    }
}
```

While shifting is done efficiently, by calling push(), the new item can be added without moving data around, shown as follows:

```
#[inline]
#[stable(feature = "rust1", since = "1.0.0")]
pub fn push(&mut self, value: T) {
    // This will panic or abort if we would allocate > isize::MAX bytes
    // or if the length increment would overflow for zero-sized types.
    if self.len == self.buf.cap() {
        self.reserve(1);
    }
    unsafe {
        let end = self.as_mut_ptr().offset(self.len as isize);
        ptr::write(end, value);
        self.len += 1;
    }
}
```

The main drawback of regular Vec<T> is the inability of efficiently adding data to the front, which is where VecDeque<T> excels. The code for doing this is nice and short, shown as follows:

```
#[stable(feature = "rust1", since = "1.0.0")]
pub fn push_front(&mut self, value: T) {
    self.grow_if_necessary();

    self.tail = self.wrap_sub(self.tail, 1);
    let tail = self.tail;
    unsafe {
        self.buffer_write(tail, value);
    }
}
```

With the use of `unsafe {}` in these functions, the code is much shorter and faster than it would be using safe Rust exclusively.

Look up

One major upside of using array-type data allocation is the simple and fast element access, which `Vec<T>` and `VecDeque<T>` share. The formal way to implement the direct access using brackets (`let my_first_element= v[0];`) is provided by the `Index<I>` trait.

Other than direct access, iterators are provided to search, fold, map, and so on the data. Some are equivalent to the `LinkedList<T>` part of this section.

As an example, the `Vec<T>`'s owning iterator (`IntoIter<T>`) owns the pointer to the buffer and moves a pointer to the current element forward. There is also a catch though: if the size of an element is zero bytes, how should the pointer be moved? What data is returned? The `IntoIter<T>` structure comes up with a clever solution (**ZSTs** are **zero-sized types**, so types that don't actually take up space):

```
pub struct IntoIter<T> {
    buf: NonNull<T>,
    phantom: PhantomData<T>,
    cap: usize,
    ptr: *const T,
    end: *const T,
}
// ...

#[stable(feature = "rust1", since = "1.0.0")]
impl<T> Iterator for IntoIter<T> {
    type Item = T;

    #[inline]
    fn next(&mut self) -> Option<T> {
        unsafe {
            if self.ptr as *const _ == self.end {
                None
            } else {
                if mem::size_of::<T>() == 0 {
                    // purposefully don't use 'ptr.offset' because for
                    // vectors with 0-size elements this would return the
                    // same pointer.
                    self.ptr = arith_offset(self.ptr as *const i8, 1) as
*mut T;

                    // Make up a value of this ZST.
```

```
                    Some(mem::zeroed())
                } else {
                    let old = self.ptr;
                    self.ptr = self.ptr.offset(1);

                    Some(ptr::read(old))
                }
            }
        }
    }
    // ...
}
```

The comments already state what's happening, the iterator avoids returning the same pointer over and over again, and instead, increments it by one and returns a zeroed out memory. This is clearly something that the Rust compiler would not tolerate, so unsafe is a great choice here. Furthermore, the regular iterator (vec![].iter()) is generalized in the core::slice::Iter implementation, which works on generic, array-like parts of the memory.

Contrary to that, the iterator of VecDeque<T> resorts to moving an index around the ring until a full circle is reached. Here is its implementation, shown in the following code:

```
#[stable(feature = "rust1", since = "1.0.0")]
pub struct Iter<'a, T: 'a> {
    ring: &'a [T],
    tail: usize,
    head: usize,
}
// ...
#[stable(feature = "rust1", since = "1.0.0")]
impl<'a, T> Iterator for Iter<'a, T> {
    type Item = &'a T;

    #[inline]
    fn next(&mut self) -> Option<&'a T> {
        if self.tail == self.head {
            return None;
        }
        let tail = self.tail;
        self.tail = wrap_index(self.tail.wrapping_add(1), self.ring.len());
        unsafe { Some(self.ring.get_unchecked(tail)) }
    }
    //...
}
```

Among other traits, both implement the `DoubleEndedIterator<T>` work on both ends, a special function called `DrainFilter<T>`, in order to retrieve items in an iterator only if a predicate applies.

Remove

`Vec<T>` and `VecDeque<T>` both remain efficient when removing items. Although, they don't change the amount of memory allocated to the data structure, both types provide a function called `shrink_to_fit()` to readjust the capacity to the length it has.

On `remove`, `Vec<T>` shifts the remaining elements toward the start of the sequence. Like the `insert()` function, it simply copies the entire remaining data with an offset, shown as follows:

```
#[stable(feature = "rust1", since = "1.0.0")]
pub fn remove(&mut self, index: usize) -> T {
    let len = self.len();
    assert!(index < len);
    unsafe {
        // infallible
        let ret;
        {
            // the place we are taking from.
            let ptr = self.as_mut_ptr().add(index);
            // copy it out, unsafely having a copy of the value on
            // the stack and in the vector at the same time.
            ret = ptr::read(ptr);

            // Shift everything down to fill in that spot.
            ptr::copy(ptr.offset(1), ptr, len - index - 1);
        }
        self.set_len(len - 1);
        ret
    }
}
```

For `VecDeque<T>`, the situation is much more complex: since the data can wrap around the ends of the underlying buffer (for example, the tail is on index three, head on index five, so the space from three to five is considered empty), it can't blindly copy in one direction. Therefore, there is some logic that deals with these different situations, but it is much too long to add here.

LinkedList<T>

Rust's `std::collection::LinkedList<T>` is a doubly linked list that uses an `unsafe` pointer operation to get around the `Rc<RefCell<Node<T>>>` unpacking we had to do in `Chapter 4`, *Lists, Lists, and More Lists*. While unsafe, this is a great solution to that problem, since the pointer operations are easy to comprehend and provide significant benefits. Let's look at the following code:

```
#[stable(feature = "rust1", since = "1.0.0")]
pub struct LinkedList<T> {
    head: Option<NonNull<Node<T>>>,
    tail: Option<NonNull<Node<T>>>,
    len: usize,
    marker: PhantomData<Box<Node<T>>>,
}

struct Node<T> {
    next: Option<NonNull<Node<T>>>,
    prev: Option<NonNull<Node<T>>>,
    element: T,
}
```

`NonNull` is a structure that originates from `std::ptr::NonNull`, which provides a non-zero pointer to a portion of heap memory in unsafe territory. Hence, the interior mutability pattern can be skipped at this fundamental level, eliminating the need for runtime checks.

Architecture

Fundamentally, `LinkedList` is built just the way we built the doubly linked list in `Chapter 4`, *Lists, Lists, and More Lists*, with the addition of a `PhantomData<T>` type pointer. Why? This is necessary to inform the compiler about the properties of the type that contains the marker when generics are involved. With it, the compiler can determine a range of things, including drop behavior, lifetimes, and so on. The `PhantomData<T>` pointer is a zero-size addition, and pretends to own type `T` content, so the compiler can reason about that.

Insert

The `std::collections::LinkedList` employs several unsafe methods in order to avoid the `Rc<RefCell<Node<T>>>` and `next.as_ref().unwrap().borrow()` calls that we saw when implementing a doubly linked list in a safe way. This also means that adding a node at either end entails the use of `unsafe` to set these pointers.

In this case, the code is easy to read and comprehend, which is important to avoid sudden crashes due to unsound code being executed. This is the core function to add a node in the front, shown as follows:

```
fn push_front_node(&mut self, mut node: Box<Node<T>>) {
    unsafe {
        node.next = self.head;
        node.prev = None;
        let node = Some(Box::into_raw_non_null(node));

        match self.head {
            None => self.tail = node,
            Some(mut head) => head.as_mut().prev = node,
        }

        self.head = node;
        self.len += 1;
    }
}
```

This code is wrapped by the publicly facing push_front() function, shown in the following code snippet:

```
#[stable(feature = "rust1", since = "1.0.0")]
pub fn push_front(&mut self, elt: T) {
    self.push_front_node(box Node::new(elt));
}
```

The push_back() function, which performs the same action but on the end of the list, works just like this. Additionally, the linked list can append another list just as easily, since it is almost the same as adding a single node, but with additional semantics (such as: is the list empty?) to take care of:

```
#[stable(feature = "rust1", since = "1.0.0")]
pub fn append(&mut self, other: &mut Self) {
    match self.tail {
        None => mem::swap(self, other),
        Some(mut tail) => {
            if let Some(mut other_head) = other.head.take() {
                unsafe {
                    tail.as_mut().next = Some(other_head);
                    other_head.as_mut().prev = Some(tail);
                }

                self.tail = other.tail.take();
                self.len += mem::replace(&mut other.len, 0);
            }
        }
```

```
            }
        }
    }
```

Adding things is one of the strong suits of a linked list. But how about looking up elements?

Look up

The `collections::LinkedList` relies a lot on the `Iterator` trait to look up various items, which is great since it saves a lot of effort. This is achieved by extensively implementing various iterator traits using several structures, like the following:

- `Iter`
- `IterMut`
- `IntoIter`

Technically, `DrainFilter` also implements `Iterator`, but it's really a convenience wrapper. The following is the `Iter` structure declaration that the `LinkedList` uses:

```
#[stable(feature = "rust1", since = "1.0.0")]
pub struct Iter<'a, T: 'a> {
    head: Option<NonNull<Node<T>>>,
    tail: Option<NonNull<Node<T>>>,
    len: usize,
    marker: PhantomData<&'a Node<T>>,
}
```

If you remember the list's declaration earlier, it will become obvious that they are very similar! In fact, they are the same, which means that when iterating over a linked list, you are essentially creating a new list that gets shorter with every call to `next()`. As expected, this is a very efficient process that is employed here, since no data is copied and the `Iter` structures' head can move back and forth with the `prev`/`next` pointers of the current head.

`IterMut` and `IntoIter` have a slightly different structure, due to their intended purposes. `IntoIter` takes ownership of the entire list, and just calls `pop_front()` or `pop_back()` as requested.

`IterMut` has to retain a mutable reference to the original list in order to provide mutable references to the caller, but other than that, it's basically an `Iter` type structure.

The other structure that also does iteration is `DrainFilter`, which as the name suggests, removes items.

Remove

The linked list contains two functions: `pop_front()` and `pop_back()`, and they simply wrap around an "inner" function called `pop_front_node()`:

```
#[inline]
fn pop_front_node(&mut self) -> Option<Box<Node<T>>> {
    self.head.map(|node| unsafe {
        let node = Box::from_raw(node.as_ptr());
        self.head = node.next;

        match self.head {
            None => self.tail = None,
            Some(mut head) => head.as_mut().prev = None,
        }

        self.len -= 1;
        node
    })
}
```

This way, removing a specific element from `LinkedList<T>` has to be done either by splitting and appending the list (skipping the desired element), or by using `drain_filter()` function, which does almost exactly that.

Wrap up

`Vec<T>` and `VecDeque<T>` both build on a heap-allocated array, and perform very well on `insert` and `find` operations, thanks to the elimination of several steps. However, the dynamic array implementation from earlier in the book can actually hold its own against these.

The doubly-linked list implemented previously does not look good against the `LinkedList<T>` provided by `std::collections`, which is built far simpler and does not use `RefCells` that do runtime borrow checking:

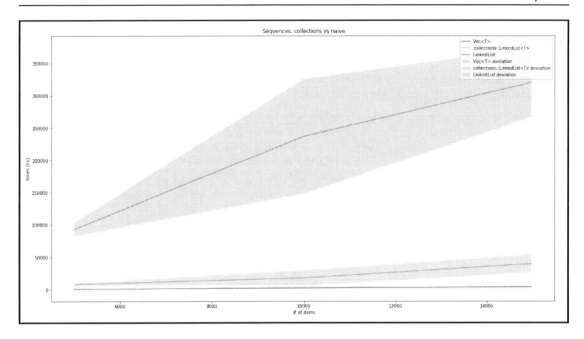

Clearly, if you need a linked list, do not implement it yourself,
`std::collections::LinkedList<T>` is excellent as far as linked lists go. Commonly,
`Vec<T>` will perform better while providing more features, so unless the linked list is
absolutely necessary, `Vec<T>` should be the default choice.

Maps and sets

Rust's maps and sets are based largely on two strategies: B-Tree search and hashing. They
are very distinct implementations, but achieve the same results: associating a key with a
value (map) and providing a fast unique collection based on keys (set).

Hashing in Rust works with a `Hasher` trait, which is a universal, stateful hasher, to create a
hash value from an arbitrary byte stream. By repeatedly calling the appropriate `write()`
function, data can be added to the hasher's internal state and finished up with the
`finish()` function.

Unsurprisingly the B-Tree in Rust is highly optimized. The `BTreeMap` documentation
provides rich details on why the regular implementation (as previously shown) is cache
inefficient and not optimized for modern CPU architectures. Hence, they provide a more
efficient implementation, which is definitely fascinating, and you should check it out in the
source code.

HashMap and HashSet

Both `HashMap` and `HashSet` use a hashing algorithm to produce the unique key required for storing and retrieving values. Hashes are created with an instance of the `Hasher` trait (`DefaultHasher` if nothing is specified) for each key that implements the `Hash` and `Eq` traits. They allow a `Hasher` instance to be passed into the `Hash` implementor to generate the required output and the data structure to compare keys for equality.

If a custom structure is to be used as a hashed key (for the map, or simply to store in the set), this implementation can be derived as well, which adds every field of the structure to the `Hasher`'s state. In case the trait is implemented by hand, it has to create equal hashes whenever two keys are equal.

Since both data structures build on keys having implemented this trait, and both should be highly optimized, one question comes up: why bother with two variants?

Let's take a look into the source, shown as follows:

```
#[derive(Clone)]
#[stable(feature = "rust1", since = "1.0.0")]
pub struct HashSet<T, S = RandomState> {
    map: HashMap<T, (), S>,
}
```

The rest of this section will only talk about `HashMap`.

Architecture

`HashMap` is a highly optimized data structure that employs a performance heuristic called **Robin Hood hashing** to improve caching behavior, and thereby lookup times.

Robin Hood hashing is best explained together with the insertion algorithm linear probing, which is somewhat similar to the algorithm used in the hash map of the previous chapter. However, instead of an array of arrays (or `Vec<Vec<(K, V)>>`), the basic data structure is a flat array wrapped (together with all unsafe code) in a structure called `RawTable<K, V>`.

The table organizes its data into buckets (empty or full) that represent the data at a particular hash. Linear probing means that whenever a collision occurs (two hashes are equal without their keys being equal), the algorithm keeps looking into ("probing") the following buckets until an empty bucket is found.

The Robin Hood part is to count the steps from the original (ideal) position, and whenever an element in a bucket is closer to its ideal position (that is, richer), the bucket content is swapped, and the search continues with the element that was swapped out of its bucket. Thus, the search takes from the rich (with only a few steps removed from their ideal spot) and gives to the poor (those that are further away from their ideal spot).

This strategy organizes the array into clusters around the hash values and greatly reduces the key variance, while improving CPU cache-friendliness. Another main factor that influences this behavior is the size of the table and how many buckets are occupied (called **load factor**). `DefaultResizePolicy` of `HashMap` changes the table's size to a higher power of two at a load factor of 90.9%—a number that provides ideal results for the Robin Hood bucket stealing. There are also some great ideas on how to manage that growth without having to reinsert every element, but they would certainly exceed the scope of this chapter. It's recommended to read the source's comments if you are interested (see *Further reading* section).

Insert

The Robin Hood hashing strategy already describes a large portion of the `insert` mechanism: hash the key value, look for an empty bucket, and reorder elements along the way according to their probing distance:

```
pub fn insert(&mut self, k: K, v: V) -> Option<V> {
    let hash = self.make_hash(&k);
    self.reserve(1);
    self.insert_hashed_nocheck(hash, k, v)
}
```

This function only does the first step and expands the basic data structure—if needed. The `insert_hashed_nocheck()` function provides the next step by searching for the hash in the existing table, and returning the appropriate bucket for it. The element is responsible for inserting itself into the right spot. The steps necessary to do that depend on whether the bucket is full or empty, which is modeled as two different structures: `VacantEntry` and `OccupiedEntry`. While the latter simply replaces the value (this is an update), `VacantEntry` has to find a spot not too far from the assigned bucket:

```
pub fn insert(self, value: V) -> &'a mut V {
    let b = match self.elem {
        NeqElem(mut bucket, disp) => {
            if disp >= DISPLACEMENT_THRESHOLD {
                bucket.table_mut().set_tag(true);
            }
            robin_hood(bucket, disp, self.hash, self.key, value)
```

```
        },
        NoElem(mut bucket, disp) => {
            if disp >= DISPLACEMENT_THRESHOLD {
                bucket.table_mut().set_tag(true);
            }
            bucket.put(self.hash, self.key, value)
        },
    };
    b.into_mut_refs().1
}
```

The call to `robin_hood()` executes the search and swap described earlier. One interesting variable here is the `DISPLACEMENT_THRESHOLD`. Does this mean that there is an upper limit of how many displacements a value can have? Yes! This value is 128 (so 128 misses are required), but it wasn't chosen randomly. In fact, the code comments go into the details of why and how it was chosen, shown as follows:

```
// The threshold of 128 is chosen to minimize the chance of exceeding it.
 // In particular, we want that chance to be less than 10^-8 with a load of
90%.
 // For displacement, the smallest constant that fits our needs is 90, //
so we round that up to 128.
 //
// At a load factor of α, the odds of finding the target bucket after
exactly n
 // unsuccessful probes[1] are
 //
// Pr_α{displacement = n} =
 //         (1 - α) / α * ∑_{k≥1} e^(-kα) * (kα)^(k+n) / (k + n)! * (1 - kα /
(k + n + 1))
 //
// We use this formula to find the probability of triggering the adaptive
behavior
 //
// Pr_0.909{displacement > 128} = 1.601 * 10^-11
 //
// 1. Alfredo Viola (2005). Distributional analysis of Robin Hood linear
probing // hashing with buckets.
```

As the comment states, the chance is *very* low that an element actually exceeds that threshold. Once a spot was found for every element, a look up can take place.

Lookup

Looking up entries is part of the insert process of `HashMap` and it relies on the same functions to provide a suitable entry instance to add data. Just like the insertion process, the lookup process does almost the same, save some steps in the end, listed as follows:

- Create a hash of the key
- Find the hash's bucket in the table
- Move away from the bucket comparing keys (linear search) until found

Since all of this has already been implemented for use in other functions, `get()` is pretty short, shown in the following code:

```
pub fn get<Q: ?Sized>(&self, k: &Q) -> Option<&V>
    where K: Borrow<Q>,
          Q: Hash + Eq
{
    self.search(k).map(|bucket| bucket.into_refs().1)
}
```

Similarly, the `remove` function requires `search`, and removal is implemented on the entry type.

Remove

The `remove` function looks a lot like the `search` function, shown as follows:

```
#[stable(feature = "rust1", since = "1.0.0")]
pub fn remove<Q: ?Sized>(&mut self, k: &Q) -> Option<V>
    where K: Borrow<Q>,
          Q: Hash + Eq
{
    self.search_mut(k).map(|bucket| pop_internal(bucket).1)
}
```

There is one major difference: `search` returns a mutable bucket from which the key can be removed (or rather, the entire bucket since it's now empty). `HashMap` turns out to be an impressive piece of code; can `BTreeMap` compete?

BTreeMap and BTreeSet

Talking about B-Trees in `Chapter 5`, *Robust Trees*, their purpose is storing key-value pairs—ideal for a map-type data structure. Their ability to find and retrieve these pairs is achieved by effectively minimizing the number of comparisons required to get to (or rule out) a key. Additionally, a tree keeps the keys in order, which means iteration is going to be implicitly ordered. Compared to `HashMap`, this can be an advantage since it skips a potentially expensive step.

Since—just like `HashSet`—`BTreeSet` simply uses `BTreeMap` with an empty value (only the key) underneath, only the latter is discussed in this section since the working is assumed to be the same. Again, let's start with the architecture.

Architecture

Rust's `BTreeMap` chose an interesting approach to maximize performance for search by creating large individual nodes. Recalling the typical sizes of nodes (that is, the number of children they have), they were more than two (root only), or half the tree's level to the tree's level number of children. In a typical B-Tree, the level rarely exceeds 10, meaning that the nodes stay rather small, and the number of comparisons within a node do too.

The implementors of the Rust `BTreeMap` chose a different strategy in order to improve caching behavior. In order to improve cache-friendliness and reduce the number of heap allocations required, Rusts' `BTreeMap` stores from *level - 1* to *2 * level - 1* number of elements per node, which results in a rather large array of keys.

While the opposite—small arrays of keys—fit the CPU's cache well enough, the tree itself has a larger number of them, so more nodes might need to be looked at. If the number of key-value pairs in a single node is higher, the overall node count shrinks, and if the key array still fits into the CPU's cache, these comparisons are as fast as they can be. The downside of larger arrays to search the key in is mitigated by using more intelligent searches (like binary search), so the overall performance gain of having fewer nodes outweighs the downside.

In general, when comparing the B-Tree from earlier in this book to `BTreeMap`, only a few similarities stand out, one of them being inserting a new element.

Insert

Like every B-Tree, inserts are done by first searching a spot to insert, and then applying the split procedure in case the node has more than the expected number of values (or children). Insertion is split into three parts and it starts with the first method to be called, which glues everything together and returns an expected result:

```
#[stable(feature = "rust1", since = "1.0.0")]
pub fn insert(&mut self, key: K, value: V) -> Option<V> {
    match self.entry(key) {
        Occupied(mut entry) => Some(entry.insert(value)),
        Vacant(entry) => {
            entry.insert(value);
            None
        }
    }
}
```

The second step is finding the handle for the node that the pair can be inserted into, shown as follows:

```
#[stable(feature = "rust1", since = "1.0.0")]
pub fn entry(&mut self, key: K) -> Entry<K, V> {
    // FIXME(@porglezomp) Avoid allocating if we don't insert
    self.ensure_root_is_owned();
    match search::search_tree(self.root.as_mut(), &key) {
        Found(handle) => {
            Occupied(OccupiedEntry {
                handle,
                length: &mut self.length,
                _marker: PhantomData,
            })
        }
        GoDown(handle) => {
            Vacant(VacantEntry {
                key,
                handle,
                length: &mut self.length,
                _marker: PhantomData,
            })
        }
    }
}
```

Once the handle is known, the entry (which is either a structure modeling a vacant or occupied spot) inserts the new key-value pair. If the entry was occupied before, the value is simply replaced—no further steps required. If the spot was vacant, the new value could trigger a tree rebalancing where the changes are bubbled up the tree:

```rust
#[stable(feature = "rust1", since = "1.0.0")]
pub fn insert(self, value: V) -> &'a mut V {
    *self.length += 1;

    let out_ptr;

    let mut ins_k;
    let mut ins_v;
    let mut ins_edge;

    let mut cur_parent = match self.handle.insert(self.key, value) {
        (Fit(handle), _) => return handle.into_kv_mut().1,
        (Split(left, k, v, right), ptr) => {
            ins_k = k;
            ins_v = v;
            ins_edge = right;
            out_ptr = ptr;
            left.ascend().map_err(|n| n.into_root_mut())
        }
    };

    loop {
        match cur_parent {
            Ok(parent) => {
                match parent.insert(ins_k, ins_v, ins_edge) {
                    Fit(_) => return unsafe { &mut *out_ptr },
                    Split(left, k, v, right) => {
                        ins_k = k;
                        ins_v = v;
                        ins_edge = right;
                        cur_parent = left.ascend().map_err(|n|
n.into_root_mut());
                    }
                }
            }
            Err(root) => {
                root.push_level().push(ins_k, ins_v, ins_edge);
                return unsafe { &mut *out_ptr };
            }
        }
    }
}
```

Looking up keys is already part of the insert process, but it deserves a closer look too.

Look up

In a tree structure, inserts and deletes are based on looking up the keys that are being modified. In the case of BTreeMap, this is done by a function called search_tree() which is imported from the parent module:

```
pub fn search_tree<BorrowType, K, V, Q: ?Sized>(
    mut node: NodeRef<BorrowType, K, V, marker::LeafOrInternal>,
    key: &Q
) -> SearchResult<BorrowType, K, V, marker::LeafOrInternal, marker::Leaf>
        where Q: Ord, K: Borrow<Q> {

    loop {
        match search_node(node, key) {
            Found(handle) => return Found(handle),
            GoDown(handle) => match handle.force() {
                Leaf(leaf) => return GoDown(leaf),
                Internal(internal) => {
                    node = internal.descend();
                    continue;
                }
            }
        }
    }
}

pub fn search_node<BorrowType, K, V, Type, Q: ?Sized>(
    node: NodeRef<BorrowType, K, V, Type>,
    key: &Q
) -> SearchResult<BorrowType, K, V, Type, Type>
        where Q: Ord, K: Borrow<Q> {

    match search_linear(&node, key) {
        (idx, true) => Found(
            Handle::new_kv(node, idx)
        ),
        (idx, false) => SearchResult::GoDown(
            Handle::new_edge(node, idx)
        )
    }
}
```

The code itself is very easy to read, which is a good sign. It also avoids the use of recursion and uses a `loop{}` construct instead, which is a benefit for large lookups since Rust does not expand tail-recursive calls into loops (yet?). In any case, this function returns the node that the key resides in, letting the caller do the work of extracting the value and key from it.

Remove

The `remove` function wraps the occupied node's `remove_kv()` function, which removes a key-value pair from the handle that `search_tree()` unearthed. This removal also triggers a merging of nodes if a node now has less than the minimum amount of children.

Wrap up

As shown in this section, maps and sets have a lot in common and there are two ways that the Rust collections library provides them. `HashMap` and `HashSet` use a smart approach to finding and inserting values into buckets called Robin Hood hashing. Recalling the comparison benchmarks from Chapter 6, *Exploring Maps and Sets*, it provided a more stable and significantly better performance over a naive implementation:

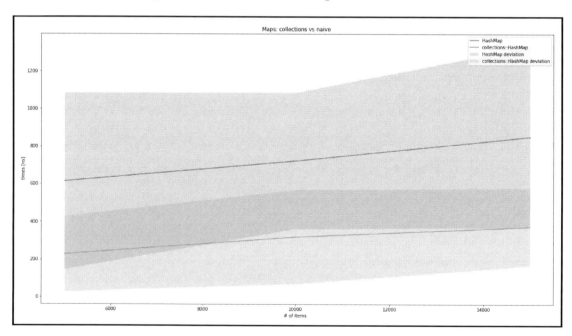

`BTreeMap` and `BTreeSet` are based on a different, more efficient implementation of a B-Tree. How much more efficient (and effective)? Let's find out!

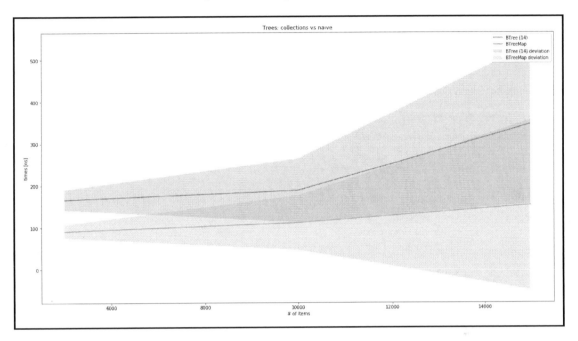

For a naive implementation of a B-Tree (from `Chapter 5`, *Robust Trees*), the performance is not that bad. However, while there might be some tweaks to be added here and there, evidence shows that there is a better and faster tree out there, so why not use that?

Summary

The Rust standard library features a great collections part, providing a few highly optimized implementations of basic data structures.

We started with `Vec<T>` and `VecDeque<T>`, both based on a heap-allocated array and wrapped in the `RawVec<T>` structure. They show excellent performance while memory efficiency remains high, thanks to the array base and `unsafe` operations based on pointers.

`LinkedList<T>` is a doubly-linked list that performs really well, thanks to direct data manipulation and the lack of runtime checking. While it excels at splitting and merging, most other operations are slower than `Vec<T>` and it lacks some useful features.

`HashSet` and `HashMap` are based on the same implementation (`HashMap`) and—unless specified differently—use `DefaultHasher` to generate a hashed key of an object. This key is stored (and later retrieved) using the Robin Hood hashing method, which provides major performance benefits over a naive implementation.

Alternatively, `BTreeSet` and `BTreeMap` use a B-Tree structure to organize keys and values. This implementation is also specialized and geared towards CPU-cache friendliness, and reducing the number of nodes (thereby minimizing the number of allocations) in order to create the high performance data structure that it is.

In the next chapter, we will decrypt the O notation, something that has been used sparingly up until this point, but is necessary for what follows: algorithms.

Questions

- Which `std::collections` data structure is not discussed here?
- How does `Vec<T>` or `VecDeque<T>` grow as of 2018?
- Is `LinkedList<T>` a good default data structure?
- What hashing implementation does the 2018 `HashMap` use by default?
- What are three benefits of `BTreeMap` over a `HashMap`?
- Is a `BTreeMap` internal tree wider or higher?

Further reading

You can refer to the following links for more information on topics covered in this chapter:

- https://doc.rust-lang.org/std/collections/index.html
- http://cglab.ca/~abeinges/blah/rust-btree-case/
- https://doc.rust-lang.org/src/std/collections/hash/map.rs.html#148

8
Algorithm Evaluation

When looking at algorithms as defined entities, what makes one algorithm better than the other? Is it the number of steps required to finish? The amount of memory that is committed? CPU cycles? How do they compare across machines and operating systems with different memory allocators?

There are a lot of questions here that need answers, since comparing work with others is important in order to find the best approach possible to solve a given problem. In this chapter, you can look forward to learning about the following:

- Evaluating algorithms in practice
- Classifying algorithm and data structure behaviors
- Estimating the plausibility of a better algorithm

The Big O notation

Physics is not a topic in this book, but its influence is far-reaching and powerful enough to be obeyed everywhere, even by virtual constructs such as algorithms! However great their design, they still are constrained by two important factors: time and space.

Time? Whenever anything needs to be done, a sequence of steps is required. By multiplying the number of steps by the time for each step, the total—absolute—time is easy to calculate. Or so we think. For computers, this is *mostly* true, but many questions make it very hard to really know, since modern CPUs go way beyond what previous generations were able to achieve. Is that only thanks to higher clock rates? What about the additional cores? SIMD? Simply taking the absolute time won't achieve real comparability between algorithms. Maybe the number of steps is what we should use.

Space (as in memory) has become a commodity in many domains over the last few years, even in the embedded space. While the situation has improved, it still pays to be mindful of how many bytes are stored in memory and how much that contributes to the goal of the algorithm. Or in other words, is this worth it? Many algorithmic tasks face a trade-off between what's stored in memory and what's computed on demand. The latter might be just enough to solve the problem, or it might not be; this is a decision the developer has to make.

Other people's code

Consequently, every algorithm must have a "number of steps required" and "bytes of memory required" property, right? Close: since they are ever-changing variables, a universal way of describing what other people have achieved is necessary.

Typically, programmers instinctively know how to do that: "is this thing really doing everything twice?!" should be a familiar outcry. What has been said here? Assuming it's a function that has an input parameter x, it sounds like the function is doing something with x twice. Mathematically speaking, this would be expressed as $f(x) = 2x$.

What this is really saying is that for every input, the required number of steps to fully execute the function is twice the input—isn't this exactly what we have been looking for? What would be a better way to write it down?

The Big O

Looking at that issue from a (mathematical) function perspective, this is a shared need across mathematics, computer science, physics, and so on: they all want to know how expensive a function is. This is why a common notation was invented by Edmund Landau: the Big O notation (or Landau notation) consisting of the uppercase letter O, which declares the *order* of a function. The main growth factor is then put into parentheses following the letter O.

There are other, related notations that use small *o*, Omegas, Theta, and others, but those are less relevant in practical terms. Check the *Further reading* section for an article by Donald Knuth on this.

Asymptotic runtime complexity

For computer science, the exact, absolute runtime is typically not important when implementing algorithms (you can always get a faster computer). Instead, the runtime complexity is more important since it directly influences performance as an overall measure of work, independent of details.

Since this is not an exact measurement and the actual performance is influenced by other factors, sticking with an asymptotic (read: rough) measure is the best strategy. In addition to that, algorithms have best and worst cases. Unless you are trying to improve on a particular case, the worst case is what's typically compared:

```
let my_vec = vec![5,6,10,33,53,77];
for i in my_vec.iter() {
    if i == 5 {
        break;
    }
    println!("{}", i);
}
```

Iterating over this, Vec<T> has a runtime complexity of $O(n)$ where n is the length of Vec<T>, regardless of the fact that the loop will break right away. Why? Because of pessimism. In reality, it is often hard to say what the input vector looks like and when it will actually exit, so the worst case is that it goes over the entire sequence without breaking, that is, n times. Now that we have seen how to write this down, let's see how to find out the runtime complexity of our own algorithms.

Making your own

There are only a few aspects that change the complexity of an algorithm, those that have been shown to proportionally increase the total time required of an algorithm.

These are as follows:

- An arithmetic operation (`10 + 30`)
- An assignment (`let x = 10`)
- A test (`x == 10`)
- A read or write of a basic type (`u32`, `bool`, and so on)

If a piece of code only does one of these operations, it is one step, that is, *O(1)*, and whenever there is a choice (`if` or `match`), the more complex branch has to be picked. Regardless of any input parameters, it will be the same number of steps—or constant time. If they are run in a loop, things get more interesting.

Loops

When in a loop, and the number of iterations is not known at compile time, it will be a major influence on runtime complexity. If an operation mentioned earlier is executed in the loop (for example, a `sum` operation), one could declare the complexity as *O(1 * n)* for the arithmetic operation. After adding another operation, we could express it as *O(2 * n)* and, while this would be correct, these are not the driving forces of the loop. Regardless of the number of operations that are executed *n* times, the main growth factor remains *n*. Hence, we simply say *O(n)*, unless you are trying to compare the same algorithm, where the number of iterations actually makes a difference. If there are subsequent loops, the most expensive one is picked.

However, upon nesting loops, the complexity changes considerably. Consider this (really bad) algorithm for comparing two lists:

```
let my_vec = vec![1,1,1,4,6,7,23,4];
let my_other_vec = vec![66,2,4,6,892];


for i in my_vec.iter() {
    for j in my_other_vec.iter() {
        if i == j {
            panic!();
        }
    }
}
```

For each element in the first collection, the second collection is fully iterated. In other words, each element is looked at $n * m$ times, resulting in a runtime complexity of $O(n*m)$, or, if both collections are the same size, $O(n^2)$.

Can it get even worse? Yes!

Recursion

Since all recursive algorithms can be unrolled into a loop, they can achieve the same results. However, recursion, or more specifically backtracking (which will be discussed in more detail in Chapter 11, *Random and Combinatorial*), makes it easier to create higher runtime complexities.

Typical combinatorial problems result in exponential runtimes, since there are a number of variations (such as different colors) that have to be enumerated n times so that a constraint is satisfied, which is only evaluated at the end. If there are two colors, the runtime complexity will therefore be $O(2^n)$ for a sequence of n colors, if no two colors can be adjacent to each other in a graph (graph coloring problem).

Recursive algorithms also make it hard to estimate runtime complexity quickly, since the branch development is hard to visualize.

Complexity classes

In general, all algorithms fall into one of a few classes. Let's look at these classes ordered by their growth speed. Depending on the literature, there might be more or fewer classes, but this is a good set to start with since they represent the major directions of growth behavior.

O(1)

Constant time, which means everything will take the same amount of time. Since this chart would be a horizontal line at the y value of 1, we will skip it in favor of sparing a tree.

O(log(n))

Growth is defined by the logarithmic function (in general, base 2), which is better than linear growth.

Here is the plot of the mathematical function:

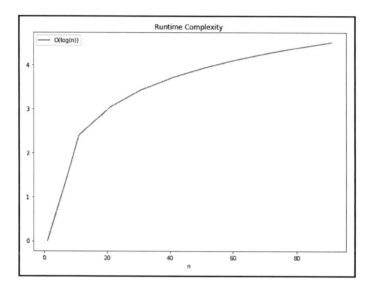

O(n)

Linear time, which means that the solution performance depends on the input in a linear way:

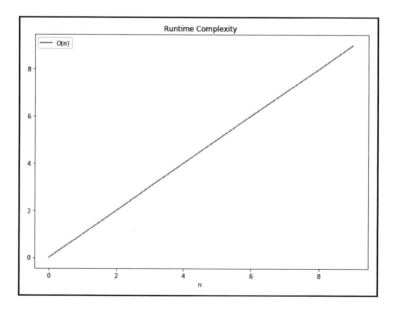

O(n log(n))

This is sometimes called quasilinear time and is the best achievable complexity for sorting:

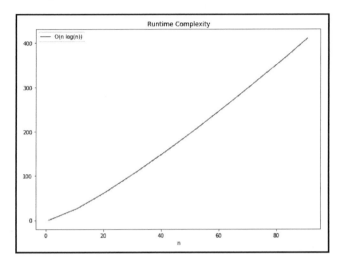

O(n²)

The squared runtime is typical for the naive implementation of search or sorting algorithms:

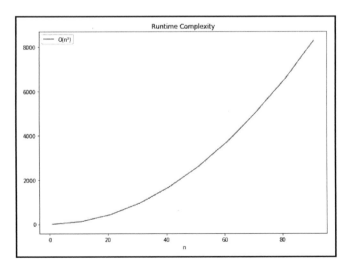

O(2^n)

This is among the most expensive classes and can often be found in really hard-to-solve problems. This plot has a significantly smaller *x* value (*0 - 10*) and generates a higher *y* value (or runtime) than the `O(n log(n))` chart:

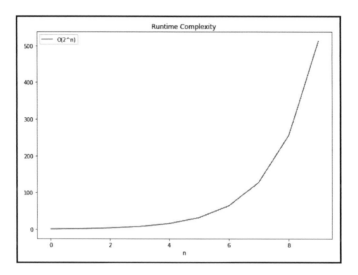

Comparison

Having individual charts is great for imagining the projected runtime and estimating what a task's performance could look like when its input is increased. If we plot all of these lines into a single chart, however, their performance will become obvious.

The typical comparison is against the linear time complexity ($O(n)$), since most naive solutions would be expected to achieve this performance:

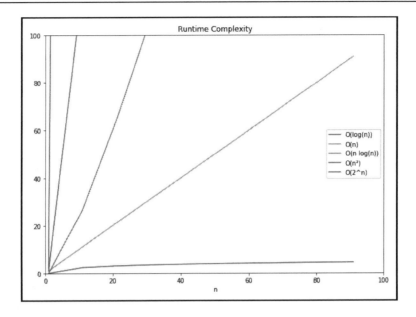

With this chart in mind, we can look at problems and their expected performance in the next section.

In the wild

In reality, there are a lot of factors that may influence the choice of space and runtime complexity. Typically, these factors are forms of resource constraints, such as power consumption on embedded devices, clock cycles in a cloud-hosted environment, and so on.

Since it is difficult to find out the complexities of a particular algorithm, it is helpful to know a few, so the choice comes intuitively. Often, the runtime complexity is not the only important aspect, but the absolute execution time counts. Under these conditions, a higher runtime complexity can be preferable if *n* is sufficiently small.

This is best demonstrated when Vec<T> contains only a few elements, where a linear search is a lot faster than sorting and then running a binary search. The overhead of sorting might just be too much compared to searching right away.

Getting this trade-off and the overall implementation right is hugely beneficial for the entire program and will outweigh any other optimizations. Let's take a look at a few runtime complexities that can be found in everyday life.

Data structures

Algorithms on lists of all kinds almost always exhibit $O(n)$ behavior, since most actions involve shifting or going through other elements. Hence, operations such as insert at or remove from a position, as well as finding elements (when unsorted), are $O(n)$. This is very visible, particularly in linked lists, with only a few exceptions: a dynamic array's element access ($O(1)$), prepending/appending elements or lists, and splitting lists appending elements in a linked list ($O(1)$).

Special cases of lists, such as **stacks** and **queues**, make use of these exceptions and let a user insert to or remove from only the ends of that list. **Skip lists** on the other hand employ a tree-like strategy for achieving great search performance, which speeds up inserts and removals too. But this comes at the expense of memory, since the additional elements are proportional ($log(n)$) to the list length.

For search, **trees** are great. Regular trees (that is, anything that can be a B-Tree) exhibit $O(log(n))$ complexities on many operations, including insert, remove, and find. This is particularly great since difference to $O(n)$ actually increases the more elements there are in the collection.

The only thing potentially better are **maps** and **sets**, if the underlying implementation uses an appropriate hashing algorithm. Any operation *should* be completed in constant time ($O(1)$), if there are no collisions. Typically, there will be some collisions, but the runtime complexity will not exceed $O(n)$ because, if all else fails, a linear search works. Consequently, real performance will be somewhere in between, with the hashing algorithm being the most important influence. For most libraries, hash maps (and sets) are faster than their tree-based counterparts.

Everyday things

Whenever something needs sorting, there are a lot of ways to achieve that, but the baseline is $O(n^2)$. It's the same way most people order their socks: pick one and find the match, then repeat (called **selection sort**). How else would one compare all elements to find their order? Better approaches, such as heap sort, merge sort, and so on, all exhibit $O(n\ log(n))$ behavior in the worst case, which is the best possible (consistent) performance for sorting algorithms. Additionally, since the best case for any sorting algorithm is $O(n)$—making sure everything was already in order—the average case matters the most. We will get into strategies about that later in this book.

Search (or lookup) is another topic that we will get into in `Chapter 10`, *Finding Stuff*, but the associated runtime complexities are great examples. Searching on any unsorted data structure will be $O(n)$ most of the time, while sorted collections can utilize binary search (a tree's search strategy) and achieve $O(log(n))$. In order to save the cost of sorting, ideal hash tables provide the absolute best case for search: $O(1)$.

Exotic things

One class that was omitted from the earlier list is **polynomial time** (**P** in short). This class is quicker to solve than the exponential time class, but worse than $O(n^3)$. These problems include checking whether a number is a prime number, or solving a Sudoku. However, there are other problems in this class as well that actually have *no* "quick" (that is, solvable in P) solution, but a solution can be verified in P time. These are called **NP** (an abbreviation of **non-deterministic polynomial time**) problems and the hardest of them are NP-hard (see the information box).

The distinction between P, NP, NP-complete, and NP-hard is not intuitive. NP problems are problems that can be solved using a non-deterministic Turing machine in P time. **NP-hard** problems are problems without a solution that, if solved, would have a polynomial time solution and if it is also an NP problem, it is also considered NP-complete. Additionally, finding a solution for one of either class (NP-hard or NP-complete) would imply a solution for *all* NP-hard/NP-complete problems.

While there are no known algorithms to solve these problems quickly, there typically are naive approaches that result in *very* long runtimes. Popular problems in this space include the traveling salesman problem ($O(n!)$), the knapsack problem ($O(2^n)$), and the subset sum problem ($O(2^{n/2})$), all of which are currently solved (or approximated) using heuristics or programming techniques. For those interested, check the further reading section for links.

Summary

The Big O notation is a way to describe the time and space requirements of an algorithm (or data structure). This is not an exact science, however; it's about finding the primary growth factor of each of the things mentioned to answer this question: what happens when the problem space grows bigger?

Any algorithm will fall within a few relevant classes that describe that behavior. By applying the algorithm to one more element, how many more steps have to be taken? One easy way is to visualize the individual charts and think of whether it will be linear ($O(n)$), quasilinear ($O(n \log(n))$), quadratic ($O(n^2)$), or even exponential ($O(2^n)$). Whatever the case may be, it is always best to do less work than there are elements to be looked at, such as constant ($O(1)$) or logarithmic ($O(\log(n))$) behaviors!

Selecting the operations is typically done based on the worst-case behavior, that is, the upper limit of what is going to happen. In the next chapter, we will take a closer look at these behaviors in the cases of popular search algorithms.

Questions

- Why estimate runtime complexity over, for example, number of statements?
- How does runtime complexity relate to math functions?
- Is the complexity class that is typically provided the best or worst case?
- Why are loops important in estimating complexity?
- Is $O(n \log(n))$ a better or worse runtime complexity than $O(\log(n))$?
- What are some commonly known complexity classes?

Further reading

You can refer to the following links to get more information on the topics covered in this chapter:

- Wikipedia's list of best-, worst-, and average-case complexities (https://en.wikipedia.org/wiki/Best,_worst_and_average_case)
- Big O Cheatsheet (http://bigocheatsheet.com/)
- Heuristic algorithms at Northwestern University (https://optimization.mccormick.northwestern.edu/index.php/Heuristic_algorithms)
- Heuristic design and optimization at MIT (http://www.mit.edu/~moshref/Heuristics.html)
- *Big Omicron And Big Omega And Big Theta* by Donald Knuth (http://www.phil.uu.nl/datastructuren/10-11/knuth_big_omicron.pdf)

9
Ordering Things

Tidy house, tidy mind is a saying that, as in its German variation, implies that order plays an important part in our lives. Anyone who wants to maximize efficiency has to rely on order, or risk the occasional time-consuming search through the chaos that has slowly unfolded. Having things in a particular order is great; it's the process of getting there that is expensive.

This often does not feel like a good use of our time, or simply may not be worth it. While a computer does not exactly feel, the time required to sort things is of a similar cost. Minimizing this time is the goal of inventing new algorithms and improving their efficiency, which is necessary for a task as common as sorting. A call to `mycollection.sort()` is not expected to take seconds (or minutes or even hours), so this is also a matter of usability. In this chapter, we will explore several solutions for that, so you can look forward to learning about the following:

- Implementing and analyzing sorting algorithms
- Knowing more about (in)famous sorting strategies

From chaos to order

There are many sorting algorithms (and their individual variations), each with their individual characteristics. Since it is impossible to cover every algorithm in a single chapter, and considering their limited usefulness, this chapter covers a selected few.

The selection should show the different strategies that are common in sorting a collection of items, many of which have been implemented in various libraries across different languages. Since many of you will never implement any sorting algorithms for productive use, this section is supposed to familiarize you with what's behind the scenes when a call to `mycollection.sort()` is issued, and why this could take a surprising amount of time.

Sorting algorithms fall into a group on each of these properties:

- **Stable**: Maintains a relative order when comparing equal values
- **Hybrid**: Combines two or more sorting approaches (for example, by collection length)
- **In-place**: Uses indices instead of full copies for passing collections around

While stable and hybrid algorithms are more complex and, in many cases, at a higher level (because they combine various approaches), in-place sorting is common and reduces the space and amount of copying an algorithm has to do.

We have touched on a very basic sorting algorithm already: **insertion sort**. It is the exact algorithm most real life things are done with: when adding a new book to a bookshelf, most people will pick up the book, look at the property to order by (such as the author's last name), and find the spot in their current collection, starting from the letter *A*. This is a very efficient approach and is used to build a new collection with minimal overhead, but it does not warrant its own section.

Let's start off with an absolute classic that is always a part of any university's curriculum because of its simplicity: bubble sort.

Bubble sort

Bubble sort is the infamous algorithm that university students often learn as their first sorting algorithm. In terms of performance and runtime complexity, it is certainly among the worst ways to sort a collection, but it's great for teaching.

The principle is simple: walk through an array, scanning two elements and bringing them into the correct order by swapping. Repeat these steps until no swaps occur. The following diagram shows this process on the example array `[8, 9, 7, 6]`, where a total of four swaps establishes the order of `[6, 7, 8, 9]` by repeatedly comparing two succeeding elements:

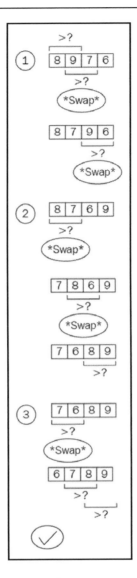

This diagram also shows an interesting (and name-giving) property of the algorithm: the "bubbling up" of elements to their intended position. The number 6 in the diagram travels, swap by swap, from the last position to the first position in the collection.

When this is transformed into Rust code, the simplicity remains: two nested loops iterate over the collection, whereas the outer loop could just as well run till infinity, since the inner portion does all the comparing and swapping.

Bubble sort is, infamously, a short snippet of code:

```rust
pub fn bubble_sort<T: PartialOrd + Clone>(collection: &[T]) -> Vec<T> {
    let mut result: Vec<T> = collection.into();
    for _ in 0..result.len() {
        let mut swaps = 0;
        for i in 1..result.len() {
            if result[i - 1] > result[i] {
                result.swap(i - 1, i);
                swaps += 1;
            }
        }
        if swaps == 0 {
            break;
        }
    }
    result
}
```

For easier handling, the algorithm creates a copy of the input array (using the Into<T> trait's into() method) and swaps around elements using the swap() method provided by Vec<T>.

The nested loops already hint toward the (worst case) runtime complexity: $O(n^2)$. However, thanks to the early stopping when there are no swaps in a run, a partially ordered collection will be sorted surprisingly quickly. In fact, the best case scenario is really fast with bubble sort, since it's basically a single run-through (in other words, $O(n)$ in this case).

The following chart shows three cases: sorting an already sorted collection (ascending numbers and descending numbers), as well as sorting a randomly shuffled array of distinct numbers:

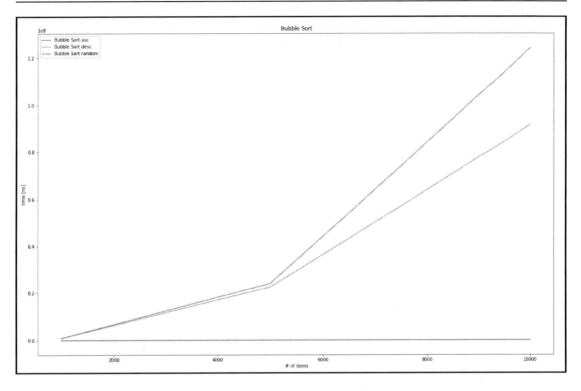

The output graph comparison between Bubble sort ascending, descending, and randomly sorted arrays

The algorithm will produce an ascending sequence, yet the shuffled collection shows a worse absolute runtime than the traditional worst case: a collection sorted in descending order. In any case, the exponential nature of these runtimes shows why bubble sort is not fit for real-world use.

Shell sort is sometimes dubbed as an optimized version of bubble sort!

Shell sort

Bubble sort always compares an element to the neighboring element, but is this important? Many would say that it depends on the pre-existing order of the unsorted collection: are these future neighbors far apart or close together?

Donald Shell, the inventor of shell sort, must have had a similar idea and used a "gap" between elements to make further jumps with the swapping approach adopted by bubble sort. By utilizing a specified strategy to choose those gaps, the runtime can change dramatically. Shell's original strategy is to start with half the collection's length and, by halving the gap size until zero, a runtime of $O(n^2)$ is achieved. Other strategies include choosing numbers based on some form of calculation of the current iteration k (for example, $2^k - 1$), or empirically collected gaps (http://sun.aei.polsl.pl/~mciura/publikacje/ shellsort.pdf), which do not have a fixed runtime complexity yet!

The following diagram explains some of the workings of shell sort. First, the initial gap is chosen, which is n / 2 in the original paper. Starting at that gap (2, in this particular example), the element is saved and compared to the element *at the other end of the gap*, in other words, the current index minus the gap:

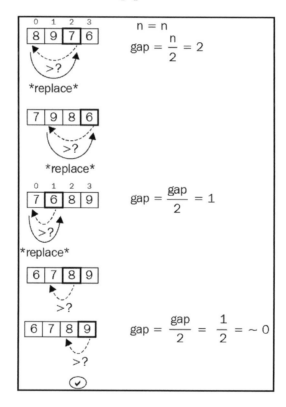

If the element at the other end of the gap is greater, it replaces the origin. Then, the process walks toward index zero with gap-sized steps, so the question becomes: what is going to fill that hole (7 is overwritten by 8, so the hole is where 8 was)—the original element, or element "gap" steps before it?

In this example, it's 7, since there is no preceding element. In longer collections, a lot more moving around can occur before the original element is inserted. After this insertion process has finished for index 2, it's repeated for index 3, moving from the gap toward the end of the collection. Following that, the gap size is reduced (in our case, by half) and the insertion steps are repeated until the collection is in order (and the gap size is zero).

Words, and even an image, make it surprisingly hard to understand what is going on. Code, however, shows the workings nicely:

```
pub fn shell_sort<T: PartialOrd + Clone>(collection: &[T]) -> Vec<T> {
    let n = collection.len();
    let mut gap = n / 2;
    let mut result: Vec<T> = collection.into();

    while gap > 0 {
        for i in gap..n {
            let temp = result[i].clone();

            let mut j = i;
            while j >= gap && result[j - gap] > temp {
                result[j] = result[j - gap].clone();
                j -= gap;
            }
            result[j] = temp;
        }
        gap /= 2;
    }
    result
}
```

This snippet shows the value of shell sort: with the correct gap strategy, it can achieve results that are similar to more sophisticated sorting algorithms, but it is a lot shorter to implement and understand. Because of this, it can be a good choice for embedded use cases, where no library and only limited space is available.

The actual performance on the test sets is good:

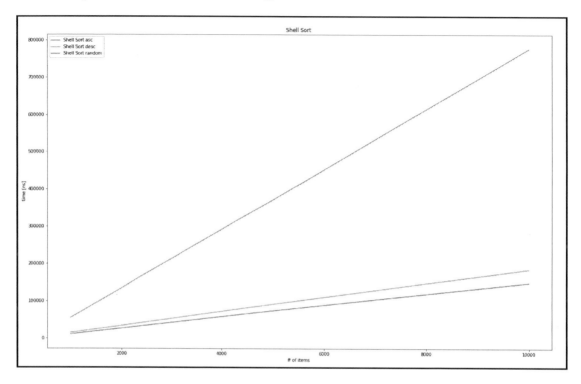

The output graph comparison between shell sort ascending, descending, and randomly sorted arrays

Even with the original gap strategy that is said to produce $O(n^2)$ runtimes, the random set produces something more akin to linear behavior. Definitely a solid performance, but can it compare to heap sort?

Heap sort

Ordering numbers was already a topic that we covered earlier in this book (Chapter 5, *Robust Trees*) while discussing trees: with heaps. A heap is a tree-like data structure with the highest (max-heap) or lowest number (min-heap) at the root that maintains order when inserting or removing elements. Hence, a sorting mechanism could be as simple as inserting everything into a heap and retrieving it again!

Since a (binary) heap has a known runtime complexity of *O(log n)*, and the entire array has to be inserted, the estimated runtime complexity will be *O(n log n)*, among the best sorting performances in sorting. The following diagram shows the binary heap in tree notation on the right, and the array implementation on the left:

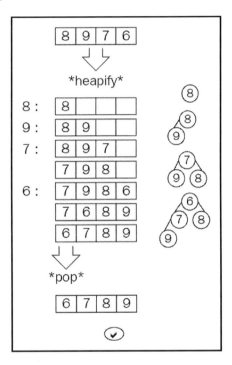

In the Rust standard library, there is a `BinaryHeap` structure available, which makes the implementation quick and easy:

```
pub fn heap_sort<T: PartialOrd + Clone + Ord>(collection: &[T]) -> Vec<T> {
    let mut heap = BinaryHeap::new();
    for c in collection {
        heap.push(c.clone());
    }
    heap.into_sorted_vec()
}
```

The fact that a heap is used to do the sorting will generate fairly uniform outcomes, making it a great choice for unordered collections, but an inferior choice for presorted ones. This is due to the fact that a heap is filled and emptied, regardless of the pre-existing ordering. Plotting the different cases shows almost no difference:

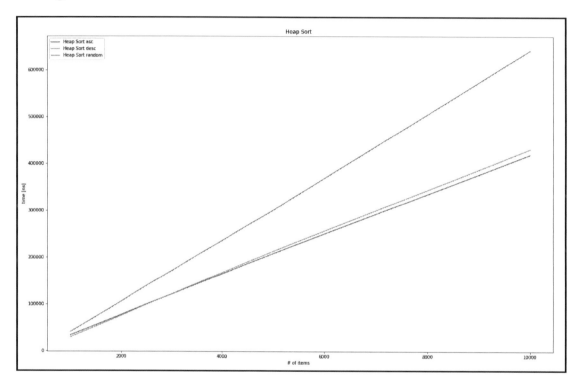

The output graph comparison between heap sort ascending, descending, and randomly sorted arrays

A very different strategy, called *divide and conquer*, is employed by an entire group of algorithms. This group is what we are going to explore now, starting with merge sort.

Merge sort

One fundamental strategy in battle, as well as in sorting collections, is to divide and conquer. Merge sort does exactly that, by splitting the collection in half recursively until only a single element remains. The merging operation can then put these single elements together in the correct order with the benefit of working with presorted collections.

What this does is reduce the problem size (in other words, the number of elements in the collection) to more manageable chunks that come presorted for easier comparison, resulting in a worst case runtime complexity of *O(n log n)*. The following diagram shows the split and merge process (note that comparing and ordering only starts at the merge step):

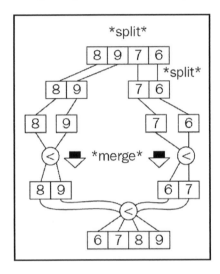

There are various implementations of this principle: bottom up, top down, using blocks, and other variations. In fact, as of 2018, Rust's default sorting algorithm is Timsort, a stable, hybrid algorithm that combines insertion sort (up until a certain size) with merge sort.

Implementing a vanilla merge sort in Rust is, again, a great place to use recursion. First, the left half is evaluated, then the right half of a sequence, and only then does merging begin, first by comparing the two sorted results (left and right) and picking elements from either side. Once one of these runs out of elements, the rest is simply appended since the elements are obviously larger. This result is returned to the caller, repeating the merging on a higher level until the original caller is reached.

Here's the Rust code for a typical merge sort implementation:

```rust
pub fn merge_sort<T: PartialOrd + Clone + Debug>(collection: &[T]) ->
Vec<T> {
    if collection.len() > 1 {
        let (l, r) = collection.split_at(collection.len() / 2);
        let sorted_l = merge_sort(l);
        let sorted_r = merge_sort(r);
        let mut result: Vec<T> = collection.into();
        let (mut i, mut j) = (0, 0);
        let mut k = 0;
        while i < sorted_l.len() && j < sorted_r.len() {
            if sorted_l[i] <= sorted_r[j] {
                result[k] = sorted_l[i].clone();
                i += 1;
            } else {
                result[k] = sorted_r[j].clone();
                j += 1;
            }
            k += 1;
        }

        while i < sorted_l.len() {
            result[k] = sorted_l[i].clone();
            k += 1;
            i += 1;
        }

        while j < sorted_r.len() {
            result[k] = sorted_r[j].clone();
            k += 1;
            j += 1;
        }

        result
    } else {
        collection.to_vec()
    }
}
```

This behavior also pays off, creating a quasi-linear runtime complexity, as shown in the following plot:

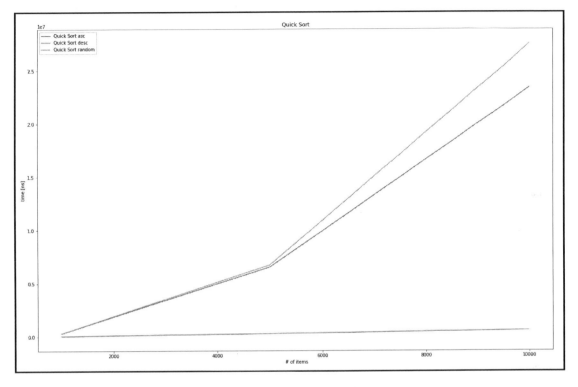

The output graph comparison between Quicksort asc, desc, and random

Another divide-and-conquer-type algorithm is Quicksort. It's a very interesting way to sort a list for a variety of reasons.

Quicksort

This algorithm significantly outperformed merge sort in best case scenarios and was quickly adopted as Unix's default sorting algorithm, as well as in Java's reference implementation. By using a similar strategy to merge sort, Quicksort achieves faster average and best case speeds. Unfortunately, the worst case complexity is just as bad as bubble sort: $O(n^2)$. How so? you might ask.

Quicksort operates, sometimes recursively, on parts of the full collection, and swaps elements around to establish an order. Hence, the critical question becomes: how do we choose these parts? This choosing bit is called the partitioning scheme and typically includes the swapping as well, not just choosing a split index. The choice is made by picking a pivot element, the value of which is what everything is compared with.

Everything less than the pivot value goes to one side, and everything greater goes to the other—by swapping. Once the algorithm detects a nice ascending (on the one side) and descending (from the other side) order, the split can be made where the two sequences intersect. Then, the entire process starts anew with each of the partitions.

The following illustration shows the picking and ordering of the elements based on the previous example collection. While the partitions in this example are only length one versus the rest, the same process would apply if these were longer sequences as well:

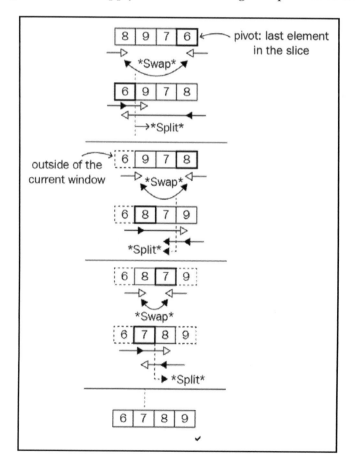

The partitioning scheme used here is called the Hoare scheme, named after the inventor of Quicksort, Sir Anthony Hoare, in 1959. There are other schemes (Lomuto seems to be the most popular alternative) that may provide better performance by trading off various other aspects, such as memory efficiency or the number of swaps. Whatever the partition scheme, picking a pivot value plays a major role in performance as well and the more equal parts it produces (like the median), the better the value is. Potential strategies include the following:

- Choosing the median
- Choosing the arithmetic mean
- Picking an element (random, first, or last, as chosen here)

In Rust code, Quicksort is implemented in three functions:

- The public API to provide a usable interface
- A wrapped recursive function that takes a low and high index to sort in-between
- The partition function implementing the Hoare partition scheme

This implementation can be considered in-place since it operates on the same vector that was provided in the beginning, swapping elements based on their indices. Here is the code:

```rust
fn partition<T: PartialOrd + Clone + Debug>(
    collection: &mut [T],
    low: usize,
    high: usize,
) -> usize {
    let pivot = collection[high].clone();
    let (mut i, mut j) = (low as i64 - 1, high as i64 + 1);

    loop {
        'lower: loop {
            i += 1;
            if i > j || collection[i as usize] >= pivot {
                break 'lower;
            }
        }

        'upper: loop {
            j -= 1;
            if i > j || collection[j as usize] <= pivot {
                break 'upper;
            }
        }

        if i > j {
```

```
            return j as usize;
        }
        collection.swap(i as usize, j as usize);
    }
}

fn quick_sort_r<T: PartialOrd + Clone + Debug>(collection: &mut [T], low:
usize, high: usize) {
    if low < high {
        let pivot = partition(collection, low, high);
        quick_sort_r(collection, low, pivot);
        quick_sort_r(collection, pivot + 1, high);
    }
}

pub fn quick_sort<T: PartialOrd + Clone + Debug>(collection: &[T]) ->
Vec<T> {
    let mut result = collection.to_vec();
    quick_sort_r(&mut result, 0, collection.len() - 1);
    result
}
```

Another new aspect in this implementation is the use of loop labels, which allow for better structure and readability. This is due to Hoare's use of a do-until type loop, a syntax that is not available in Rust, but that required the algorithm to avoid an infinite loop.

> The `break`/`continue` instructions are relatives of the infamous go-to instruction, so they should only be used sparingly and with great care for the purpose of readability. Loop labels provide a tool to achieve that. They allow a reader to track exactly which loop is being exited or continued. The syntax leans slightly on that of the lifetimes: `'mylabel: loop { break 'mylabel; }`.

Quicksort's performance characteristics are definitely interesting. The rare worst case behavior or $O(n^2)$ has triggered many optimizations over the decades since its invention, the latest of which is called Dual-Pivot Quicksort from 2009, which has been adopted in Oracle's library for Java 7. Refer to the *Further reading* section for a more detailed explanation.

Running the original Quicksort on the previous dataset, the worst case and best case behaviors are clearly visible. The performance on the descending and (curiously) the ascending datasets is clearly $O(n^2)$, while the randomized array is quickly processed:

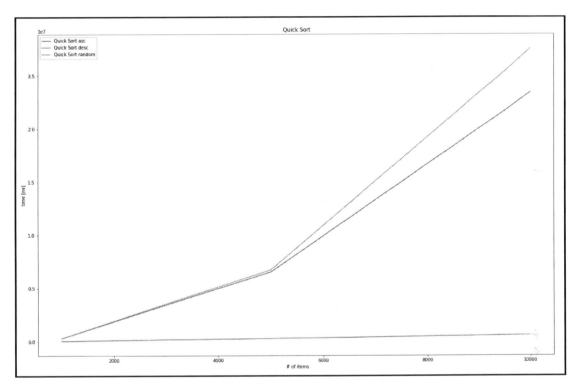

The output graph comparison between Quicksort ascensding, descending and randomly sorted arrays

This behavior speaks for the Quicksort's strong sides, which are more "real-world" type scenarios, where the worst case rarely appears. In current libraries around various programming languages though, sorting is done in a hybrid fashion, which means that these generic algorithms are used according to their strengths. This approach is called **Introsort** (from introspective sort) and, in C++'s `std::sort`, relies on Quicksort up to a certain point. Rust's standard library, however, uses Timsort.

Summary

Putting things in order is a very fundamental problem that has been solved in many different ways, varying in aspects such as worst-case runtime complexity, memory required, the relative order of equal elements (stability), as well as overall strategies. A few fundamental approaches were presented in this chapter.

Bubble sort is one of the simplest algorithms to implement, but it comes at a high runtime cost, with a worst-case behavior of $O(n^2)$. This is due to the fact that it simply swaps elements based on a nested loop, which makes elements "bubble up" to either end of the collection.

Shell sort can be seen as an improved version of bubble sort, with a major upside: it does not start off by swapping neighbors. Instead, there is a gap that elements are compared and swapped across, covering a greater distance. This gap size changes with every round that shows worst-case runtime complexities of $O(n^2)$ for the original scheme to $O(n \log n)$ in the fastest variant. In fact, the runtime complexity of some empirically derived gaps cannot even be measured reliably!

Heap sort makes use of a data structure's property to create a sorted collection. The heap, as presented earlier, retains the largest (or smallest) element at its root, returning it at every `pop()`. Heap sort therefore simply inserts the entire collection into a heap, only to retrieve it one by one in a sorted fashion. This leads to a runtime complexity of $O(n \log n)$.

Tree-based strategies are also found in **merge sort**, a divide-and-conquer approach. This algorithm recursively splits the collection in half to sort the subset before working on the entire collection. This work is done when returning from the recursive calls when the resulting sub-collections have to be merged, hence the name. Typically, this will exercise a runtime complexity of $O(n \log n)$.

Quicksort also uses a divide-and-conquer approach, but instead of simply breaking the collection in half every time, it works with a pivot value, where the other values are swapped before looking at each sub-collection. This results in a worst-case behavior of $O(n^2)$, but Quicksort is often used for its frequent average complexity of $O(n \log n)$.

Nowadays, standard libraries use hybrid approaches such as Timsort, Introsort, or pattern-defeating Quicksort to get the best absolute and relative runtime performance. Rust's standard library provides either a stable sorting function for slices (`slice::sort()` versus `slice::sort_unstable()`) based on merge sort, and an unstable sorting function based on the pattern-defeating Quicksort.

This chapter aimed to be the basis for the next chapter, which will cover how to find a specific element, something that typically requires a sorted collection!

Questions

- Why is sorting an important aspect of programming?
- What makes values bubble up in bubble sort?
- Why is shell sort useful?
- Can heap sort outperform bubble sort in its best case scenario?
- What do merge sort and Quicksort have in common?
- What are hybrid sorting algorithms?

Further reading

Here is some additional reference material that you may refer to regarding what has been covered in this chapter:

- *Dual-Pivot Quicksort* (https://web.archive.org/web/20151002230717/http://iaroslavski.narod.ru/quicksort/DualPivotQuicksort.pdf)
- C++ sorting explained (https://medium.com/@lucianoalmeida1/exploring-some-standard-libraries-sorting-functions-dd633f838182)
- Wikipedia on Introsort (https://en.wikipedia.org/wiki/Introsort)
- Wikipedia on Timsort (https://en.wikipedia.org/wiki/Timsort)
- Pattern defeating Quicksort (https://github.com/orlp/pdqsort)

10
Finding Stuff

The issue with searching for *something* is always directly related to the space in which you are searching. You will certainly have experienced looking for your keys in your house: the search space contains anything from jackets worn the previous day to the sock drawer into which the key might have slipped the last time you did the washing. Upon finding the item (and after a lot of wasted time spent running up and down stairs and searching in various rooms), you then swear to keep things tidier in the future....

We have encountered this issue more often than we are comfortable with admitting, but it illustrates a fundamental issue that we can solve algorithmically without any particular order to build on. In this chapter, we'll explore how to do the following:

- Finding items in an unordered array of chaos
- Making a trade-off between preparation and search

Finding the best

The search domain is present on various levels of abstraction: finding a word in a body of text is typically more complex than simply calling the `contains()` function, and if there are several results, which is the one that was searched for? This entire class of problem is summed up under the umbrella of **information retrieval**, where problems of ranking, indexing, understanding, storing, and searching are solved in order to retrieve the optimum result (for all definitions). This chapter focuses only on the latter part, where we actually look through a collection of items (for example, an index) in order to find a match.

This means that we will compare items directly ($a = b$) to determine closeness, rather than using something such as a distance - or locally-sensitive hashing function. These can be found in more specific domains such as a fuzzy search or matching bodies of text, which is a field of its own. To learn more about hashing, please check out `Chapter 6`, *Exploring Maps and Sets* or the *Further reading* section in this chapter.

Starting off with the most naive implementation, let's look at linear searches.

Linear searches

Linear searching is a fancy name for something that we do in almost every program and our everyday lives: going through a collection of items to find the first match. There is no need for any preprocessing or similar steps; the collection can be used as-is, which means that standard libraries commonly provide a generic implementation already. In Rust's case, the iterator trait offers this feature with functions called `position()` (or `rposition()`), `find()`, `filter()`, or even `any()`. `fold()` can also be used to find the thing you are looking for. The following is a diagram of the process:

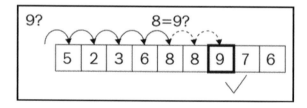

Fundamentally, however, it's a loop over each item that either exits or collects all items where a predicate (an evaluation function that takes in an item of a type to return a Boolean value) matches:

```
pub fn linear_search<T: Eq + Clone>(haystack: &[T], needle: &T) ->
Option<usize> {
    for (i, h) in haystack.iter().enumerate() {
        if h.eq(needle) {
            return Some(i);
        }
    }
    None
}
```

This algorithm obviously exhibits $O(n)$ runtime complexity, growing with the collection size. Iterating over 10,000 items will take a while, even if the predicate executes quickly, so how can this strategy be improved?

Jump search

Going linearly over a collection one-by-one is only efficient if you are already close to a potential match, but it is very hard to determine—what does *close to a match* mean? In unordered collections, this is indeed impossible to know this since any item can follow. Consequently, what about sorting the collection first? As discussed in Chapter 9, *Ordering Things*, sorting at quasi-linear runtime complexity can be significantly faster than going over each item of a long collection past a certain size.

A jump search makes use of knowing about the range it jumps over, not unlike a skip list:

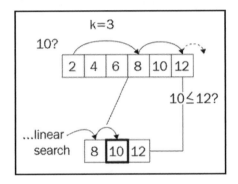

After sorting, a search can be significantly faster and a number of elements can be skipped in order to search in a linear fashion once the algorithm is close to a match. How many elements can be skipped at each jump? This is something to be tested, but first here is the code that does the work:

```
pub fn jump_search<T: Eq + PartialOrd + Clone>(
    haystack: &[T],
    needle: &T,
    jump_size: usize,
) -> Option<usize> {
    if jump_size < haystack.len() {
        let mut i = 0;
        while i < haystack.len() - 1 {
            if i + jump_size < haystack.len() {
                i += jump_size
            } else {
                i = haystack.len() - 1;
```

```
            }
            if &haystack[i] == needle {
                return Some(i);
            } else if &haystack[i] > needle {
                return linear_search(&haystack[
                                 (i - jump_size)..i], needle);
            }
        }
    }
  None
}
```

The API expects a pre-sorted slice, which means that sorting, strictly speaking, is not part of the algorithm's runtime. Without the sorting, the runtime complexity might be something around $O(n / k + k)$, with k being the step size, which can be reduced to $O(n)$ in a worst-case scenario.

Including the sorting mechanism, the sorting algorithm will trump the search's runtime complexity easily, raising it to $O(n\ log\ n)$. While various choices for the jumps can improve the absolute runtime of this search algorithm by a significant amount, it will not perform as well as something like a tree structure. Binary searching as a strategy achieves that nicely, however.

Binary searching

Binary trees greatly reduce the number of comparison operations by creating branches from the collection, just like a binary tree would. This creates a tree on-the-fly, resulting in superior search performance. The significance is predictability, which allows us to build the tree and provides the options for what branch the algorithm can expect the result in.

A binary search, just like a jump search, requires the incoming slice to be ordered for it to work. Then the algorithm splits the array in half and chooses the side that will most likely contain the item. Once there are two collections, the behavior is very similar to that of a binary tree walk, as follows:

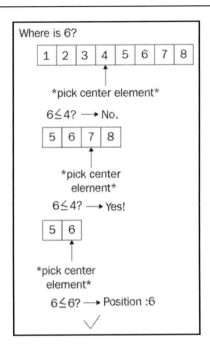

Again, given that the sorting effort trumps the algorithm's runtime complexity, it's that of the sorting algorithm that will be considered the outcome: *O(n log n)*. However, we should also be interested in the real performance, if the collection is already sorted; it's significantly lower! First, let's look at some code to make this easier to understand:

```
pub fn binary_search<T: Eq + PartialOrd>(
    haystack: &[T],
    needle: &T,
) -> Option<usize> {
    let (mut left, mut right) = (0, haystack.len() - 1);
    while left <= right {
        let pivot = left + (right - left) / 2;
        if needle < &haystack[pivot] {
            right = pivot - 1;
        } else if needle > &haystack[pivot] {
            left = pivot + 1;
        } else {
            return Some(pivot); // lucky find
        }
    }
    None
}
```

While the recursive implementation of the algorithm would have worked too, though it is not significantly shorter it harbors the risk of a stack overflow, hence the iterative approach.

After choosing a pivot (center) element, the algorithm has to determine the collection for the next iteration by one of the following three scenarios:

- The left part containing smaller values
- The right chunk with larger values
- Not at all; the pivot element is the result too

This tree-like behavior allows for a great runtime complexity of *O(log n)*, since the number of items searched keeps halving until the desired element has been found. However, how does all this compare?

Wrap up

The three approaches differ somewhat, with the binary search being the established state-of-the-art type algorithm. In fact, it can be used on any Rust slices (if they are sorted, of course) and used to find whatever is required.

Comparing these algorithms is tricky: a linear search works well on unordered datasets and is the only way to search those if sorting is not an option. If sorting is an option, then a binary search is faster by a large margin (`asc` is the sorting direction: ascending):

```
test tests::bench_binary_search_10k_asc ... bench: 80 ns/iter (+/- 32)
test tests::bench_binary_search_1k_asc ... bench: 63 ns/iter (+/- 17)
test tests::bench_binary_search_5k_asc ... bench: 86 ns/iter (+/- 28)
test tests::bench_jump_search_10k_asc ... bench: 707 ns/iter (+/- 160)
test tests::bench_jump_search_1k_asc ... bench: 92 ns/iter (+/- 10)
test tests::bench_jump_search_5k_asc ... bench: 355 ns/iter (+/- 46)
test tests::bench_linear_search_10k_asc ... bench: 2,046 ns/iter (+/- 352)
test tests::bench_linear_search_1k_asc ... bench: 218 ns/iter (+/- 22)
test tests::bench_linear_search_5k_asc ... bench: 1,076 ns/iter (+/- 527)
test tests::bench_std_binary_search_10k_asc ... bench: 93 ns/iter (+/- 10)
test tests::bench_std_binary_search_1k_asc ... bench: 62 ns/iter (+/- 7)
test tests::bench_std_binary_search_5k_asc ... bench: 89 ns/iter (+/- 27)
```

When plotted, the difference is clearly visible, with the linear search showing its linear characteristics. Taking the absolute runtime out of the game will show the runtime complexity as well, as demonstrated in the following chart:

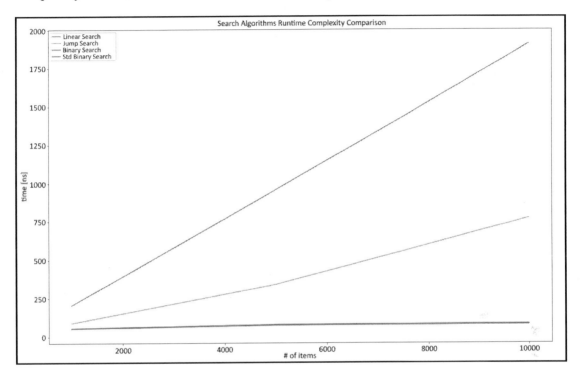

This chart shows the relative behavior of each algorithm in order to show its runtime complexities: a binary search with *O(log n)*, a linear search with *O(n)*, and a jump search, which is almost linear because of the parameter choice (the jump size is one-third of the length of the array):

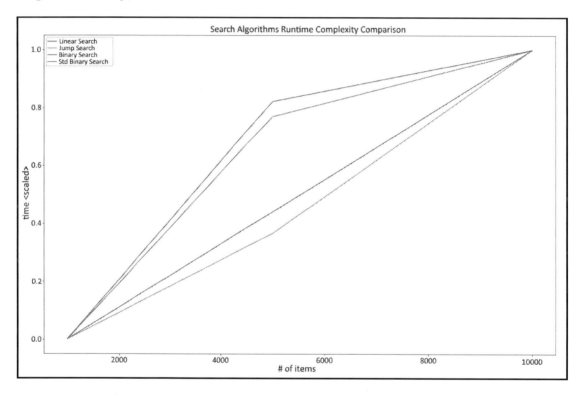

And that is it—a short introduction to search algorithms. Typically, it's more about the data, and having some way to sort beforehand creates a powerful opportunity to quickly find the item you are looking for.

Summary

Search, as a part of the information retrieval (among others) process, is an elementary way of finding something independently of the data structure being used. There are three popular types of algorithm: linear search, jump search, and binary search. Completely different approaches (such as locally-sensitive hashing) have been discussed in an earlier chapter about maps and sets, but they still need a mechanism to compare quickly.

A linear search is the least complex approach: iterate over a collection and compare the items with the element that is to be found. This has also been implemented in Rust's iterator and exhibits $O(n)$ runtime complexity.

Jump searches are superior. By operating on a sorted collection, they can use a step size that is greater than 1 (like a linear search) in order to skip to the required parts faster by checking whether the relevant section has already passed. While faster in absolute terms, the worst-case runtime complexity is still $O(n)$.

The (at the time of writing) fastest approach is a binary search, which also operates on a sorted collection and repeatedly splits the desired sections in half to work with a tree-like strategy. In fact, the runtime complexity of the algorithm itself is $O(\log n)$ as well.

In the next chapter, we will explore some more exotic algorithms: backtracking, random number generation, and more!

Questions

1. What is information retrieval?
2. Do modern search engines and databases use simple search algorithms?
3. Why do linear searches have $O(n)$ runtime complexity?
4. What does a jump search do better than a linear search?
5. What is a binary search and why is it comparable to a tree?

Further reading

Here is some additional reference material that you may refer to regarding what has been covered in this chapter: `https://www.aaai.org/ocs/index.php/AAAI/AAAI14/paper/view/8357/8643`.

11
Random and Combinatorial

While sorting and searching are two very fundamental problems in computer science, they are far from the only ones. In fact, those problems have been thoroughly solved by people who deeply specialize in such things. In today's world, it is more likely that a solution to a real-world problem involves generating random numbers, the best possible combination of several items (combinatorics) , "rolling up" several time periods into single numbers, and visualizing the results. Random number generation algorithms and solving combinatorial problems efficiently have become very important. Especially for the latter, the implementation will be specific to the solution, but there are fundamental approaches that remain. In this chapter, we will discuss a few of these fundamental approaches and learn about the following:

- Implementing backtracking algorithms
- Utilizing dynamic programming techniques
- How a pseudo-random number generator works

Pseudo-random numbers

In the last few years, random number generation has seen an interesting rise in popularity, yet many developers simply accept the generator provided by whatever technology they use. However, good random numbers are critical for many applications, such as encryption and security (or the lack thereof; see 2010's Sony PlayStation 3 security incident that prompted a famous XKCD—`https://xkcd.com/221/`), simulation, games, statistics, and biology.

As a basic principle: the more random a sequence is, the better. The reason for this is obvious. If any number in a sequence of random numbers is statistically dependent on one of the others, it becomes a pattern that can be predicted, and there is no such thing as predictable randomness. Thus, the numbers in a random sequence have to be statistically independent to qualify as good random numbers.

To get these random numbers, either a pseudo-random number generator or a true random number generator can be used (or you can buy a book—https://www.rand.org/pubs/ monograph_reports/MR1418.html). Since computers are deterministic machines, the latter is impossible without an external influence, which is why there have actually been (unsuccessful) devices to try and achieve truly random numbers. **Pseudo-random number generators** (**PRNGs**), on the other hand, are deterministic, but start off using fairly random input (mouse pointer movements, network traffic, and so on) and periodically produce numbers based on that seed.

PRNGs also enjoy a speed advantage (since there is no physical interaction required, such as measuring atmospheric noise) and the output is often good enough for many applications. In fact, if the seed is very close to random, PRNGs do a great job, as can be seen in modern cryptography.

There are a range of institutions researching PRNGs and their effectiveness at producing cryptographically saved random numbers, for example, Germany's BSI provides an in-depth analysis paper (https://bit.ly/2AOIcB1). This is a fascinating topic with a close relationship to IT security. For non-security researchers, however, there is a simple way to appraise the quality of a random number generator at a glance: visual inspection. When randomly deciding whether to plot each single pixel in a scatter plot, there should not be any visible pattern.

The following graph is of Python's numpy.random random generator, which was created to provide the same number from the same seed:

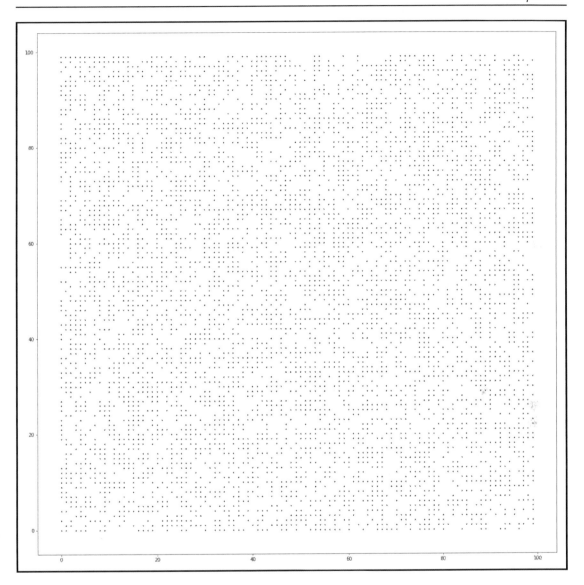

It fares well enough for statistical work and some simulations, but should not be relied upon for cryptographic work.

Regardless of the type of work, a bad random generator should never look like this:

As the pattern indicates, there are systemic errors that can be found in this random generator! Unfortunately, this is not unheard of, even in widely used technologies such as PHP on Windows (`https://boallen.com/random-numbers.html`).

Thanks to the seed, PRNGs can create reproducible as well as close-to-random numbers, which comes in handy for simulations or simply drawing a random sample for data science purposes. One very old and well researched method is the **linear congruential generator,** or **LCG.**

LCG

The LCG is one of the oldest ways of generating a pseudo-random number sequence. It follows a simple, recursive formula:

$$X_n = (a * X_{n-1} + c) \bmod m$$

X denotes the random number (or, more precisely, the nth random number in the sequence). It is based on its predecessor multiplied by a factor, a, and offset by a constant, c. The modulo operator makes sure that there is no overflow. What's the first X? The seed! So a random number sequence will start with the seed, providing determinism if needed.

These parameter settings are subject to significant testing; in fact, many library and compiler developers have different settings. The Wikipedia page provides an overview (https://en.wikipedia.org/wiki/Linear_congruential_generator):

```
pub struct LCG {
    xn: f32,
    m: f32,
    c: f32,
    a: f32,
}

impl LCG {
    fn seeded(seed: u32) -> LCG {
        LCG {
            xn: seed as f32,
            m: 2e31,
            a: 171f32,
            c: 8f32,
        }
    }

    fn new(seed: f32, m: f32, a: f32, c: f32) -> LCG {
        LCG {
            xn: seed,
            m: m,
            a: a,
            c: c,
```

```
        }
    }

    fn next_f32(&mut self) -> f32 {
        self.xn = (self.a * self.xn + self.c) % self.m;
        self.xn / self.m
    }
}
```

This parameter setting, while chosen at random, does not look terrible:

The bitmap that was generated as a bad example previously also used the LCG, but with another random parameter setting:

```
impl LCG {
    fn seeded(seed: u32) -> LCG {
        LCG {
            xn: seed as f32,
            m: 181f32,
            a: 167f32,
            c: 0f32,
        }
    }
    ...
}
```

Since the result is obviously bad, this goes to show how important the parameters are here. Typically, these are not settings you should adjust (or you'd know about them). Similarly, two scientists came up with a particular set of magic numbers that allow for a better random number generator: the Wichmann-Hill PRNG.

Wichmann-Hill

An extended approach to the LCG was taken by Brian Wichmann and David Hill when they invented their random number generator. It is based on the LCG, but uses three of them modified and combined by (magic) prime numbers.

These numbers, when added together, produce a sequence that is 6,953,607,871,644 (or 6.95 * 10^{12}) numbers long, which means that calling the PRNG after this number of calls will make it start over:

```
const S1_MOD: f32 = 30269f32;
const S2_MOD: f32 = 30307f32;
const S3_MOD: f32 = 30323f32;

pub struct WichmannHillRng {
    s1: f32,
    s2: f32,
    s3: f32,
}

impl WichmannHillRng {
    fn new(s1: f32, s2: f32, s3: f32) -> WichmannHillRng {
        WichmannHillRng {
            s1: s1,
            s2: s2,
```

```
            s3: s3,
        }
    }

    pub fn seeded(seed: u32) -> WichmannHillRng {
        let t = seed;
        let s1 = (t % 29999) as f32;
        let s2 = (t % 29347) as f32;
        let s3 = (t % 29097) as f32;
        WichmannHillRng::new(s1, s2, s3)
    }

    pub fn next_f32(&mut self) -> f32 {
        self.s1 = (171f32 * self.s1) % S1_MOD;
        self.s2 = (172f32 * self.s2) % S2_MOD;
        self.s3 = (170f32 * self.s3) % S3_MOD;
        (self.s1 / S1_MOD + self.s2 / S2_MOD + self.s3 / S3_MOD) % 1f32
    }
}
```

The generator does well, as the visual inspection shows. In fact, the Wichmann-Hill generator was used in various technologies and applications in the past, so this is not surprising.

Here is the visual analysis:

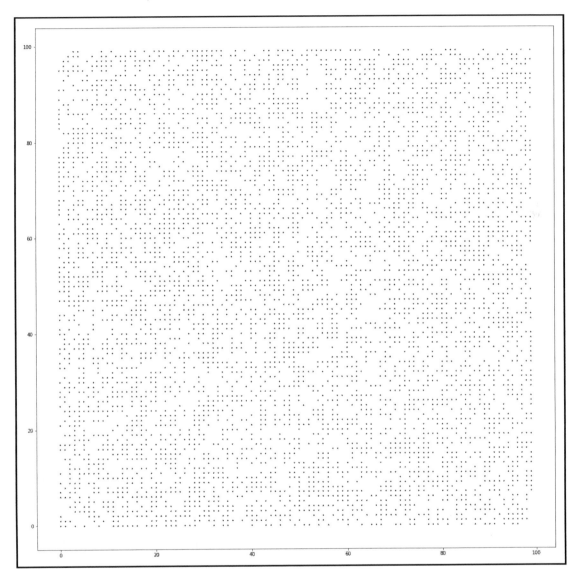

Clearly, implementing every variation of the random generator is not efficient for every project. Luckily, there is an excellent crate on `https://crates.io/` called `rand`.

The rand crate

When talking about random number generators, there is an excellent crate that cannot be skipped: `rand`. Since Rust's standard library does not include a random function, this crate provides that, and more.

In particular, there are several implementations that come with the `rand` crate, ranging from regular PRNGs, to an interface to the OS number generator (`/dev/random` on Unix-like systems), including a compatible interface for other targets, such as web assembly!

The features are impossible to describe in this chapter, so more information on these can be found in their own book (`https://rust-random.github.io/book/`).

Back to front

There are types of problems that humans can solve a lot easier than computers. These are typically somewhat spatial in nature (for example, a traveling salesman, knapsack problem) and rely on patterns, both of which are domains humans are great at. Another name for this class of problems is optimization problems, with solutions that minimize or maximize a particular aspect (for example, a minimum distance or maximum value). A subset of this class is constraint satisfaction problems, where a solution has to conform to a set of rules while minimizing or maximizing another attribute.

The brute force approach that's used to create these solutions is an algorithmic class called backtracking, in which many small choices are recursively added together to form a solution. Fundamentally, this search for the optimal solution can run to find all possible combinations (*exhaustive* search) or stop early. Why recursion? What makes it better suited than regular loops?

A typical constraint satisfaction problem requires incrementally adding items to a set of existing items and then evaluating their quality. A backtracking algorithm is such that it can backtrack once it encounters a bad solution early on so that it can skip at the best possible time. This is much clearer when talking about an example, so here are two famous problems that can be solved with regular backtracking algorithms: the 0-1 knapsack problem, and the N queens problem.

Packing bags or the 0-1 knapsack problem

The knapsack problem is very real: any time you fly with a cheap airline with cabin baggage only, things get complicated. Do I really need *this*? I could just leave my DSLR at home and use my phone for pictures, right?

These are statements that express the potential value of an item and the considerations regarding its weight (or volume on these flights), and we typically want to bring the most valuable (to us) items on a trip. While this smells like an algorithmic problem, it's far from simple. Let's start with the goal:

Given n items (with weights and values), find the subset of items providing the highest value without exceeding the knapsack's capacity, W.

Derived from this, the way to implement the solution can be constructed as follows: as an exhaustive search algorithm, every possible solution can be the best solution. However, this will only become clear once all solutions are evaluated. Thus, let's generate every possible solution first and then worry about the best one.

For any recursive scenario, it's important to worry about the exit condition first: when should the recursion stop and what will it return? In the case of the knapsack problem, the stopping condition is built around the current weight:

- The weight exceeds the capacity
- The current weight is at capacity
- There are no items left

If the capacity is already exceeded, the algorithm returns the data type's minimum value and "backtracks" on this execution branch. However, if the weight is exactly the same as the capacity, or there are no more items left, a neutral value is returned.

What does the return value indicate, then? It's the total value of the items and, since this is a search for maximum value, the return value of the two possibilities are compared:

- Including the item
- Excluding the item

Thus, we'll take the maximum of the return values of a recursive call either with or without the current item, thereby excluding any combination that exceeds the capacity provided:

```
pub trait Backtracking {
    fn fill(&self, items: Vec<&Item>) -> u64;
    fn fill_r(&self, remaining: &[&Item], current_weight: usize) -> i64;
}
```

A note on architecture: since this example is going to be improved using dynamic programming (refer to the following code), a nice way to structure this is to create and implement a trait for either technique:

```
#[derive(Debug, PartialEq)]
pub struct Item {
    pub weight: u32,
    pub value: u32,
}

pub struct Knapsack {
    capacity: usize,
}

impl Knapsack {
    pub fn new(capacity: usize) -> Knapsack {
        Knapsack { capacity: capacity }
    }
}

impl Backtracking for Knapsack {

    fn fill(&self, items: Vec<&Item>) -> u64 {
        let value = self.fill_r(&items, 0);
        if value < 0 {
            0
        } else {
            value as u64
        }
    }

    fn fill_r(&self, remaining: &[&Item], current_weight: usize)
     -> i64 {
        let w = current_weight;

        if w > self.capacity {
            return i64::min_value();
        }
```

```
    if remaining.len() > 0 && w < self.capacity {
        let include = remaining[0].value as i64
            + self.fill_r(&remaining[1..], current_weight
            + remaining[0].weight as usize);
        let exclude = self.fill_r(&remaining[1..], current_weight);
        if include >= exclude {
            include
        } else {
            exclude
        }
    } else {
        0
    }
}

}
```

One question about the runtime complexity of this algorithm remains—and it's not very clear cut this time. Some people suggest that it's $O(2^n)$, but there are two main growth factors: the capacity, as well as the number of available items. In this book, the graphs will focus on the number of items to be added to the bag, which exercises (pseudo) polynomial complexity (greater than $O(n^2)$). Regardless, you should know that this is an expensive problem to solve using backtracking.

Another popular example in universities for backtracking is the 8 queens problem (or, in its general form, the N queens problem).

N queens

The N queens chess problem (the generalized version of the 8 queens problem/puzzle) is defined as follows:

On a chessboard with N by N squares, place N queens so that they cannot attack each other.

As a first step, it's important to understand the ways a queen can move in chess, which is luckily straightforward: they can move in a straight line up, down, left, right, and diagonally, as demonstrated in the following diagram:

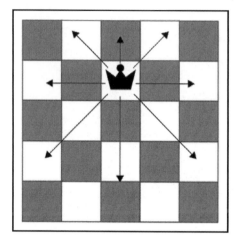

With this known, the rest is very similar to the preceding knapsack problem, but with a few more possibilities caused by various placement options. There are a number of strategies to tackle that:

- Each cell individually, which would result in a large number of recursive calls quickly
- Each row (or column) individually, and iterate over the cells within

The latter is clearly the preferred method, since a 10 by 10 board results in 100 recursive calls for each individual cell (including allocations, for example) and thereby quickly results in a stack overflow. Hence, the second option (by row) is the best trade-off, since each row/column has to have at least one queen placed and it rules out any other queen placements there:

```
pub struct ChessBoard {
    board: Vec<Vec<bool>>,
    n: usize,
}

impl ChessBoard {
    pub fn new(n: usize) -> ChessBoard {
        ChessBoard {
            n: n,
            board: vec![vec![false; n]; n],
        }
```

```
    }

    pub fn place_queens(&mut self) -> bool {
        self.place_queens_r(0)
    }

    pub fn place_queens_r(&mut self, column: usize) -> bool {
        if column < self.n {
            for r in 0..self.n {
                if self.is_valid(r, column) {
                    self.board[r][column] = true;
                    if self.place_queens_r(column + 1) {
                        return true;
                    }

                    self.board[r][column] = false;
                }
            }
            false
        }
        else {
            true
        }
    }

    fn is_valid(&self, row: usize, col: usize) -> bool {
        for i in 0..self.n {
            if self.board[i][col] {
                return false;
            }
            if self.board[row][i] {
                return false;
            }
        }
        let mut i = 0;
        let (mut left_lower, mut left_upper, mut right_lower,
            mut right_upper) =
            (true, true, true, true);

        while left_lower || left_upper || right_lower || right_upper {
            if left_upper && self.board[row - i][col - i] {
                return false;
            }
            if left_lower && self.board[row + i][col - i] {
                return false;
            }
            if right_lower && self.board[row + i][col + i] {
                return false;
```

```
    }
    if right_upper && self.board[row - i][col + i] {
        return false;
    }
    i += 1;
    left_upper = row as i64 - i as i64 >= 0
                 && col as i64 - i as i64 >= 0;
    left_lower = row + i < self.n && col as i64 - i
                 as i64 >= 0;

    right_lower = row + i < self.n && col + i < self.n;
    right_upper = row as i64 - i as i64 >= 0
                  && col + i < self.n;
}
true
    }
// ...
}
```

The strategy is simple: for each cell in a row, check whether a valid queen can be placed under the current conditions. Then, descend deeper into the recursion and end it as soon as a valid setting has been found. The result looks as follows ($n = 4$):

However, the computational complexity of this algorithm grows exponentially ($O(2^n)$), which means that for large n, it will not finish in any reasonable amount of time:

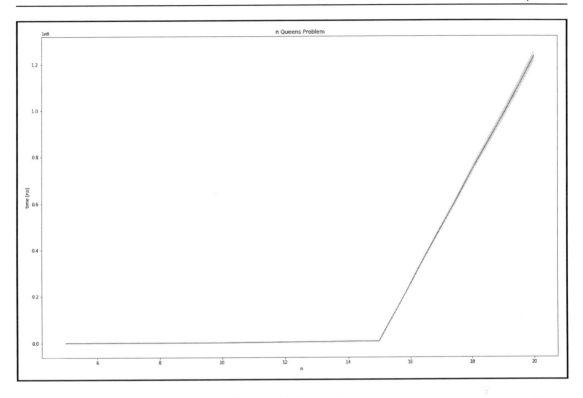

The output graph for N queens problems

While this particular problem is probably more like a teaching problem, this approach can certainly be applied to other (similar) use cases, especially in the spatial domain.

Advanced problem solving

Backtracking calculates and finds the best overall solution to a particular problem. However, as described in `Chapter 8`, *Algorithm Evaluation*, there are problems that have a really large computational complexity, which leads to a really long running time. Since this is unlikely to be solved by simply making computers faster, smarter approaches are required.

With several strategies and techniques available, the choice is yours to find an approach that best solves your problem. The position of Rust in this space can be critical, thanks to its great speed and memory efficiency, so keeping an eye on solutions for complex problems might pay off in the future (in the author's opinion).

First up is a surprising programming technique that is aimed at improving the complexities of backtracking algorithms: dynamic programming.

Dynamic programming

The concept of dynamic programming is one of these techniques that you thought had a different name: caching. The fundamental idea is to save relevant temporary results to a cache and use this precomputed result instead of recalculating something over and over again!

This means that a problem and a potential solution have to be examined to find relevant sub-problems, so any result can be cached. The main upside of this approach is that it finds the globally best solution possible, but at the price of a potentially high runtime complexity.

The knapsack problem improved

As an example, let's examine the recursive calls of the knapsack solver. For brevity, this knapsack is to be filled using a list of three items where the weight is uniformly one and has a capacity of two. Since the backtracking algorithm walks through the list of items in order (and tries either to include or exclude a particular item), the knapsack solver can be seen as a function *K* that maps any items that are remaining as well as capacity remaining to a particular value:

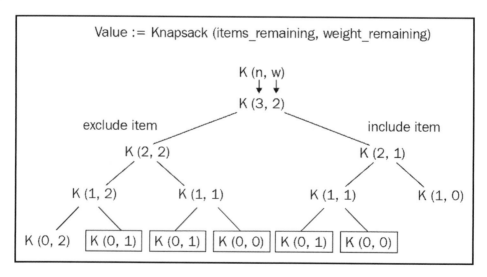

Therefore, at the same level, the same input parameter leads to the same value and this is easy to cache. In the preceding diagram, the nodes marked by the rectangle are calculated at least twice. This example was taken from the GeeksforGeeks' article (https://www.geeksforgeeks.org/0-1-knapsack-problem-dp-10/) regarding the 0-1 knapsack problem.

Before anything else, we can now implement a different trait to the backtracking:

```
pub trait DynamicProgramming {
    fn fill(&self, items: Vec<&Item>) -> u64;
}
```

Implementation then follows and, as a function with two input parameters, each combination of input parameters can be saved in a two-dimensional array, which reduces the runtime complexity to walking this matrix, leading to a *O(n * W)* runtime complexity:

```
impl DynamicProgramming for Knapsack {
    fn fill(&self, items: Vec<&Item>) -> u64 {
        let mut cache = vec![vec![0u64; self.capacity + 1];
                        items.len() + 1];
        for i in 1..items.len() + 1 {
            for w in 1..self.capacity + 1 {
                if items[i -1].weight as usize <= w {
                    let prev_weight =
                        w - (items[i - 1].weight as usize);
                    cache[i][w] = max(
                        items[i - 1].value as u64
                        + cache[i - 1][prev_weight],
                        cache[i - 1][w],
                    );
                } else {
                    cache[i][w] = cache[i - 1][w]
                }
            }
        }
        cache[items.len()][self.capacity]
    }
}
```

The code went from a recursive call chain to constructing a matrix where the maximum value for a particular combination is just a lookup, which seriously improves the absolute and relative runtime (20 items take 41,902 +/- 10,014 ns when using backtracking and 607 +/- 138 ns for dynamic programming):

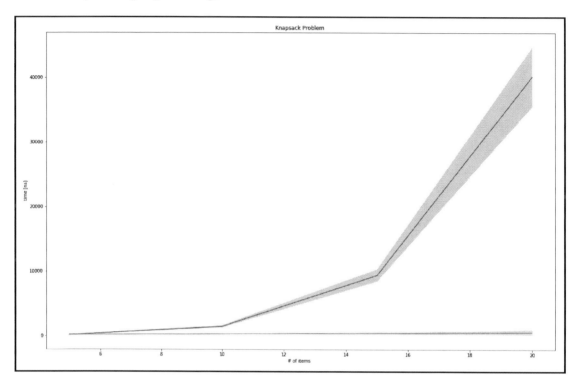

The output graph for Knapsack problems

In relative terms, the runtime complexity improved significantly:

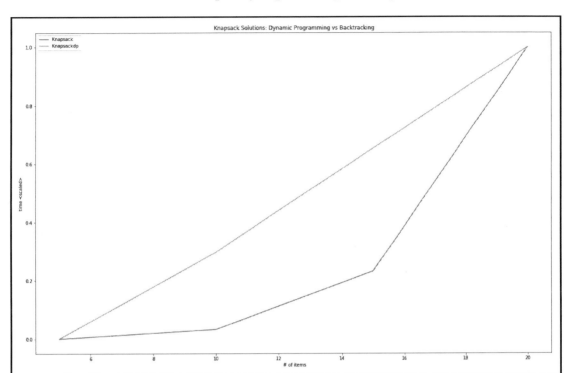

The runtime complexity graph comparison between dynamic programming and backtracking

Employing this strategy (or similar) to problems that allow for that kind of optimization permits far higher input parameters and therefore enable it to solve real-world problems! Imagine an airline trying to work out the most valuable cargo it can bring, but it's limited to 40 different items at once.

Since there are many harder problems (for example, a problem class called NP-hard problems), people came up with ways to find good solutions as well.

Metaheuristic approaches

Dynamic programming is great for constraint satisfaction problems. However, better solutions can be found using something akin to systematic guessing, or metaheuristics. These problem-agnostic solution generators can be classified in several ways, for instance, whether they are population-based, inspired by nature, and searching globally or locally.

Whichever optimization algorithm is chosen, it will treat the problem like a search problem, trying to find the best possible solution within the solutions provided. Absent of any guarantees to find the best solution possible, it will typically find a good enough solution. Thanks to the expensive runtimes of NP-hard problems, a wide variety of ways can lead to a better solution than a more specific solution.

Popular metaheuristics include the following:

- Simulated annealing
- Genetic algorithms
- Particle swarm optimization
- Ant colony optimization
- Tabu search

Rust's ecosystem features several crates that implement these metaheuristic strategies. The progress of some of these crates can be tracked on `http://www.arewelearningyet.com/metaheuristics/`.

Example metaheuristic – genetic algorithms

Examples include the traveling salesman problem, where a tour of the shortest path connecting n cities has to be found. With a $O(n!)$ runtime complexity, only 20 cities prove to be computationally very expensive, but it can be solved well enough for a very large n by starting off with a random order of cities (tour), and then repeatedly recombining or randomly changing (mutating) several of these tours only to select the best ones and restarting the process with these.

Using the `rsgenetic` crate (`https://crates.io/crates/rsgenetic`), implementing the solution becomes a matter of implementing the `TspTour` trait, which requires a `fitness()` function to be supplied so that a solution can be evaluated, the `crossover()` function to recombine two parents into a new offspring tour, and the `mutate()` function to apply random changes to a tour:

```
impl Phenotype<TourFitness> for TspTour {
    ///
    /// The Euclidean distance of an entire tour.
    ///
    fn fitness(&self) -> TourFitness {
        let tour_cities: Vec<&City> = self.tour.iter().map(|t|
                                        &self.cities[*t]).collect();
        let mut fitness = 0f32;
        for i in 1..tour_cities.len() {
```

```
            fitness += distance(tour_cities[i], tour_cities[i - 1]);
        }
        -(fitness.round() as i32)
    }

    ///
    /// Implements the crossover for a TSP tour using PMX
    ///
    fn crossover(&self, other: &TspTour) -> TspTour {
        // ...

        TspTour {
            tour: offspring,
            cities: self.cities.clone(),
            rng_cell: self.rng_cell.clone(),
        }
    }

    ///
    /// Mutates the solution by swapping neighbors at a chance
    ///
    fn mutate(&self) -> TspTour {
        let mut rng = self.rng_cell.borrow_mut();
        if rng.gen::<f32>() < MUTPROB {
            let mut mutated: Tour = self.tour.clone();
            for i in 0..mutated.len() {
                if rng.gen::<f32>() < INDPB {
                    let mut swap_idx = rng.gen_range(0,
                                        mutated.len() - 2);
                    if swap_idx >= i {
                        swap_idx += 1;
                    }
                    let tmp = mutated[i];
                    mutated[i] = mutated[swap_idx];
                    mutated[swap_idx] = tmp;
                }
            }
            TspTour {
                tour: mutated,
                cities: self.cities.clone(),
                rng_cell: self.rng_cell.clone(),
            }
        } else {
            self.clone()
        }
    }
}
```

Once these are implemented, the framework allows you to set a selector to select the best *n* solutions in each generation to create the next generation's population. These steps are repeated until the fitness values stagnate (converge) and the highest fitness in the last generation can be considered a good solution for the problem.

Over several generations, a solution like this one can be found:

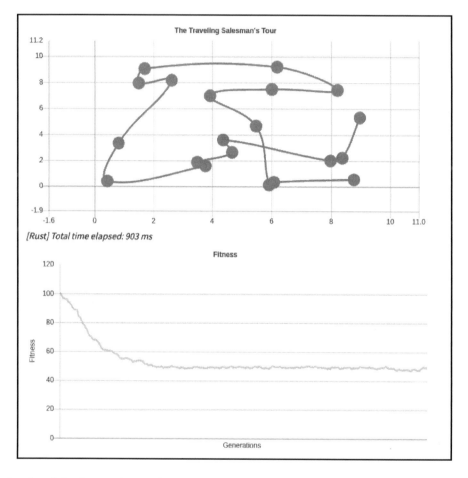

A more in-depth look at solving this problem in JavaScript, as well as in Rust (and Wasm), can be found on my blog at https://blog.x5ff.xyz. A similar approach can be taken to arrange a highly valuable combination of items in a knapsack, which is left for you to find out.

Summary

Other than regular data structures and sorting, as well as searching methods, there are several other problems that arise. This chapter talks about a small subset of those: generating random numbers and solving constraint satisfaction problems.

Random number generation is useful in lots of ways: encryption, gaming, gambling, simulations, data science—all require good random numbers. Good? There are two important types: pseudo-random numbers and "real" random numbers. While the latter has to be taken from the physical world (computers are deterministic), the former can be implemented with the LCG or the Wichmann-Hill generator (which combines LCGs using magic numbers).

Constraint satisfaction problems are problems that find the best combination that conform to a set of constraints. A technique called backtracking builds a state of the current permutation by using recursion to generate all combinations, but tracking back on those that do not satisfy the required constraints. Both the 8 queens (or N queens) problem and the 0-1 knapsack problem are examples of backtracking algorithms that exhibit expensive runtime behavior.

Advanced techniques such as dynamic programming or metaheuristics (that return good enough solutions) can lead to a significant improvement in solving these challenges quicker (or for larger sizes). Rust, as a fast and efficient language, can play a significant role in these techniques in the future.

In the next chapter, we will look into algorithms that the Rust standard library provides.

Questions

- What is the difference between PRNGs and RNGs?
- What crate provides random number generators in Rust?
- How can backtracking solve combinatorial problems?
- What is dynamic programming?
- How are metaheuristics a problem-agnostic approach to solving hard problems?

Further reading

Here is some additional reference material that you may refer to regarding what has been covered in this chapter:

- https://en.wikipedia.org/wiki/Random_number_generator_attack
- https://blog.x5ff.xyz
- https://en.wikipedia.org/wiki/Metaheuristic

12
Algorithms of the Standard Library

Rust's standard library provides a few fundamental data types that cover the basic needs of many projects and, typically, there is no need to implement your own algorithms if the appropriate data structure is available. If, for some reason, the data type is not perfectly suited to the task, the standard library has you covered as well. In this quick round-up, you can look forward to learning about the following:

- The `slice` primitive type
- The `Iterator` trait
- `binary_search()`
- `sort()`, stable, and unstable

Slicing and iteration

Similar to how interfaces standardize access to functionality in the libraries of other languages, Rust's standard library utilizes a type and a trait to provide fundamental implementations. The trait, `Iterator<T>`, has been looked at and used over the course of this book several times. The slice type, however, was not explicitly used a lot, especially since the Rust compiler automatically uses slices when `Vec<T>` is borrowed for a function call. How can you leverage this type, though? We have seen the `Iterator<T>` implementation in action, but does it provide more than that?

Iterator

To recap: an iterator is a pattern to traverse a collection, providing a pointer to each element in the process. This pattern is mentioned in the book *Design Patterns*, by Erich Gamma, Richard Helm, Ralph Johnson, and John Vlissides (the Gang of Four), in 1994 and can be found in basically every language one way or another.

In Rust, the term pointer to each element gets a new dimension: is it a borrowed or owned item? Can this be mutably borrowed as well?

Using the standard library's Iterator<T> trait makes a lot of sense, since it provides a serious amount of useful functions, which are all based around a single implementation of next().

next() returns an Option<Self::Item>, which is the associated type that has to be declared when implementing the trait—and it can be anything you like!

Therefore, using &MyType, &mut MyType, and MyType can all be implemented separately to achieve the desired functionality. IntoIter<T> is a trait that is specifically designed to facilitate this workflow and to integrate it neatly with the for loop syntax. The following code is from the Rust standard library's source code:

```
impl<T> IntoIterator for Vec<T> {
    type Item = T;
    type IntoIter = IntoIter<T>;

    /// Creates a consuming iterator, that is,
    /// one that moves each value out of
    /// the vector (from start to end).
    /// The vector cannot be used after calling
    /// this.
    ///
    /// # Examples
    ///
    /// ```
    /// let v = vec!["a".to_string(), "b".to_string()];
    /// for s in v.into_iter() {
    /// // s has type String, not &String
    /// println!("{}", s);
    /// }
    /// ```
    #[inline]
    fn into_iter(mut self) -> IntoIter<T> {
        unsafe {
            let begin = self.as_mut_ptr();
            assume(!begin.is_null());
```

```
let end = if mem::size_of::<T>() == 0 {
    arith_offset(begin as *const i8, self.len()
                    as isize) as *const T
} else {
    begin.add(self.len()) as *const T
};
let cap = self.buf.cap();
mem::forget(self);
IntoIter {
    buf: NonNull::new_unchecked(begin),
    phantom: PhantomData,
    cap,
    ptr: begin,
    end,
}
            }
        }
    }
```

Rust's Vec<T> implements precisely this pattern, but with a nice twist. The preceding code consumes the original data structure, potentially transforming the original into something that's easier to iterate, in the same way as trees can be expanded into a sorted Vec<T> or a stack. To return to the original theme, the Iterator<T> provides functions (implemented in further structures) that add many possible ways to search and filter through a collection.

Any Rust user will be aware of the iter() function of Vec<T>, however, which is actually provided by the slice type that Vec is implicitly converted into?

Slices

Slices are views into sequences to provide a more unified interface for accessing, iterating, or otherwise interacting with these memory areas. Consequently, they are available through Vec<T>, especially since they implement the Deref trait to implicitly treat Vec<T> as a [T]—a slice of T.

The Vec<T> implementation also hints at that for the IntoIterator implementation for immutable and mutable references:

```
impl<'a, T> IntoIterator for &'a Vec<T> {
    type Item = &'a T;
    type IntoIter = slice::Iter<'a, T>;

    fn into_iter(self) -> slice::Iter<'a, T> {
        self.iter()
```

```
        }
    }

    impl<'a, T> IntoIterator for &'a mut Vec<T> {
        type Item = &'a mut T;
        type IntoIter = slice::IterMut<'a, T>;

        fn into_iter(self) -> slice::IterMut<'a, T> {
            self.iter_mut()
        }
    }
```

The slice itself is only a view, represented by a pointer to the memory part and its length. Since the compiler knows the nature of the data contained within, it can also figure out individual elements to provide type safety.

A more detailed explanation of slices and the way they work would warrant its own book, so it is recommended at least reading the documentation (or the source code) of the slice module (https://doc.rust-lang.org/std/slice/index.html).

Search

Finding things in a collection has been discussed throughout this book, and the Rust standard library provides a few ways by default. These functions are attached to the Iterator<T> trait or slice types and work regardless of the actual type, provided that a function to compare two elements is furnished.

This can either be the Ord trait or a custom comparator function, such as the position() function on the Iterator<T>.

Linear search

The classic linear search is provided via position() (or rposition()) on the Iterator<T> trait, and it even utilizes other iterator functions that are implemented on the trait itself:

```
fn position<P>(&mut self, mut predicate: P) -> Option<usize> where
    Self: Sized,
    P: FnMut(Self::Item) -> bool,
{
    // The addition might panic on overflow
    self.try_fold(0, move |i, x| {
```

```
        if predicate(x) { LoopState::Break(i) }
        else { LoopState::Continue(i + 1) }
    }).break_value()
}
```

`try_fold()` is a short-circuit variation on the `fold()` (or `reduce()`, following the map/reduce pattern) function that returns whenever `LoopState::Break` is returned. The call to `break_value()` transforms the result from the value returned in the `LoopState::Break` enumeration into `Option` and `None` if it ran through the entire collection.

This is the brute-force approach to searching and can be useful if the collection is unsorted and short. For anything longer, sorting and using the binary search function might pay off.

Binary search

A generic fast search function is provided through slices as well, called `binary_search()`. As discussed in `Chapter 10`, *Finding Stuff*, a binary search returns the index of an element after closing in on its position by repeatedly choosing a half.

To achieve that, there are two prerequisites that the input slice has to satisfy:

- It's sorted
- The element type implements the `Ord` trait

`binary_search()` cannot check whether the collection that's provided is sorted, which means that if an unordered collection returns the expected result, it can only be coincidental. Additionally, if there are multiple elements with the same value, any of those can be the result.

Other than using the implicitly provided comparison function (by implementing `Ord`), `binary_search()` also has a more flexible sibling—`binary_search_by()`, which requires a comparison function to be supplied.

Under the hood, this function is comparable to the naive implementation we created in `Chapter 10`, *Finding Stuff*; on occasion, it was even faster by a nanosecond or two. The code is just as simple, however:

```
pub fn binary_search_by<'a, F>(&'a self, mut f: F) -> Result<usize, usize>
    where F: FnMut(&'a T) -> Ordering
{
    let s = self;
    let mut size = s.len();
```

```
        if size == 0 {
            return Err(0);
        }
        let mut base = 0usize;
        while size > 1 {
            let half = size / 2;
            let mid = base + half;
            // mid is always in [0, size),
            // that means mid is >= 0 and < size.
            // mid >= 0: by definition
            // mid < size: mid = size / 2 + size / 4 + size / 8 ...
            let cmp = f(unsafe { s.get_unchecked(mid) });
            base = if cmp == Greater { base } else { mid };
            size -= half;
        }
        // base is always in [0, size) because base <= mid.
        let cmp = f(unsafe { s.get_unchecked(base) });
        if cmp == Equal { Ok(base) } else {
                    Err(base + (cmp == Less) as usize) }

}
```

Other variants of the function include searching by key or by the comparator function of the Ord trait (as mentioned previously). One major caveat can be the requirement to provide a sorted collection to the binary search function, but luckily, Rust provides sorting in its standard library.

Sorting

Sorting is an important feature in user interfaces, but also provides the predictability that's necessary for many algorithms. Whenever there is no way to use an appropriate data structure (such as a tree), a generic sorting algorithm can take care of creating that order. One important question arises regarding equal values: will they end up at the same exact spot every time? When using a stable sorting algorithm, the answer is *yes*.

Stable sorting

The key to stable sorting is not reordering equal elements, so in [1, 1, 2, 3, 4, 5], 1s never change their positions relative to each other. In Rust, this is actually used when sort() is called on Vec<T>.

The current (2018 edition) implementation of Vec<T> uses a merge sort variation based on Timsort. Here is the source code:

```
pub fn sort(&mut self)
    where T: Ord
{
    merge_sort(self, |a, b| a.lt(b));
}
```

The code is quite verbose, but can be split into smaller parts. The first step is to sort smaller (20 elements or less) slices by deleting and reinserting the elements in order (in other words, insertion sort):

```
fn merge_sort<T, F>(v: &mut [T], mut is_less: F)
    where F: FnMut(&T, &T) -> bool
{
    // Slices of up to this length get sorted using insertion sort.
    const MAX_INSERTION: usize = 20;
    // Very short runs are extended using insertion sort
    // to span at least this many elements.
    const MIN_RUN: usize = 10;

    // Sorting has no meaningful behavior on zero-sized types.
    if size_of::<T>() == 0 {
        return;
    }

    let len = v.len();

    // Short arrays get sorted in-place via insertion
    // sort to avoid allocations.
    if len <= MAX_INSERTION {
        if len >= 2 {
            for i in (0..len-1).rev() {
                insert_head(&mut v[i..], &mut is_less);
            }
        }
        return;
    }
}
```

If the collection is longer, the algorithm resorts to traversing the items back to front, identifying natural runs. The constant MIN_RUN (10 in the preceding code) defines a minimum length of such a run, so a shorter run (such as 5, 9, 10, 11, 13, 19, 31, 55, 56 in [5, 9, 10, 11, 13, 19, 31, 55, 56, 1, ...]) is expanded by doing an insertion sort on the 1 to get to 10 elements. The metadata of the resulting block (for [1, 5, 9, 10, 11, 13, 19, 31, 55, 56], it would start at 0, with a length of 10) is then pushed onto a stack for subsequent merging (note: we recommend reading the comments from the code authors):

```
// Allocate a buffer to use as scratch memory.
// We keep the length 0 so we can keep in it
// shallow copies of the contents of `v` without risking the dtors
// running on copies if `is_less` panics.
// When merging two sorted runs, this buffer holds a copy of the
// shorter run, which will always have length at most `len / 2`.
let mut buf = Vec::with_capacity(len / 2);

// In order to identify natural runs in `v`, we traverse it
// backwards. That might seem like a strange decision, but consider
// the fact that merges more often go in the opposite direction
// (forwards). According to benchmarks, merging forwards is
// slightly faster than merging backwards. To conclude, identifying
// runs by traversing backwards improves performance.
let mut runs = vec![];
let mut end = len;
while end > 0 {
    // Find the next natural run,
    // and reverse it if it's strictly descending.
    let mut start = end - 1;
    if start > 0 {
        start -= 1;
        unsafe {
            if is_less(v.get_unchecked(start + 1),
                    v.get_unchecked(start)) {
                while start > 0 && is_less(v.get_unchecked(start),
                        v.get_unchecked(start - 1)) {
                    start -= 1;
                }
                v[start..end].reverse();
            } else {
                while start > 0 && !is_less(v.get_unchecked(start),
                        v.get_unchecked(start - 1)) {
                    start -= 1;
                }
            }
        }
    }
}
```

```
    // Insert some more elements into the run if it's too short.
    // Insertion sort is faster than
    // merge sort on short sequences,
    // so this significantly improves performance.
    while start > 0 && end - start < MIN_RUN {
        start -= 1;
        insert_head(&mut v[start..end], &mut is_less);
    }

    // Push this run onto the stack.
    runs.push(Run {
        start,
        len: end - start,
    });
    end = start;
```

To conclude the iteration, some pairs on the stack are already merged, collapsing them in an insertion sort:

```
    while let Some(r) = collapse(&runs) {
        let left = runs[r + 1];
        let right = runs[r];
        unsafe {
            merge(&mut v[left.start .. right.start + right.len],
                  left.len, buf.as_mut_ptr(), &mut is_less);
        }
        runs[r] = Run {
            start: left.start,
            len: left.len + right.len,
        };
        runs.remove(r + 1);
    }
}
```

This `collapse` loop ensures that there is only a single item left on the stack, which is the sorted sequence. Finding out which runs to collapse is the essential part of Timsort, since merging is simply done using insertion sort. The collapse function checks for two essential conditions:

- The lengths of the runs are in descending order (the top of the stack holds the longest run)
- The length of each generated run is greater than the sum of the next two runs

With this in mind, let's look at the collapse function:

```
// [...]
fn collapse(runs: &[Run]) -> Option<usize> {
    let n = runs.len();
    if n >= 2 && (runs[n - 1].start == 0 ||
                  runs[n - 2].len <= runs[n - 1].len ||
                  (n >= 3 && runs[n - 3].len <=
                   runs[n - 2].len + runs[n - 1].len) ||
                  (n >= 4 && runs[n - 4].len <=
                   runs[n - 3].len + runs[n - 2].len)) {
        if n >= 3 && runs[n - 3].len < runs[n - 1].len {
            Some(n - 3)
        } else {
            Some(n - 2)
        }
    } else {
        None
    }
}
// [...]
```

It returns the index of the run that is to be merged with its successor (`r` and `r + 1`; refer to the `collapse` loop for more information). The collapse function checks the top four runs to satisfy the aforementioned conditions if the topmost run (at the highest index) does not start at the beginning. If it does, the end is almost reached and a merge is necessary, regardless of any conditions that are violated, thereby ensuring the final sequence to be merged last.

Timsort's combination of insertion sort and merge sort make it a really fast and efficient sorting algorithm that is also stable and operates on "blocks" by building these naturally occurring runs. Unstable sorting, on the other hand, uses a familiar Quicksort.

Unstable sorting

Unstable sorting does not retain the relative position of equal values, and can therefore achieve better speeds thanks to the lack of additionally allocated memory that stable sorting requires. The slice's `sort_unstable()` function uses a Quicksort variation that is called a pattern-defeating Quicksort by Orson Peters, combining heap sort and Quicksort to achieve an excellent performance in most cases.

The slice implementation simply refers to it as Quicksort:

```
pub fn sort_unstable_by<F>(&mut self, mut compare: F)
    where F: FnMut(&T, &T) -> Ordering
{
    sort::quicksort(self, |a, b| compare(a, b) == Ordering::Less);
}
```

Looking at the Quicksort implementation, it spans the entire module—about 700 lines of code. Therefore, let's look at the highest level function to understand the basics; curious readers should dive into the source code (https://doc.rust-lang.org/src/core/slice/sort.rs.html) to find out more.

The Quicksort function performs a few preliminary checks to rule out invalid cases:

```
/// Sorts `v` using pattern-defeating quicksort, which is `O(n log n)`
worst-case.
pub fn quicksort<T, F>(v: &mut [T], mut is_less: F)
    where F: FnMut(&T, &T) -> bool
{
    // Sorting has no meaningful behavior on zero-sized types.
    if mem::size_of::<T>() == 0 {
        return;
    }
    // Limit the number of imbalanced
    // partitions to `floor(log2(len)) + 1`.
    let limit = mem::size_of::<usize>() * 8 - v.len()
                    .leading_zeros() as usize;

    recurse(v, &mut is_less, None, limit);
}
```

The `recurse` function is at the heart of this implementation and is even a recursive function:

```
/// Sorts `v` recursively.
///
/// If the slice had a predecessor in the original array,
/// it is specified as `pred`.
///
/// `limit` is the number of allowed imbalanced partitions
///  before switching to `heapsort`. If zero,
/// this function will immediately switch to heapsort.
fn recurse<'a, T, F>(mut v: &'a mut [T], is_less: &mut F, mut pred:
Option<&'a T>, mut limit: usize)
    where F: FnMut(&T, &T) -> bool
{
```

```
// Slices of up to this length get sorted using insertion sort.
const MAX_INSERTION: usize = 20;

// True if the last partitioning was reasonably balanced.
let mut was_balanced = true;
// True if the last partitioning didn't shuffle elements
// (the slice was already partitioned).
let mut was_partitioned = true;

loop {
    let len = v.len();
    // Very short slices get sorted using insertion sort.
    if len <= MAX_INSERTION {
        insertion_sort(v, is_less);
        return;
    }
    // If too many bad pivot choices were made,
    // simply fall back to heapsort in order to
    // guarantee `O(n log n)` worst-case.
    if limit == 0 {
        heapsort(v, is_less);
        return;
    }
    // If the last partitioning was imbalanced,
    // try breaking patterns in the slice by shuffling
    // some elements around.
    // Hopefully we'll choose a better pivot this time.
    if !was_balanced {
        break_patterns(v);
        limit -= 1;
    }
    // Choose a pivot and try guessing
    // whether the slice is already sorted.
    let (pivot, likely_sorted) = choose_pivot(v, is_less);

    // If the last partitioning was decently balanced
    // and didn't shuffle elements, and if pivot
    // selection predicts the slice is likely already sorted...
    if was_balanced && was_partitioned && likely_sorted {
        // Try identifying several out-of-order elements
        // and shifting them to correct
        // positions. If the slice ends up being completely sorted,
        // we're done.
        if partial_insertion_sort(v, is_less) {
            return;
        }
    }
    // If the chosen pivot is equal to the predecessor,
```

```
            // then it's the smallest element in the
            // slice. Partition the slice into elements equal to and
            // elements greater than the pivot.
            // This case is usually hit when the slice contains many
            // duplicate elements.
            if let Some(p) = pred {
                if !is_less(p, &v[pivot]) {
                    let mid = partition_equal(v, pivot, is_less);

                    // Continue sorting elements greater than the pivot.
                    v = &mut {v}[mid..];
                    continue;
                }
            }
            // Partition the slice.
            let (mid, was_p) = partition(v, pivot, is_less);
            was_balanced = cmp::min(mid, len - mid) >= len / 8;
            was_partitioned = was_p;

            // Split the slice into `left`, `pivot`, and `right`.
            let (left, right) = {v}.split_at_mut(mid);
            let (pivot, right) = right.split_at_mut(1);
            let pivot = &pivot[0];

            // Recurse into the shorter side only in order to
            // minimize the total number of recursive
            // calls and consume less stack space.
            // Then just continue with the longer side (this is
            // akin to tail recursion).
            if left.len() < right.len() {
                recurse(left, is_less, pred, limit);
                v = right;
                pred = Some(pivot);
            } else {
                recurse(right, is_less, Some(pivot), limit);
                v = left;
            }
        }
    }
}
```

Thankfully, the standard library's source has many helpful comments. Therefore, it's highly recommended to read through all the comments in the preceding snippet. In short, the algorithms make a lot of guesses to avoid making a bad choice for the pivot. If you recall, when Quicksort chooses a bad pivot element, it will split into uneven partitions, thereby creating very bad runtime behavior. Therefore, choosing a good pivot is critical, which is why so many heuristics around that process are employed and, if all else fails, the algorithm runs heap sort to at least have *O(n log n)* runtime complexity.

Summary

Rust's standard library includes several implementations for basic things such as sorting or searching on its primitive slice type and the `Iterator<T>` trait. The slice type in particular has many highly important functions to offer.

`binary_search()` is a generic implementation of the binary search concepts provided on the slice type. `Vec<T>` can be quickly and easily (and implicitly) converted into a slice, making this a universally available function. However, it requires a sorting order to be present in the slice to work (and it won't fail if it's not) and, if custom types are used, an implementation of the `Ord` trait.

In case the slice cannot be sorted beforehand, the `Iterator<T>` variable's implementation of `position()` (of `find()`) provides a basic linear search that returns the first position of the element.

Sorting is provided in a generic function, but comes in two flavors: stable and unstable. The regular `sort()` function uses a merge sort variation called Timsort to achieve an efficient and stable sorting performance.

`sort_unstable()` utilizes a pattern-defeating Quicksort to combine the efficiency of heap sort and Quicksort in a smart way, which typically leads to a better absolute runtime than `sort()`.

This was the final chapter of this book and, if you made it to here, you finally deserve some answers! You can find the answers to all of the questions that have been asked in the *Assessments* section.

Questions

- Where is Rust's implementation of generic algorithms on collections?
- When is a linear search better than a binary search?
- *Potential job interview question:* What are stable and unstable sorting algorithms?
- What is a bad behavior exhibited by Quicksort that pattern-defeating Quicksort mitigates?

Further reading

Here is some additional reference material that you may refer to regarding what has been covered in this chapter:

- *Design Patterns,* by Erich Gamma, Richard Helm, Ralph Johnson, and John Vlissides
- Iterator pattern on Wikipedia (`https://en.wikipedia.org/wiki/Iterator_pattern`)
- *OpenJDK's java.utils.Collection.sort() is broken: The good, the bad and the worst case,* by de Gow et al. (`http://envisage-project.eu/wp-content/uploads/2015/02/sorting.pdf`)
- Pattern-defeating Quicksort (`http://envisage-project.eu/wp-content/uploads/2015/02/sorting.pdf`)

Assessments

Chapter 1

What are traits and how are they different from interfaces?

Traits are pieces of functionality shared across components. They can contain code as well as associated types, and can be implemented for any type and generics independently. Interfaces, on the other hand, describe the public methods a class provides, without an implementation and typically with inheritance. Rust only has traits.

Why doesn't Rust have a garbage collector?

Garbage collection is required to free up unused heap memory that is generated from a running the program. Rust avoids this by providing a static code analysis at compile-time that forces the user to think of variable lifetimes. These lifetimes are very strictly defined and require a lifetime scope to own or borrow memory so that the compiler knows when it's not being used without an explicit statement.

Name three examples of how lifetimes are created in Rust (explicitly and implicitly)!

Any three that you can come up with are great, but here are mine: Functions, scopes (simply create one using { }), and closures (lambda functions).

Why is immutability for variables important?

It guarantees that only read operations take place, thereby avoiding any side effects.

What does the Sync marker trait do?

It marks a structure as safe to access from multiple threads.

Where can you go to participate in the Rust community?

Go to `https://github.com/rust-lang` (opening issues, submitting code, discussions, and so on) or `www.rust-lang.org/community`, where all the current community resources (such as the forum and chats) are kept.

Why are RFCs preferred over PRs?

To contribute changes to the Rust programming language, `cargo`, or `crates.io`, the traditional fork-then-change-and-PR (pull request) won't work (especially if there are major changes). RFCs are the formal process required for substantial changes to either of the three projects and allow the wider community to discuss and evaluate the proposed changes, as well as contribute to them. This is the Rust community's effort to effectively govern something as fundamental as a programming language.

Chapter 2

What does cargo do?

Read and write access to repositories, run tests, dependency management (download, update, and managing the dependency tree), executing the build process, and providing a central interface for additional tooling.

Does cargo provide linting support?

`cargo` itself doesn't, but there are additional tools, such as `clippy` (https://github.com/rust-lang/rust-clippy), that work seamlessly with `cargo`.

In which cases is the Cargo.lock file important to publish?

For libraries. The file is used by cargo to determine the exact versions of the dependency tree. As a consequence, there should not be any version issues caused by unintentionally updated dependencies.

What are the requirements to publish to crates.io?

Passing tests, no uncommitted files in the repository, a valid account, and an available spot on `crates.io`.

What is Wasm and why should you care?

Wasm is a compilation target that can be executed in traditional JavaScript environments, such as browsers or the Node runtime. This skips the compilation steps required for JavaScript as well as its garbage collection, so Wasm binaries are better suited for (near-) real-time applications with a browser UI component. They can be simply run in the JavaScript world.

How are tests organized in a Rust project?

Tests can either be added to each file in a module, annotated by # [tests] and # [test], as well as # [bench]. These can also be placed into their own file structure under test/ in the component's directory. Additionally, Rust supports doctests, which are executed when the docstring (///) has an example section that contains code.

Chapter 3

How are Sized types different from other types?

Sized means that the size of a type instance is known at runtime, so it doesn't contain a growing data type. For example, str is typically not a sized type – String is.

How does Clone differ from Copy?

Clone is an explicit call to the clone() function; copy happens implicitly, for example, at assignments. Since Clone is explicitly called, it usually does a deep copy on the underlying data structure.

What are the main drawbacks of immutable data structures?

Immutable data structures can have worse absolute performances since they can't use the optimizations that regular data structures provide. Additionally, updates on the data that's contained is impossible, making it a very inefficient choice for constantly changing data.

How can applications benefit from immutable data structures?

They implicitly keep track of changes and work well across threads without side effects or the need for locking.

Think about an immutable list that you want to work on—how would you distribute it across multiple threads?

Depending on the task, it can be split into *n* chunks, where *n* is the number of threads. However, this requires you to create *n* copies of the list—or at least a move per each. Alternatively, the list can be made accessible across threads, providing only the indices to represent the chunks to work on.

Chapter 4

Why is a linked list tricky to implement in Rust?

Rust's ownership principle makes it hard to implement non-hierarchical structures, such as the doubly-linked list. There, it's unclear which node owns which area of the memory, since both neighbors hold a reference that can't be invalid.

How does Rust's standard library, LinkedList<T>, work?

It's a doubly-linked list: individual nodes are interlinked, just like the implementation in this chapter.

What is the difference between a doubly-linked list and a skip list?

A skip list has multiple levels where nodes are linked together to achieve a tree-like search performance. Therefore, the skip list has to be ordered and stores multiple pointers to successors and predecessors. The doubly-linked list has only two links (forward and backward), doesn't need to be sorted, and achieves linear search performance at best.

Does a dynamic array outperform a skip list for element access?

Yes, if the skip list doesn't use a dynamic array as a base!

Why is a dynamic array a great choice for CPU caching?

The data is stored in a large continuous portion of the memory, with the elements stored one after the other. Caching always builds on blocks of memory, which is why caching several elements that are likely processed after each other makes the dynamic array well-suited for that.

What is another growth strategy for dynamic arrays?

Memory can be doubled, increased by a certain amount each time, or logarithmically so that it grows fast in the beginning and slows down later on.

Rust takes arrays seriously, so what does the dynamic array use internally?

It uses a boxed slice.

Chapter 5

How does a binary search tree skip several nodes when searching?

By following one branch, it skips one subtree every time the decision for one branch is made. A subtree can be anything from a single node to all nodes except one.

What are self-balancing trees?

Trees that use some kind of logic to (roughly) equalize the number of nodes in each subtree. This ensures that all tree algorithms work at the best possible efficiency.

Why is balance in a tree important?

If a tree is skewed, any algorithm operating on it will encounter an uneven amount of work depending on the subtree it works on. The mismatch is the assumption that every branch of the tree leads to the same amount of work (for example, the same number of comparisons to make), which is what makes the tree data structure efficient.

Is a heap a binary tree?

Yes. Each node has two children.

What are good use cases for tries?

Here are mine: A trie set is a very efficient data structure for guaranteeing uniqueness, there are sequence prediction methods based on tries, and they can do a lossless data compression.

What is a B-Tree?

A B-Tree is a tree with a defined level that relates to the number of children in each node. Thus, it is a self-balancing generalization of all trees: a level 2 B-Tree is akin to a binary tree, but more children will make the data structure more efficient and avoid unnecessary heights.

What are the fundamental components of a graph?

Graphs are nodes that are connected with edges. These nodes typically have a value; the value on the edges is referred to as weights. In a general graph, there are no directions on the edges, but further constraints can make it directed, acyclic, or otherwise limited. Graphs are the superstructure of all lists and trees.

Chapter 6

What makes a good hash function?

It depends on the use case. Cryptography should minimize collisions, message digests should maximize hash differences on minor input differences, and bloom filters should do the reverse.

How can you estimate the suitability of a hash function for a particular task?

By using plots and tests to get a sense of how the output hashes are distributed and whether that's what you're looking for. Histograms and scatter plots work well to see the distribution of values. Also, search the internet for potential breaches or weaknesses and the original paper.

Is a checksum hash useful in other ways?

They can also be useful to determine whether two texts or files are equal, which can be used for finding matches quickly or to check whether the content is the content that was transferred or whether the content has been tampered with.

What are two ways to implement a map?

Using trees or using hashing.

What are buckets?

Buckets are the hash values that are mapped onto the underlying data structure. Hashes might output u64, but Vec<T> only has a length of 100. Therefore, multiple hashes share an index in Vec<T>, which is called a bucket.

Can a set replace a list?

Only if uniqueness is a required constraint for the contents.

What makes a set useful?

Quick and specialized set operations, such as union, intersect, difference, and fast "contains" lookups, as well as the ability to guarantee uniqueness with better efficiency.

Chapter 7

Which std::collections data structure is not discussed here?

BinaryHeap (https://doc.rust-lang.org/std/collections/struct.BinaryHeap.html).

How does Vec<T> or VecDeque<T> grow, as of 2018?

They double (or more) their size when more space is required.

Is LinkedList<T> a good default data structure?

No. It doesn't provide index access and is generally slower than Vec<T>, thanks to the internal memory structure, but provides the same basic features.

What hashing implementation does the 2018 HashMap<T> use by default?

SipHashing. There are others that are on their way into the standard library, such as the hashbrown crate (https://github.com/Amanieu/hashbrown).

What are three benefits of BTreeMap<T> over HashMap<T>?

Use any three, but here are some suggestions:

- Ordered keys
- Lower computational intensity (no hashing required)
- No hash function required—good performance regardless

Is the internal tree of BTreeMap<T> wider or higher?

Wider, thanks to a larger number of children (up to *2 * level - 1*) for efficient CPU caching.

Chapter 8

Why estimate runtime complexity over something such as the number of statements?

Runtime complexity is more about the projected growth alongside the main input parameter. In a way, it *is* counting the number of statements and you would likely arrive at the same conclusion. The statements that are being counted are the subset that matters most.

How does runtime complexity relate to math functions?

In two ways: mathematical functions can be described the same way as functions in programming, since they rest on the same fundamental construct; and math functions are used to express the runtime complexity itself, in particular the logarithmic and exponential functions.

Is the complexity class that is typically provided the best or worst case?

The worst case, since this will be the slowest/most inefficient case.

Why are loops important in estimating complexity?

Loops are great constructs that repeatedly execute statements and, depending on the growth parameter, will drive the function's runtime complexity.

Is O(n log(n)) a better or worse runtime complexity than O(log(n))?

O(log(n)) is clearly a better runtime complexity. Try replacing the *n* with three numbers of your choice and calculate *log(n)* versus *n * log(n)*.

What are some common known complexity classes?

$O(n)$, $O(log(n))$, $O(n^2)$, and $O(2^n)$.

Chapter 9

What is information retrieval?

All disciplines surrounding storage, search, ranking, tokenization, analysis, and a general understanding of an information structure. It's everything that a good search engine does well.

Do modern search engines and databases use simple search algorithms?

Yes. Regardless of the abstraction on top of the search index, the storing of tokens is often done in a linear, append-only fashion that allows for efficient search (binary search) on these segments.

Why does the linear search have O(n) runtime complexity?

In case an element doesn't exist in the sequence, it has to walk over all *n* items to be sure.

What does jump search do better than linear search?

It skips parts of the list since, in an ordered list, certain locations can be ruled out based on the sorting. Therefore, it significantly reduces the number of elements that are searched for linearly.

What is binary search and why is it comparable to a tree?

Binary search splits the input sequence in half and only continues on the part that has to contain the element. Drawing these parts visually (including those that have been skipped) looks just like a binary tree, which is why the two parts are effectively branches.

Chapter 10

Why is sorting an important aspect of programming?

Establishing a predictable order so that algorithms can make assumptions based on the content (for example, for search) will enable it to perform much better. Another important aspect is user experience in user interfaces, or to establish a semantic link between data points (for example, a time series can now have trends).

What makes values bubble up in bubble sort?

By repeatedly swapping a pair of elements when going through the sequence, elements that belong on the opposite end (or close to it) will have to swap places with every other element on the way. Therefore, the large number "bubbles up."

Why is shell sort useful?

It achieves solid sorting performances, yet it's not as complex as merge sort and uses less computational resources. This makes it great in scenarios where hardware can be bottlenecked (embedded devices) or other sorting approaches aren't available (for example, if the standard library is not supported).

Can heap sort outperform bubble sort in its best case?

No. Bubble sort's best case is simply iterating the list – $O(n)$. Heap sort, on the other hand, always has to build a heap, regardless of the sequence being already sorted or not – $O(n \log n)$.

What do merge sort and quicksort have in common?

The divide-and-conquer approach: both split the sequence into smaller pieces so that they can work on those separately.

What are hybrid sorting algorithms?

Hybrid sorting algorithms use the strengths of at least two different approaches. Timsort, for example, uses insertion sort for smaller sequences (for example, under 20 items) but merge sort for larger ones.

Chapter 11

What is the difference between PRNGs and RNGs?

Pseudo-random number generators (PRNGs) use a process to generate a close-to-random sequence of numbers that are as statistically independent as possible. Random number generators (RNGs) try to use true randomness (for example, phenomena from the physical world that cannot be predicted) to generate random numbers.

What crate provides random number generators in Rust?

`rand` is the most important one.

How can backtracking solve combinatorial problems?

Backtracking recursively tries out possible combinations and evaluates their validity as soon as possible. This allows you to backtrack the bad solutions and save good solutions.

What is dynamic programming?

A programming technique that saves and uses common intermediate solutions to improve the algorithm's runtime complexity.

How are metaheuristics a problem-agnostic approach to solving hard problems?

Metaheuristics use generally applicable strategies to find the best solution. These strategies can be inspired by nature (natural selection, animal behavior, physical processes) and repeatedly generate and evaluate parameters to improve the next solution. If the generation and validation of a problem is supplied by the user, the approach can be problem-agnostic and since the strategies take care of converging toward the best solution, they can provide a best guess in predictable time.

Chapter 12

Where is Rust's implementation of generic algorithms on collections?

The slice primitive type.

When is linear search better than binary search?

If the sequence is short and not sorted—the time it takes to sort it would be longer than a simple linear search.

Potential job interview question: **What are stable and unstable sorting algorithms?**

Stable sorting algorithms maintain a relative order between equal elements, while unstable sorting algorithms don't. This means that if there are sequences of the same number, the entire block will show up in the sorted collection exactly in the same order.

What is a bad behavior of Quicksort that pattern-defeating Quicksort mitigates?

The choice of bad pivots is the most important problem that is mitigated. This is done by employing strategies to improve the selection or, if all else fails, use heap sort to achieve at least a $O(n\ log\ n)$ runtime complexity (instead of quicksort's $O(n^2)$).

Other Books You May Enjoy

If you enjoyed this book, you may be interested in these other books by Packt:

Hands-On Concurrency with Rust
Brian L. Troutwine

ISBN: 978-1-78839-997-5

- Probe your programs for performance and accuracy issues
- Create your own threading and multi-processing environment in Rust
- Use coarse locks from Rust's Standard library
- Solve common synchronization problems or avoid synchronization using atomic programming
- Build lock-free/wait-free structures in Rust and understand their implementations in the crates ecosystem

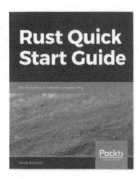

Rust Quick Start Guide
Daniel Arbuckle

ISBN: 978-1-78961-670-5

- Install Rust and write your first program with it
- Understand ownership in Rust
- Handle different data types
- Make decisions by pattern matching
- Use smart pointers
- Use generic types and type specialization
- Write code that works with many data types
- Tap into the standard library

Leave a review - let other readers know what you think

Please share your thoughts on this book with others by leaving a review on the site that you bought it from. If you purchased the book from Amazon, please leave us an honest review on this book's Amazon page. This is vital so that other potential readers can see and use your unbiased opinion to make purchasing decisions, we can understand what our customers think about our products, and our authors can see your feedback on the title that they have worked with Packt to create. It will only take a few minutes of your time, but is valuable to other potential customers, our authors, and Packt. Thank you!

Index

Made in the USA
San Bernardino, CA
09 April 2019